DEAR PRINCESS GRACE, DEAR BETTY

The Memoir of a
Romantic Feminist

ALIDA BRILL

**schaffner
press**

Tucson, Arizona

Also by Alida Brill

Dancing at the River's Edge:
A Patient and Her Doctor Negotiate Life with Chronic Illness
Co-author

A Rising Public Voice: Women in Politics Worldwide
Editor

Nobody's Business: The Paradoxes of Privacy

Dimensions of Tolerance: What Americans
Believe About Civil Liberties
Co-author

First Hardcover Edition
Printed in the United States

Cover photo: Betty Friedan, courtesy of Susan Wood
Cover image: envelope courtesy of Alida Brill
Cover and book design: Darci Slaten

Permission to print from the lyrics of "Gigi" (Lyrics by ALAN JAY
LERNER/ Music by FREDERICK LOEWE),
Copyright (c) 1957 (Renewed) CHAPPELL & CO., INC. All Rights
Reserved. Used by Permission of ALFRED MUSIC.

An additional list of copyrighted source material may be found in the
back of this book.

For permissions and copyright information, contact the publisher,
Schaffner Press, POB 41567, Tucson, Az 85717. No part of this book
may be excerpted or reprinted without the publisher's written consent.

Library of Congress Cataloging-in-Publication Data

Names: Brill-Scheuer, Alida, author.
Title: Dear Princess Grace, dear Betty : the memoir of a romantic
feminist /
  Alida Brill.
Description: Tucson, Az : Schaffner Press, [2016]
Identifiers: LCCN 2016000771 (print) | LCCN 2016005861 (ebook)
| ISBN
  9781936182848 (hardback) | ISBN 9781936182848 (Hardcover
Edition) | ISBN
  9781936182855 (Mobi/Kindle) | ISBN 9781936182862 (Epub) |
ISBN
  9781936182879 (Pdf)
Subjects: LCSH: Brill-Scheuer, Alida. | Feminists--United States--
Biography.
  | Feminism--United States--History. | BISAC: BIOGRAPHY &
AUTOBIOGRAPHY /
  Women. | SOCIAL SCIENCE / Feminism & Feminist Theory.
Classification: LCC HQ1413.B75 A3 2016 (print) | LCC HQ1413.
B75 (ebook) | DDC
  305.42092--dc23
LC record available at http://lccn.loc.gov/2016000771

*Some names and identifying details have been changed to protect the privacy of
individuals who have crossed paths with the author.*

For "the daughters"
Anne, Jennifer, Olivia and Emma
and for:
Elizabeth and Kim

— All women of the 21st century —

— And in memory of my parents, a
new old couple of the 20th —

DEAR PRINCESS GRACE,
DEAR BETTY
The Memoir of a
Romantic Feminist

ALIDA BRILL

CONTENTS

Author's Note:

I grew up a regular girl in a regular Southern California suburb. My adolescence and then my adulthood were interrupted by chronic illness, which gave me my understanding of fairness and unfairness, and from there, feminism. I was fortunate to participate in the Second Wave of the Women's Movement. And although I am not among the fairly small group of feminists who really changed America, I was changed by those women--transformed by what I witnessed, by the powerful influence of the leaders of the feminist movement, and by what I read. When I was thirty, I left Northern California for Manhattan and began working in the world of women's research. It was then that Betty Friedan stepped into my life.

My mother's own engagement with the feminist conversation began with the publication of Friedan's The Feminine Mystique. *Because of the BOOK, Friedan was a presence in my childhood. Later she became a close friend and colleague—another mother for me—and an intimate part of my life.*

This is a memoir. It is not a research project, not a scholarly treatise, not a biography of famous feminists, not a work of quantitative social science. It is a personal reflection of a girl's, and then a woman's, life during a time of enormous expansion of the ways we women could choose to compose our lives. It begins with a letter I sent to Princess Grace of Monaco, and it moves through to the first years of the 21st century.

1956 - 6 of MARCH

Dear Miss Kelly

On Sunday I Will
Be Seven Years
Old. I am Going To
Start A Stamp
Collection. I
Would Like To Begin
With YOUR STAMP
I Dont Know How To
Get one. Can You
Tell Me How. Thank
You Very Much

I Hope You Will Be
Happy For Ever and
Ever.

Alida Brill

3542 Arbor Rd.
Lakewood 11
California

Alida's draft of letter to Grace Kelly

2 *Alida Brill*

I

Dear Princess Grace...

When I was six, I fell in love with Grace Kelly. I wanted to become Miss Grace Kelly, Actress, and I wanted to ascend the throne, where I, too, would be recognized worldwide as *Her Serene Highness*. Nothing deterred me from this fantasy. What did I really want—to be a movie star—to be the chosen princess of a romanticized kingdom? My adult self insists that my childhood delusions incorporated both: a working career as well as a handpicked princess-bride. I indulge this notion because it suggests a nascent, if fuzzy, concept of feminist thinking in a girl's brain.

My infatuation with Grace could not protect me from illness. There were frequent and unexplained episodes of high fevers and weakness. I was hospitalized and diagnosed with rheumatic fever. It was the prologue to later troubles. I was released and prescribed the maximum dose of penicillin and bed rest. My world shrank to my frilly lavender and white bedroom. It was in there that Grace consoled me. When in Grace-mode, I was powerful and beautiful; fears disappeared. Grace made me larger than life, made me think beyond illness, beyond the confinement of the bedroom. I dreamed of a prince, a kingdom and movie roles. As a Serene Princess I would rule as co-monarch—my Prince would permit me to do so. I didn't know that the Principality of Monaco (about half the size of New York's Central Park) was smaller than the incorporated city of Lakewood, CA. I could not know that Grace's life would end in a car accident, with a daughter as both witness and injured passenger.

I had no idea Princess Grace was also keeping house, in a manner of speaking, and that she was more like our own mothers than I imagined. Grace had taken on a new career, of good wife and mother. Her job was to ensure that her husband the Prince was happy and satisfied. She had an enormous additional task: at all times and in all places she was to appear to be the perfect woman. It was the only way to be an appropriate spouse for a monarch. While Grace's lavish lifestyle diverged dramatically from that of Lakewood's moms, far less separated the Serene Princess of Monaco from many of our mothers. Grace fought boredom, depression, and her weight. She was confined by cultural norms and rules, just as were the era's traditional wives and mothers.

If the history of American women in the 20th century hadn't taken the turn it did, my preoccupation with Grace might have turned into a more harmful obsession. There were a number of serious flaws with my plan to follow in Grace's steps. There were few—as in, *not one*—available princes who would have found me on the corner of Arbor and Downey and would have gone on to choose me as the fairest of them all. I disliked boys who insisted they were in charge. I already questioned why doctors and school principals were men. Nonetheless I longed to be the ethereal Grace dressed in elaborate ball gowns waltzing with her prince, without a hair out of place, adored by everyone. It took a long time for me to admit that my impressions of Grace's life were influenced more by her Hollywood life than her married one in Monaco.

Grace Kelly was a woman with a career, a working actress. The life of that Grace Kelly ended when she emerged from the wedding ceremony in Monaco on April 19th, 1956. From then on she lived as a monarch's wife and then a mother. She was ruled and controlled by ritual, custom, and the expectations and laws of her adopted country. Laws enacted at the time of her marriage specifically prohibited her films from being shown in Monaco. Grace Kelly got her prince, but paid a high price. Women throughout history have become transfixed by the power of romantic illusions, royal and otherwise. Some of us want to be chosen more than we want anything else, despite the costs and sacrifices.

During my exile in my sickroom of a bedroom, I discovered how to run away. I turned the bed into a cruise ship. Old shoeboxes became cabins. I was the cruise director; my dolls were the passengers, assigned to the boxes. The cabins were outfitted with scraps of cloth and other small items. Though I had little concept of social class, I decided the cabins were first-class, which I did understand meant pretty and fancy.

The cruise idea came from the Matson Steamship line, which took passengers from the West Coast to Hawaii. Mother had only one travel fantasy: to take a Matson ship to Hawaii. My parents weren't going anywhere--their life together didn't include a travel budget. She never boarded that ship but it was her dream. My parents went several times to the port to see a Matson steamer sail off to its destination. Watching the ship depart was probably enough for her. Financial considerations aside, my mother's fears about travel and leaving her home often kept her from taking excursions. The Matson steamer was an adventure of my mother's mind, and so it became mine as well.

Mother's friend, Tina, regularly sent postcards from her worldwide trips. I didn't know who Tina was or how she was able to travel in luxury, but she caught my attention. The postcards came in a steady stream and in every season. I envisioned transporting myself to the dreamy destinations from which she wrote. Her handwriting was a beautiful script, in teal blue fountain pen ink.

I never met Tina. She was an old friend who came from a different time and place in Mother's life, a time when she was something other than Mother. Tina flew on Pan Am or TWA, and her postcards arrived in my room of confinement like a trail of fairy dust. There was never much news on the cards, only a few lines about the place she was visiting, Paris, Nice, Capri, Lisbon, London, Zurich. The signature never changed: *Love always, Tina.* My mother loaned the cards to me. After I pronounced the ship-bed and its cardboard boxes seaworthy, the dolls and I set sail, arriving at fantasy destinations determined by Tina's postcards.

Who was Tina? What happened to her? Why and how was she able to travel? What was the meaning of those evocative cards she sent addressed only to my mother? How did my mother feel about them? Did she ever respond?

These are questions without answers which, had I obtained them, might have dissolved the magic dust. I didn't ask, because I didn't want to risk breaking the spell. I didn't question my mother because it seemed too private, and not my business. But Tina was the first evidence I had that female independence existed out there somewhere.

I knew she was not an airline attendant; they were prohibited from marrying or from weighing over a certain amount. Air travel then had the patina of glamour. Even the airports themselves were exciting destinations, but I wasn't seduced by the appeal of being a stewardess. My head was filled with stories of the waitresses who worked for and with my father. Many had hard, sad lives. I knew several of them quite well. I did not intend a career requiring me to walk up and down an airplane's crowded aisle serving drinks and food. This was not part of the Princess Grace agenda.

My rheumatic fever extended its stay. Confined to my bed, my imaginary travels unlocked my girlish prison cell. I shuffled through the shoeboxes where I hoarded Tina's cards. Alone, I quietly planned trips for the dolls. Perhaps I was readying myself for the itinerary of a life where travel was used as an attempt to escape from the reality of my disease. It would be behavior that lasted well beyond middle age.

Tentatively I finally emerged from the ship-bed. We began with evenings at the local drive-in. On Sunday nights, off we went with a packed dinner. My parents bundled me up in layers of clothing and brought blankets, as if we were living in the tundra.

I had encountered Grace Kelly on television and at indoor theaters, but not in the drive-in. It was there I saw her full magnificence. The movie was *High Society*, released three months before her marriage. Her personal trajectory was tailor-made for me. Her life as a princess was unfolding before my eyes, on the television and in the newspapers and magazines. Grace's idealized adventures into monarchy inspired my flights to the land of Let's Pretend. All I needed to do was pay close attention.

At almost seven, I was reading considerably well. *The Long Beach Independent Press Telegram* was filled with news of the upcoming wedding. Her wedding gown was designed by the costume designer Helen Rose of MGM and was a gift from the studio to Grace. There was news about *The U.S. Constitution*, the ship they were all on—the bridesmaids, bridal party guests, and of course, Grace and her whole family. When the ship docked, the Prince himself came aboard to escort his bride, or as one news report said, to *claim* her. There were parties onboard and events before the wedding. The pre-wedding and wedding coverage was an enormous amount of hype for the time. I wasn't the only person who wanted to immerse myself in the enchanted tale, it seemed the entire world did as well.

I had taken action the month before the wedding. Days before my seventh birthday, I decided to write to Grace. My mother was not enamored of fairy tales or of my ideas about a future on the screen or as a princess. I had to come up with a plausible reason to correspond with Grace. I announced my intention to begin a stamp collection. I would request a *first day cover* of the wedding. One of my teachers was an avid stamp collector and I had seen her extensive collection. My ploy worked. I wrote to

Grace and she, the Palace, did write back, enclosing a first day cover as well as extra stamps. For all the dreams in my seven-year-old kingdom, the one I wanted most was for her to be happy forever and ever, and ever. And *I* wanted to be happy in the present and in the future.

When the small package from Monaco arrived, my mother took me, along with my precious mail, to the *Press Telegram* to meet the editor of the *Lakewood Today* column. I told him about the letter, and likely showed him my last draft. He wrote a few words about it in his column. Mother impressed upon me that the important event was that I wrote the letter.

Here's what I thought my mother's lesson was:

You wrote something. A reporter found out, your name appeared in the newspaper, and with that came instant local fame.

1, 2, 3, it was simple arithmetic.

Eventually I would turn away from my obsession with Grace and decide to become a famous writer. I quickly discovered the long odds against attaining celebrity through writing.

* * *

Lakewood bordered the city of Long Beach, which was larger and more diverse. Hollywood was a few miles up the freeway, and it had a powerful influence on childhood activities. I wrote plays and cast girlfriends in backyard productions. On weekends there were acting classes at the Peppermint Playhouse, and another long-forgotten children's acting studio. I diligently prepared for theatre studies, convinced Hollywood was in my future.

On the eve of adolescence, I anticipated doing *big-girl* things. My parents, Ida and Alfred, gave me a twelfth birthday party. My father turned our den into a makeshift soda fountain where he made root-beer floats and ice cream sundaes. We played hit songs on the record player, and took turns changing the singles. No boys wanted or invited. We danced with each other.

A teacher encouraged me to play basketball. I hadn't expected to be any good but surprisingly I was. It was a sport suitable for the *tall girls*. On the courts, *tall girls* called the shots, not the popular smaller girls who reigned supreme at recess and school dances. Basketball was the territory of girls who looked like me. I belonged. It took me out of my head, out of my books and expanded the horizons of a lonely, only child.

A few more months of this magic passed. Then the year of being twelve ended, at a full stop. I did not yet know that my twelfth birthday marked the last time I would be free from disease. What became a chronic illness began fleetingly. One morning my ankles were stiff and they hurt, but the symptoms vanished by the time I was dressed and ready for school. A few mornings later one knee was swollen and red. Over the next few weeks there were surges of pain, and then more enduring ailments. I was less able to hide the symptoms. My mother watched, as I stood still for several minutes, unable to take a step. It was difficult to walk without a noticeable limp. There were persistent fevers. I developed methods of disguise and denial and employed the readily available lie that I had injured myself dancing or playing basketball.

When I was thirteen a doctor concluded something was wrong, but he did not focus on my aching body. Perhaps I was *crazy*, though he wasn't quite that blunt. He announced: *Maybe it's all in her head*. I knew what he meant. But something was very wrong and I wasn't making it up or pretending. His arrogance was the last straw for my mother. Infuriated, she screamed at him and didn't care if he thought we were both crazy. In rapid-fire she spit out: *It's in her bones, not in her brain*. It was one of the few times I enjoyed a maternal outburst. In the quest to reach a diagnosis, more doctors followed and offered their opinions. They used unfamiliar words: *Hysterical Tendencies, Psychosomatic*

Disorder, Hormonal Surges. I was unsure of the definitions but what I saw in their eyes told me what they thought.

I was: A Crazy Girl. They think I'm crazy and I'm not. And I will never convince them otherwise.

I viewed my teenage years through this prism. I first became a feminist as a sick girl. Although the women's movement was emerging, I didn't fully understand what it meant. What I did comprehend was that doctors, all older men, had the power, and that they might well harm me. The medical establishment, with its entrenched system of male authority, was a constant presence. I learned early that male doctors did not take the stories of a girl seriously. I gave detailed descriptions of what was happening based on what I wrote in my diary. Despite the precision of my recordings, they did not believe my accounts. They only believed me when I presented visible symptoms. Medical schools later did change their approach, but not soon enough to rescue my adolescence.

The practice of rheumatology didn't have the research knowledge or tools it now has. I was thirty before I found Michael Lockshin, a doctor who listened and believed, even when there wasn't much to see. Slowly I realized my childhood doctors were not so much cruel as clueless. They were also sexist. An understanding of sexism had not yet been integrated into our cultural ethos, so their attitudes and behaviors weren't considered inappropriate. I observed the way things were—and I did not like it.

Mother was barely five feet tall. Her eyes were crystalline blue, a color best depicted in antique prints of the Grand Canal in Venice. Her eyes were riveting when she was angry. She was a terrifying force. She was also smart, witty, articulate, and funny. I loved and admired her as much as I dreaded her outbursts. She bore me at forty-one, an advanced age in the 1950s. I was unplanned. Her first child William Terry (known only as Terry) died of measles meningitis. It happened in the space of one night when he was just six. I was born six years later. His sudden death would be the loss from which my mother never recovered. Her mourning dictated her rhythms and moods. The duplicated portrait of a beautiful boy sitting on a front porch next to his adoring mother, a photograph taken a few months before he died, was displayed in every room except my bedroom. Some cultures maintain elaborate shrines to dead relatives in their homes, and the parlors of the Victorian era were filled with memorial memorabilia. But in a 1950s Caucasian suburb in Southern California, it was creepy.

In the few hours before he died, Terry ran an extremely high fever. Mother took him to an emergency room, where she was cautioned against "maternal hysteria" and sent home with her sick boy. Their diagnosis: a passing virus or flu. No male authority figure was present to speak for her or on behalf of her son. The men in the family were away at war. Later that night she went to another hospital, where the explanation was essentially the same. She was being overly emotional and the boy would be fine by morning. Frantic, she went home and again tried to bring down his fever. When the first hospital finally admitted him, he was near the end. He could not have survived; in those days, measles meningitis was incurable. But how the medical community handled her was unforgivable, and avoidable.

Ida was thirty-five when Terry died. She lived one month to the day short of her 101st birthday. In those sixty-six years she remained convinced that Terry's death was her fault because she was unable to make the doctors listen, and that if a man had been present it would have changed her child's fate. It was something she never forgot and decades of persisting grief would become part of my life too. Fear and guilt held her in their grasp. Today she probably would be in therapy, or on medication, or at the least, in grief counseling. But in 1943, individual grief was not seen as a condition that required treatment.

My mother was guilty and conflicted, but she wasn't crazy. After an unwanted late pregnancy, the last thing she wanted was another child with a mysterious illness. But that's what she got. Though Terry's death often eclipsed her joy, that earlier encounter with the male medical establishment gave her the confidence and determination to advocate for me. After the Crazy Girl diagnosis, she stood up to all the doctors we saw. I would remain quiet and allow myself to be remote during medical appointments. I was delighted to watch my righteously furious mother negotiate the system. By now Mother was asking hard and smart questions. She spent hours in the medical reference section of the local library. Few physicians passed her inquisition. We moved on in our quest to find just one who might alleviate my suffering—or at the least, choose to pay attention. I believe Mother's fierceness and suspicions protected me from the worst abuses of the medical community of that era. She was a strong model of a woman who demanded to be taken seriously, and who was willing to pay the price of their disapproval.

Sometimes I would have extreme symptoms just before an appointment. I viewed this as a blessing; I felt bizarrely relieved, because then doctors would not think it was all in my head, and that at long last, I would be of interest. Part of me hated doctors. I disliked the white coats even more than the alarming events overtaking my body.

Eventually I was diagnosed with atypical Juvenile Rheumatoid Arthritis. One doctor with a prestigious university's medical diploma hanging on his wall injected me with shots of gold, a fairly common practice at the time. I was still considered "A Crazy Girl," but now one filled with gold.

My adolescence sped up sharply to accelerated adulthood. I know now that I have an incurable autoimmune disease. It has refused to take a vacation for more than brief periods. In time, the Juvenile Rheumatoid Arthritis (JRA) was ruled out, and for years I carried a Systemic Lupus (SLE) diagnosis. Eventually it was defined as *atypical Wegener's Granulomatosis*—a disease related to Lupus. (The disease is now usually referred to as Granulomatosis with polyangiitis-Wegener's, or GPA.) The essential nature of inflammatory autoimmune disease is that we are allergic to ourselves.

It has taken decades for me to concede I will always be unwell. Chronic illness and feminism describe and define much about my life. There are times when I still try to hide from illness, but not from a feminist identity. My vision of feminism is a generous one, in which individual men are not the enemies to feminist thought or the advancement of women. It is patriarchy—as ideology and as an entrenched institution—that is the enemy to our common humanity.

* * *

I am an American girl of the baby boom generation, a typical child of the 1950s when: Dads went to work; Moms stayed home; boys played sports; girls played house with baby dolls. Lakewood was a place of sameness. Everyone was white, middle class, and presumptively Christian. The idea of conformity was not discussed; it was assumed. We lived in some 17,500 identical little houses on straight, flat streets carved out from what had been bean fields. The development plans of such communities, especially Lakewood, forever altered the map of Southern California.

Lakewood was a synchronized last stage of the World War II battle plan. It represented a domestic victory lap. If Americans could triumph over tyrants and their armies, we could take care of the needs of returning veterans and their families. The goal was to provide not just housing, but also to create a town with amenities, including parks, schools, and shops. The city's design—neat, tidy, serene, secure—encompassed white-middle-class values. It also was the media's favored image of America at that moment. Many of the men worked at neighboring factories, either as white-collar workers or on the assembly lines making defense weapons as well as commercial airliners. Later, NASA's space program created more jobs. Everyone assumed the aerospace industry would be a source of lifetime employment with generous benefits.

Lakewood's seal of incorporation, which served as the official stamp for legal and public documents, depicted a church, a school, and a home. A boy playing baseball portrayed the town's children. Affirming the town's symbolic image, local parks were filled with fathers teaching sons to play baseball, and on weekends the baseball diamonds were alive with many Little League games. As girls, we primarily went to the parks to socialize, to engage in gender-approved activities, to watch the boys' sports, but in the summers we joined them in the swimming pools. I learned to swim at the Pat McCormick Pool, named after the Olympic gold medalist. She was a diver who perfected dives women were not allowed to execute during the Olympics. She was fearless. I was not, either in the water or out.

Lakewood was marketed as *Tomorrow's City Today*. In that *world* men were in charge of everything outside the home, except for school relations. Wives and mothers were thought to be content at home with their chores and parenting. Housework was not defined as working at home, nor was it considered real work. Like the rearing of children, it was expected, but not respected. It was what women were supposed to do.

Quotidian life in Lakewood had a predicable rhythm. Housewives waited to hear the familiar bell that announced the arrival of the Helms man, a figure more ubiquitous than even the Avon lady. Early each morning, hundreds of Helms trucks,— or "woody wagons" as they were known—each outfitted with bakery shelves and laden with freshly baked breads, cakes, cookies, doughnuts, and brownies, set out from headquarters in L.A. The enormous central bakery was also a destination for school outings. At the conclusion of a tour, each child was given a cardboard Helms wagon and a small loaf of bread.

Mothers bought at their curbsides what their mothers used to bake in their kitchens, and what mothers in urban settings purchased at local bakeries. When we got good grades, we might be rewarded with money to choose a special cupcake or doughnut. "A whistle-stop bakery on wheels" was the Helms motto. The Helms men who drove the trucks and sold the goods were neighborhood fixtures—part of our lives. The bakery was successful partially because Helms Men chatted with and befriended the women they saw each day. Virgil, our Helms man became a good friend, and we called him Virg. He was a crucial player in my mother's transformation from housewife to a full-time employee, as she had been before and during the war years.

The women gathered at the Helms truck to buy what they needed, including coffee cakes or doughnuts for the daily coffee *klatsch*. They met in each other's homes—it was an all-female communal breather from their solitary lives. During these informal gatherings they might discuss the town's activities, school issues, their own problems, or the problems of others. My mother was an infrequent participant, though I wanted her to blend in with the other mothers. Reluctantly, she sometimes joined a morning group. She was uncomfortable because she was considerably older than the others, and she called herself a bookworm.

Mostly she dodged becoming a regular member because she didn't want to invite others to our house, an eccentricity interpreted as rude and unacceptable. My mother hated housework. If there were regular visitors she would have to tidy up, which was something she either would not or could not do. Having a child when she was in her forties, who had a chronic illness, and without an extended family to support or assist her, was more than enough.

Mother saw nothing chic or trendsetting about being an older mother. She was often mistaken for my grandmother. These days women become pregnant well into their forties and a few beyond that. In 2011, a *New York Magazine* cover featured a naked pregnant woman in her fifties. For Mother there was nothing about late-life mothering that was suitable for the cover of a glossy magazine. She was misunderstood, underappreciated, and isolated.

2
"Gigi, Oh! What Miracle Has Made You The Way You Are..."

In March 1958, Her Serene Highness Princess Grace gave birth to a son, Prince Albert. The newspapers were filled with the news. A 101-gun salute boomed upon the news of his birth. Grace's mother said he was a "bonny, bonny prince." The one-year-old Princess Caroline's claim to the throne was superseded by her brother. According to the Treaty of 1918, if there were no natural heir to the throne after the death of Prince Rainier, Monaco would become the possession of France. News reports around the world declared the birth of a male heir ensured that the monarchy of Monaco was "doubly safe." Although Princess Caroline was the true heir to the throne, all the celebrations and jubilation upon Albert's birth suggested she no longer counted, at least in any official or important way.

Caroline's demotion had little, if any, impact on me at the time. I cut out pictures from the magazines of the birth of Princess Grace's little prince, adding them to my expanding Princess Grace scrapbooks. I was as enthralled as ever with the Princess and now she had triumphed in a most exciting way. In producing a male heir for Prince Rainier—who began his rule of Monaco the year I was born—she had successfully performed the most essential part of her job.

Princess Grace looked undiminished by her labors. An official palace portrait showed her in a strapless white gown, the royal sash across her shoulders, the tiny Prince in her arms. She still didn't look like anybody's mother. In July she appeared on the Ed Sullivan show, where clips were shown of her royal life. Grace's actual existence and her movie star life blurred. I was sure the fairy tale hype about Monaco was true, but I was disappointed that she was not making new movies. The hopeful waiting proved fruitless. She never made another film. Rainier forbade it. Not all that surprising in a country where women didn't get the franchise until 1962.

* * *

My father worked every day except Sunday. On his day off we went on adventures, often to an afternoon movie. *Gigi* was the one I chose to see on my ninth birthday in 1958. It took place in Paris, the city my father talked about as much as he did Manhattan. He longed to see Paris again, and he correctly calculated the movies were his best shot. *Gigi* was playing at The Crest, a movie theater in the Bixby Knolls section of Long Beach. It featured lavish Art Deco detailing. Large ornaments hung on the walls, which looked like giant versions of my mother's brooches. When the house lights went down, I was transported to a magical kingdom. Forget Monaco. Skip Disneyland. Finally my father's tales about the glories of Paris impressed me. Maurice Chevalier warbled the theme song "Thank Heaven for Little Girls," and I was captivated. But it's chilling to hear those lyrics today. It could be the anthem for pedophiles.

After the movie, Mother joined us at one of the most elegant restaurants in town, The Chandelier, just down the street from the theater. It was owned or managed by a pal of my father's. The interior of the restaurant was dark, and each table was set with small packs of black cigarettes stamped *The Chandelier* in gold. It wasn't Maxim's, but Paris didn't feel far away that evening. I couldn't contain my excitement about Gigi, played by Leslie Caron, and the handsome Gaston, played by Louis Jourdan. For a nine-year-old girl who flew on flights of fancy, Gigi hit all the right notes. She was an adorable French schoolgirl who ended up living like a princess of sorts. My mother wasn't alarmed initially by our movie choice. She was a fan of Colette's stories and that had been her focus. But, as she listened to my jabbering, my mother ignited, and there were domestic fireworks at our dinner. It remains one of the only times I recall my parents exchanging critical words in public. Mother was emphatic. It wasn't a wholesome movie choice for a girl of nine: "She is only a child."

My father insisted I didn't know what the movie was about. Assuming the role of Grand and Frightening Inquisitor, Mother quizzed me. I did know what happened in the story. A pretty girl named Gigi, who lived in Paris, fell in love with a handsome man named Gaston. And he loved her too. It was a more accessible version of the Grace story. I didn't understand why their argument wouldn't die down. It was ruining my birthday celebration. I quietly sang my favorite lines from Gaston's song about Gigi.

"Oh Gigi! While you were trembling on the brink was I out yonder somewhere blinking at a star? Oh Gigi! Have I been standing up too close or back too far? When did your sparkle turn to fire? And your warmth become desire? Oh what miracle has made you the way you are?"

The lyrics provided Mother more ammunition: "Alida, do you know what a courtesan is?" A new word! *Courtesan*—I didn't know what it meant. But, it was French, and sounded romantic and glamorous. Mother defined the word in age-appropriate language. A courtesan was a woman attached to a man who would not marry her—a woman who existed solely for the happiness of a man—and lived her life for his something-or-another. What exact words were used—Pleasure? Needs? Desires? I doubt those words crossed her lips. I thought sex and love involved kissing; the rest was a mystery. The question, however, helped me piece together a confusing plotline. Gigi was holding out on Gaston until he proposed. I asked if the grandmother and aunt also were courtesans. My mother said that indeed they were. Gigi was being trained to be a courtesan just like them. I needed to think things over before I responded. Being a wife represented a life of compromise—duties and chores, housekeeping, cooking, the same routine day after day. Being a courtesan looked fantastic: better than becoming a princess.

Mother wouldn't let the issue rest. A courtesan's career ended as soon as she got older. I wasn't interested in that information. I was considering practical matters. A courtesan was a semi-permanent girlfriend, and Gigi wanted to be a wife, not a courtesan. My parents wanted me to applaud Gigi for doing the smart thing by refusing Gaston's initial offer and waiting for his marriage proposal. Were they trying to instill in me the notion that Gigi possessed power even in her situation? Gigi said *Non!*—until Gaston said *marry me*. *Gigi* remained one of my favorite movies for decades, but the time came when I could no longer justify its sexist, predatory overtones. Now the film lingers as a strong childhood memory about being chosen by a man.

But during the Chandelier dinner I had an entirely different attitude. Listening to my parents voice opinions about Gigi and her wise decision to be a wife, I had urgent questions that required answers. Would Gigi still get those beautiful dresses if she were *only* a wife? Would she still live in Paris? Would she still go to Maxim's and drink champagne with Gaston? If a Frenchwoman had options other than becoming a wife, I intended to weigh them carefully before rejecting a possible career as a courtesan. There were many mental miles I had to travel before exiting the land of Princess Grace. In a surprising way, a partial liberation arrived in time for my tenth birthday. The beginnings of my deliverance came in the shape of a wholly new kind of doll.

3
Barbie, My Liberator

The Barbie doll was born on March 9th, 1959. She was conceived in the best American tradition of capitalistic greed married to marketing brilliance. Her human mother was Ruth Handler, whose husband was Elliott Handler, a cofounder of the Mattel Toy Company. Handler's inspiration was a German doll, but she created a doll that was compatible with American popular culture and named her after their daughter.

My best friend Kathe and I received Barbies for our tenth birthdays, part of a first release of 300,000 dolls. Each Barbie came in standard issue—black high heels, zebra striped swimming suit, sleek pulled back ponytail, pierced earrings. She was dressed like a beauty pageant contestant in the swimsuit competition. The only difference in the dolls was hair color: brunette or blonde. Ours were brunettes. (Christie, the African-American Barbie doll, did not appear until 1968.)

I thought Barbie was glamorous. She didn't resemble any mothers we knew. She looked like a movie star. Though Barbie's overly large breast size didn't impress me, what did was that she was a *woman*-doll. I didn't jam a small water-filled bottle into Barbie's mouth and wait for the liquid to hit her bottom for the presumed thrill of changing a wet doll diaper. Kathe and I knew that the water coming out of the openings in the backsides of our baby-dolls were, anatomically, wrong. I assumed motherhood was a given, but I didn't see the use of participating in extended training sessions for the duration of my girlhood. I did notice that Barbie didn't have a vagina, but neither did the baby-dolls, or the fancy dress-up dolls.

A popular neighborhood game was *Playing House*. I had a notorious reputation as the girl who refused. I had made a secret pledge not to spend my life as a girl or woman who only played house. I wanted to be a different kind of adult woman. I didn't dream about replicating the lives of our mothers, because I didn't want to be sad and bored. Beyond that, I was confused and knew little of the world. I had vowed to do something else and go somewhere else—but what and where?

Barbie became my surrogate woman, a subversive undercover agent. I imagined her living an exciting life. I employed her to break with custom. Sometimes she was a doctor, sometimes an actress, a writer, or a fashion designer. Barbie traveled far away on her own or in the company of Kathe's Barbie. My Barbie worked as an *executive secretary* (I wasn't all that evolved). What mattered to me was that Barbie got up, got dressed, went to work, and had a full life outside the home.

Our parents couldn't invest in expensive Mattel-made costume changes so we made do with a couple each, which we shared. Kathe created their wardrobes from small scraps of fabric. We made up stories about where they were going and how they needed to dress. I chattered about what they were going to do while Kathe sketched designs and made outfits and the accessories for our dolls. Millions of mass-produced Barbie outfits later, I realize we were fortunate to be among the girls who needed to invent back-stories for Barbie.

As the 21st century progresses, Barbie is under increasing suspicion of criminal intent. Some girls and young women try to look like her, to the point of extreme surgical alterations. The Barbie doll empire is criticized for inculcating bad values and accused of contributing to the population of girls who suffer from eating disorders. But for two Lakewood girls at the end of the 1950s, she was something else: a non-maternal model of womanhood. There was no Skipper, or Midge, no fancy cars and dream houses. We were spared the mountains of manufactured Barbie-associated plastic junk. The Barbie of our moment was a solo act. On Kathe's bunk bed we invented their life situations. We didn't focus on how very thin she was. There was no discussion of anorexia in our childhood. We focused on her freedom of movement.

Princess Grace's aura dimmed with Barbie's arrival. Barbie was my liberator. She made me consider options. My scripts for Barbie did not match the "Ozzie and Harriet" surroundings, or the plots of other television sitcoms. The exceptions were those starring Ann Sothern, first in "Private Secretary" and then "The Ann Sothern Show" as a working woman. (But even those were primarily focused on Ann getting her man.) Barbie's pre-feminist appearance signaled a universe of other possibilities. She allowed us to dream about doing more than getting married and having children. With Barbie as surrogate, I now viewed myself an interesting girl/woman-in-training.

By the time Ken rolled out of Mattel's assembly lines in 1961, Kathe and I were almost too old to bother with dolls. It was a relief because I wasn't pleased with his intrusion. Kathe got her Ken immediately. After the initial run in stores, there were few Kens left, but then word went out that our local Sav-On drugstore had a new shipment. When my mother and I arrived, there was only one Ken left on the shelf. He had a nick out of his fuzzy felt blown-on hair, which was blond, not the color I preferred. He was forlorn and shopworn, and I took him, flaws and all. But I did not love him. I didn't think my Barbie did either. Ken's arrival was greeted with the consumer excitement that had been showered on Barbie. He was the doll-size symbol of the persisting female dream of being chosen, of not ending up in life without a man at your side.

But it was my Barbie who rescued me from thinking I had to wait in line for a place on the conveyor belt with only three endpoint destinations: Marriage. House. Family. A few years earlier I had written to Princess Grace, wishing her eternal happiness. With a girl's earnest heart I had believed that what happened to Grace Kelly was the greatest thing that could happen to an American woman. Barbie's appearance signaled a different message. Barbie was teaching me there were roles besides that of princess and bride. There were, for women as well as men, achievements, adventures, and experiences. I could seize new worlds and conquer stubborn stereotypes.

4
Daddy, Marilyn, and Dallas

Daddy.

My father was a validation of the cliché: tall, dark, and handsome. Women pursued him throughout his life. He appeared not to care or notice but he did appreciate being appreciated. He was flirtatious, but not seductive. He was charismatic and engaging. Without warning, his conversation would veer into a version of the gambler's riff. *Five will get you ten, ten will get you twenty, and twenty will get you killed. Guaranteed not to rip, ravel, tear, roll down at the ankles, or pull apart at the seams.* The routine was part gambler, part carnival barker—but he made it his own. People were drawn to him. Acquaintances assumed they knew all about him. In truth, he revealed little. His vocal register was soft and low, with a gentle though not distinctly Southern cadence. He was usually forgiving and was slow to anger. When he was upset he would snap his fingers—you could hear it a room away. If pushed beyond patience, his voice would become all but inaudible. I don't know if he worked to check his temper or whether it came naturally. His father was prone to volcanic outbursts, and my mother was herself a volcano. Observing my father, I tried to be like him.

He was six feet tall and well built. He dressed immaculately and had a weekly manicure. My mother claimed she would dress quickly to clear mirror space for him. His eyes were brown-black. His hair was just as dark, until it turned completely white. He always had a moustache. As he got older, he kept a full (and, of course, trimmed) beard. When he was younger, women insisted he looked like William Powell. When old, he looked like a Biblical prophet or an actor playing Moses. To me he was always a Southern Jewish man with a different way of speaking and acting. In a town where conformity was embraced and not questioned, he stood out. He was not a regular guy.

He was a Jew from a liberal family in the Deep South (Charleston, SC and Augusta, GA). Though he loved the South, he didn't deny its history. There was no revisionist version of the Civil War in our home, but neither did he give a free pass issued to northern slavers. He believed the South was capable of racial harmony and that it must abide by the laws of equality and justice. In that he was bitterly disappointed—but not always. Despite his love of his ancestral home, when an opportunity came he got us out of the South. He observed the cultural rules that existed for women and girls; he said that they were damaged by Southern standards for *appropriate* female behavior. He saw early on that it wasn't in my nature to be a *go along girl*. But I called him Daddy throughout my life, in keeping with Southern tradition.

In his core he hated bigotry. He was disgusted by Jim Crow laws and with the Klan. My parents supported civil rights, which put them at odds with most neighbors in Lakewood (and with much of the country). They stressed the importance of tolerance and appreciated what is now called diversity. Their opinions encouraged me to seek a wider world. One day my father sat me down to watch the news with him. Although the Court's 1954 decision in *Brown vs. Board of Education* held that separate was not equal, for nine students in 1957 it required military protection and President Eisenhower's intervention in Little Rock, Arkansas. For me it was an early jolt of reality.

My father told me about hate crimes he had witnessed in the South—particularly the lynchings he'd witnessed in his childhood, often on the way to school. The Klan torched his father's lighting and electrical store, and they threatened all the Jewish merchants. My paternal grandfather, a short, muscular man, had his own brand of fearlessness. During Klan parades he escorted my father to the front of the crowd. In an audible voice my grandfather announced the name of each Klansman as they walked past them. They were all local men—some were town officials—my grandfather insisted he recognized them by the shoes they wore.

Daddy was regularly mistaken for a professor or a psychiatrist. He acted bemused when people refused to believe he was not. He learned to stop the questions by stating in a serious tone and with a poker face: *I am a riverboat gambler by training and trade.* I never asked him what it felt like to be mistaken for a man of distinction and achievement, when he chose to compromise to support family. While he had regret for what might have been, he refused to let it spoil the present. His well-rehearsed phrases perhaps helped move him through a long life. He taught me the basics about negotiating life with illness.

He had limited patience for consistently unhappy people, especially whiners. At times he seemed to retreat to a private mindscape. I assume he went to the past, which was populated with memories of relatives, family peach orchards, and steamy summers spent on screened porches sipping sweet tea. He would become quiet, even silent, but strangely, not remote. He could take happiness from the smallest moments. He would describe a particular sunset or a field of flowers in minute detail, down to the gradations of color and tones within the colors.

Not an overtly religious man, he was impatient with most rituals. Life was his ritual. Mother spent most of her life seeking a spiritual path, and this put him to the test. She would insist the two of us join her in a variety of theological quests she was pursuing. Most of the time we went along reluctantly—pretending it interested us. But often my repressed hostility would break through my intention of being a good daughter. Her spiritual adventures were unsuccessful attempts to muffle her grief over the death of her son Terry. My father and I understood that quietly accompanying Mother on a variety of sacred explorations made family interactions easier.

My paternal grandmother's ancestors had sailed into Charleston harbor before the American Revolution. Née Rosina Levy, my grandmother knew who she was and where she came from—an attitude that informed my father's earliest sense of self. Both grandparents were from Charleston, but moved between Augusta and Charleston, Augusta being the family's primary home. But, during the 1920s they resettled in Miami Beach. My grandfather, Alfred Lewis Brill, Sr., saw an opportunity during the city's roaring land and real estate boom. Harry Sr., my grandfather's younger brother, had established himself in Miami Beach and made plenty of money in real estate. He convinced his three older brothers, Abe, Ike (Isaac), and Alfred, to join him. My grandmother didn't think Miami Beach was genuinely Southern. She saw the city fairly accurately for what it would soon turn out to be—a sandy mirage. Gender rules firmly in place, she saw no other option but to go along with her husband's plan and leave her beloved Augusta.

Miami's great boom was over before it had begun, but not before the Brills had spent excessive sums of money on lifestyles that required constant financial refueling. All their earnings were based in real estate, and with its demise everything was lost. They were faced with the results of total financial ruin and the family's expected trajectory changed quickly and irreversibly. Wives and husbands suffered serious depression. Harry's wife, Rhea, a favorite family member, committed suicide. She turned on the gas and put her head into the oven. When her two young children returned from school they discovered her body. Her death, and the details of her story, haunted all of us for decades. Not long after, my grandfather developed serious cardiac disease, and my father had to abandon his dream of art school. He hit the road at the age of seventeen—going North to earn money for the family in Miami.

First he was a traveling salesman, working on commission for a company that supplied the popular paper *punch game*s of the era to drugstores. Eventually he got on-the-job training as a cook and ran a modest diner near Times Square. Finally, a friend's family in Hempstead, Long Island took him under their wing. There he learned the essentials of the restaurant business and spent the rest of his working life in the food and beverage industry. He owned or held partnership shares (silent and open) in bars, nightclubs, restaurants, and coffee shops—managed large and small establishments, and frequently worked for wages.

Daddy turned this line of work into a stage-worthy performance. He wore white-on-white French cuff shirts. He had suits expertly tailored—though they were "off the rack." The wardrobe served him well and it made it harder for those who looked down at what he did to be disrespectful. My father was as resolute in his commitment to live each day as it came, as my mother was devoted to her practice of daily grief. They were connected by a love that lasted almost seven decades. Their relationship thrived, despite the intrusion of my birth.

I was somewhat the spoiler of my mother's great love affair. My illness created dread; it fed the fear that she might have to bury another child. Still, she engaged as a mother with considerable enthusiasm, choosing what played to her strengths and what was consistent with her values. Mother schooled me in poetry, literature and the significance of being a person of use in the world. She taught me that jealousy was a green-eyed monster and to keep it away from my heart and mind. She was protective of my health, and encouraged what she perceived were my talents. If I was treated unfairly, she was fiercely loyal and outspoken.

Sadly for both of us, Mother was incapable of keeping her anger in check. Grief, guilt, and resentment often dominated her behavior. She had unexplained outbursts—frequently followed by spankings—for a period of time these were *de rigueur* at night, when my father was out working. But I never told on her and I will not offer possible reasons. The fact is I did not expose her. My mother gave me access to the world of words, a belief in books and ideas, an understanding of the enormous suffering caused by poverty and prejudice. Her personal sorrows and their accompanying demons taught me that love could be as imperfect as it is unconditional.

My father taught me an early feminist lesson. Mothering is not gender-specific. He was Mommy-Daddy. He bought the groceries and cooked, took me shopping for school clothes. To improve my math scores, he taught me to play blackjack. He also took me to the racetrack, where he explained the intricacies of handicapping—a further futile attempt to make numbers more agreeable to me. He explained the finer points of shooting craps or as he called it, *rolling the dice*. In our town this style of parenting was hardly considered part of a wholesome upbringing. But I loved it.

My mother's roots included suffragists. Her mother had been strongly pro-suffrage. To the ridicule of the male members of her family, my mother and grandmother walked in Votes For Women marches. My parents were proud to stand up and speak out for women's rights, but came to this belief from different roads. My father was sharply influenced by two women he loved deeply—his mother and his wife. Both had been incapacitated by their past experiences. Grandmother Rosina died on her wedding anniversary, ten years after the death of her husband, Alfred Sr. During that long decade, she had refused to let go of anything—his death, the loss of money, property, status, sense of place. Emotionally and physically hobbled by illness and depression, she settled into despair. Her life became small, dark, and impoverished. She lived in rented rooms with her daughter, Rosine, and another son, Harold. Rosine gave up her personal life, sacrificing time and intimate attachments to her mother's needs and demands. The satisfaction from a career with the Southern Pacific Railroad was blunted by worry about her mother and anxiety over her severely depressed younger brother.

Through it all, Grandmother Rosina defined herself as a matriarch of an important Southern Jewish family. The family tree testifies to the veracity of her lineage, but it does not justify what she did to her three children. My father worked to provide money enough for everyone. My grandmother lived in a dream of restored grandeur, until she gave up totally. In my earliest years, I spent a great deal of time with her. I recall her seated in an enormous chair that looked like a throne. I was too young to understand that the chair was one of a few things of worth that escaped the pawnshops or bill collectors. It was out of scale for the modest rental apartment. Our favorite game together was *Jackstones* (her name for Jacks); she played to win. There came a time when she could not leave that chair easily, because part of her leg was gone, a fact hidden from me. She did not choose to move when I visited. I didn't know until much after her death that she wore dark glasses inside because she was going blind; the light hurt her eyes.

Grandmother Rosina declined most invitations. She became increasingly isolated and eventually did not leave her rooms. Harold, who was by then too depressed to look for or find work, attended to his mother with slavish devotion. Beginning in his adolescence, he was hospitalized several times for intractable depression. This chapter of family history remained a secret. What did he experience during those institutionalizations in a time of primitive treatments for severe depression? Rosina died from the complications of untreated heart disease and diabetes which might have been controlled had she been willing to take medication or follow the advice of her doctors. She stopped going to doctors, gave up any practice of Judaism, and turned with zeal to the Christian Science Church. Rosine and Harold didn't approve, but were afraid of their mother and didn't try to stop her. My father was not afraid, and at one point assumed she had stopped it. But he was outfoxed by his siblings, who simply instructed the Christian Science readers not to come when he was expected. She was in agony before she went into a coma.

She died at about sixty. Her final vanity trumped consideration for others. As ill as she was (by then her leg had been amputated above the knee), she managed to burn all record of her existence: birth certificate, marriage license, insurance policies, and the birth certificates of her children, anything that showed her age was condemned to her private inferno. She burned all her photographs, except a professional one taken upon her engagement. There she stands, elegant, stately tall at six feet, young, beautiful, privileged, dressed as a Southern woman of means—the only way she wanted to be remembered.

While Mother's grief for Terry often preoccupied her and eclipsed many otherwise happy experiences, it never took precedent over her love for my father. Terry was not his child. My father knew Terry for a short time before he had gone to war. Terry died in 1943 when Daddy was overseas. My father loved him, but the grief was not equally shared. Terry was the child from my mother's first marriage, which was made in haste and without due diligence. Her former husband turned out to have had *another* family in a neighboring state. He'd said he was a physician, but was only a hospital orderly. My mother had married a bigamist and a liar. It seems impossible that he managed to disguise all of this. But she was young and in love. His polygamy was discovered by two of her brothers, Roy and Wally, who followed their instincts until their suspicions were confirmed. One day they appeared at her home and reported their discovery with convincing evidence. They moved their sister and her baby son back to the family home where their parents still lived. She filed for divorce, asking for nothing. Mother never forgave herself for the marriage, nor did she overcome a deep sense of humiliation. She rarely spoke of the marriage, but when she did, she called herself a *moron*, not a victim.

It was from that Detroit house, built by her carpenter father, that she agreed to accompany her mother on a winter holiday to Miami. Miami Beach for that grandmother was a magical place. She had lived a life of hardship always on the brink of poverty. She had many children and a marriage fraught with disputes, then a divorce followed by reconciliation. One of her sons had made a beneficial move to Miami; she visited each winter. Mother was a single working mom and Terry was a young child. Grandmother Martha had been working on a strategy for some time, if only she could persuade my mother and Terry to join her. Grandmother was sure my father was the right match for her daughter and small grandson. She had gotten to know him through her many winter visits because she stayed in the hotel where he had a restaurant concession.

According to family lore, their first encounter unfolded this way: My mother, Terry, her brother, sister-in-law and her mother were having lunch in my father's restaurant. He took one look at my mother and fell in love. He was struck by her lack of pretense, her Michigan accent, and her freckled face free of make-up. She had just finished a round of golf when they were introduced, and was dressed for sports, not romantic conquests. My mother was quite pretty, but my father saw her as the antithesis of flashy or glamorous. In the fairly fancy restaurant, she ordered a melted cheese sandwich. He was amused and teased her. And he fell for her. It took her longer. For another week she wasn't sure he was right. Was this story true? It became fact because it was the only one ever told and the details never varied.

Seven decades later that chemistry was still there. They didn't hold themselves up as a model couple. My father never used the vernacular of the women's movement. He didn't use the word *patriarchy* but instead described it more directly. His thoughts about women's lives were political but not cloaked in obvious ideology: *When men always get their way, women suffer.* It didn't occur to me that he viewed the world differently from other fathers. When I did come to realize this, the assumption I made was that he was unusual because he had a daughter and not a son. Eventually I understood that his strong convictions about women's roles grew from his witnessing his mother, wife, sister, aunts, and cousins suffering from a system that favored men.

My father was not the beneficiary of male advantage. He worked hard, but he believed that most women had tougher lives that demanded more sacrifice from them than from men. His childhood had held promise of considerable entitlement and some privilege. And before he was a man, he had to accept that his life would be different. He spoke often about the advantage of being a woman who was independent—economically and emotionally. My romantic fixations perplexed him. When I moped about waiting for a guy to ask me to a dance or was distraught because I wasn't asked to my senior prom, he was annoyed. *Boys are like streetcars, Alida. You might miss one, two or three—but there's always another one coming up the tracks.* My mother, who wholeheartedly agreed with this position, would often remind me of my father's words.

For me Grandmother Rosina's life was a warning sign. I see her now as the victim of an era of entrenched male dominance and inadequate medical care. She had no skills, no ability to earn a living, even if she had wished it. Rosina was raised to be a lady, an adornment, and a social asset. My father didn't blame her for the emotional paralysis that overtook her or her lifetime of dependency. He didn't suggest she was spoiled, but felt that she suffered greatly. My father did not disparage or criticize his mother, nor did he chastise his wife for her inability to put the dead to rest; he loved my mother through it all. For all the wrong reasons, as a child I thought they were a romantic couple. She was five years older. At first glance they appeared to have little in common, coming from such different places and experiences. They were great dancers. Mine was a child's list, someone who had little knowledge of relationships. When they were gone, dying within three months of each another, I came to a greater understanding. Luck had brought them together, but the secret was in their capacity to nurture what fate had given them. They understood each other and did not press each other to change. My father said often about marriage: *Take a person or leave a person, but don't try to fine-tune them.*

* * *

Being in the booze business meant late hours for my father. Sometimes we joked about what I should say he did—one week it was described as the food and beverage industry, another week as the cocktail lounge and entertainment business. But the truest description was simple: *It was the booze business.* Bars, nightclubs, and the people who drank there kept me fed and clothed. I knew kids from religious families who thought my father's work was sinful. I asked him what I should tell the ones who said that. *Tell them your father plays a piano in a house of prostitution.* I looked up the word in the dictionary and decided against mentioning this to my mother. Much later I learned this was a standard joke among bartenders, nightclub owners, bar owners, and barkeeps in general.

Books were my best friends from the time I was very young. I was an only child, unwell, frightened, and lonely, and reading was my consolation. I learned from my mother, who was hardly ever without a book in hand. One Halloween I went to the afterschool party as a bookworm while other girls dressed up as princesses. Mine was a handcrafted costume painstakingly created by my mother, for whom sewing did not come naturally. I didn't win the prize for best costume—that went to one of the princesses.

Mostly I read in the dark, staying awake long into the night reading books under the covers with a flashlight slyly borrowed from a tool shelf in the garage. Though I was motivated by a passion for books, primarily I read to ward off fear. I would read until I heard my father's key in the front door. It would be about 3 or 4 a.m. I waited for the sound of his footsteps coming down the hall. Then I listened for the sound as he turned into their bedroom. When that door closed, the flashlight, the books and I could go to sleep. If my mother woke, I could make out the few words they exchanged. My goal wasn't to eavesdrop; it was to hear my father's voice. He made me feel safe in a life that felt dangerous due to all the opinions the various doctors had about what was wrong with me.

The places where he worked or the ones he owned weren't especially targets for burglaries or hold-ups. But he did carry fairly large sums of cash each night, which courted danger. Throughout some years of my childhood, he was working at a popular destination for the Long Beach vice squad. Off-duty police officers came to relax, listen to live music, and trade war stories. They also came to hang out with my charismatic father. After closing time, they usually escorted him to his car, and if it was deemed prudent, one of their cars followed him home. I knew they were armed policemen, and though it was a less stressful time, than now, it was still the middle of the night. I never confessed my fears to him.

Marilyn.

1962 did not hold the same magical promise of the previous year. I didn't look forward to turning thirteen. I was in the grip of doctors and drugs. My mother was distraught and my father thought most doctors quacks. Neither believed the medical profession was helping me, and I was certain they were not. Still the three of us did not dare discontinue the prescribed treatments. Each morning I obediently swallowed pills. The internists argued with the rheumatologists and the rheumatologists argued among themselves. There were just too many cooks in the kitchen of my illness. While my mother's desperation was understandable, the constant doctor-shopping was not an effective route to a remedy. My father voiced concern over his growing sense of powerlessness, but as he had nothing better to offer, we proceeded with my mother's quests for medical answers.

Our primary doctor confidently continued to pronounce that it was *all in my head*. It hardly helped matters that his name was Richard Nixon and my parents were staunch Democrats. One day I announced that I intended to fire Richard Nixon, M.D. Both my parents agreed with my decision; it was all fairly bloodless. My mother called for my records to be transferred to another doctor. In my fantasy life, however, I continued to believe I had taken this action on my own. However, I continued to have a dialogue *in my head* with Dr. Nixon. I would show him I wasn't crazy. The doctors who stepped into fill his absence weren't any better.

By this time Grace Kelly had faded from the screen and my thoughts. I still watched her movies on television, but she was no longer the stuff of my dreams. On the cover of *Time*, she now looked like somebody's mother, not a princess or a movie star. Hitchcock wanted her to star in *Marnie*, but she turned it down because of negative feelings in Monaco about the script, in which she would play a kleptomaniac.

Hollywood was just a short drive up the freeway, and it influenced our ideas of beauty and glamour. Marilyn Monroe was both, and also the subject of gossip and judgments. My parents were fans of Marilyn without apology or explanation. *Some Like It Hot* topped their list. I liked Marilyn too, undoubtedly because they did.

Grace Kelly was married to a real prince. The year after her wedding, in 1957, Marilyn Monroe made *The Prince and the Showgirl* opposite the reigning king of actors, Laurence Olivier.

Just about everything went wrong for Marilyn during the making of that film, except what was captured of her on film. Watching it now saddens me. I know too much about her life, including her depressions, drug addictions, and the dismal state of her marriage to Arthur Miller. Watching it as a girl, I thought Marilyn was adorably funny. I wanted Marilyn to win the prize of a prince, if only in the movies.

On August 5th, 1962, news of Marilyn's death ripped through the Los Angeles basin like an earthquake. There was the initial shock, and then aftershocks. Her death was an international event, but in Southern California it was personal. Marilyn belonged to us. The news said she had committed suicide by barbiturate overdose—sleeping pills. The words "Marilyn" and "sleeping pills" were often used in the same sentence. When I learned that she had been under the care of doctors, I was outraged. I knew little about her personal life other than her marriage to Joe DiMaggio, which worked for me because I loved baseball. The tabloid press insisted he was the last person she talked to that night. It seemed he wanted to be remembered as her one true love, the keeper of the flame. He arranged for a fresh rose to be placed at her crypt each day.

Eventually I learned enough about DiMaggio to see that public gesture primarily as a dramatic flourish, though his grief was undoubtedly real. He was given to violent outbursts and as incapable of loving Marilyn as all the others had been, despite his fame and status as an American icon. Arthur Miller's name didn't mean much to me except that he and Marilyn stood against the Black List. Miller refused to "name names" to HUAAC. Marilyn married him despite the fact she was threatened with losing work. My parents thought Monroe and Miller were heroic. I was more fascinated with Marilyn's conversion to Judaism and with stories of Miller's mother teaching her to cook traditional Jewish recipes. But it was the indelible television image of Marilyn singing Happy Birthday to President Kennedy that got my attention: breathy, sexy, and inappropriate for the president of the United States even from a child's perspective. Beyond that I was clueless.

The day of her death was given over to listening to the radio and watching the television. Everywhere there was talk, talk, talk. Everyone needed to speak about Marilyn. *Poor Marilyn. Pathetic Marilyn.* The depths of her sorrow that she endured from childhood through the marriages were yet to be uncovered. By the time I was an adult feminist, I viewed Marilyn through the prism of child abuse, male dominance, and the need to be loved. For years I could not attend an Arthur Miller play. By the time *Fragments* was published, I thought nothing could surprise me about what Miller did to or felt about her, but I was wrong.

Reading the excerpts from her private journals about how she wanted to be and be seen as a serious person—seeing her handwriting, the photos of the books she owned and read radicalized me about Marilyn again. She wanted to be taken seriously not only as an actress but also as a thoughtful human being. She had believed that marrying Miller was a guarantee to a personal intellectual mentor. But he had far different ideas. In 1972 Gloria Steinem wrote of that other Marilyn in her essay, "Marilyn, The Woman Who Died Too Soon" in the first year of Ms. Magazine. It was the cover story that August, ten years after her death.

Now that women are changing their vision of themselves, they have begun to reevaluate the life of Marilyn Monroe. Might the new confidence in women's autonomy, without depending totally on the approval and validation of men, have helped a thirty-six-year-old woman of talent, the woman Marilyn Monroe was when she died, to stand on her own and resist the ridicule? To stop depending on sexual attractiveness for proof that she was alive and important, and therefore to face aging with confidence? To question the Freudian analysts whom she turned to in her distress? Gloria Steinem, August 1972, *Ms. Magazine*

At thirteen and a half, I believed Marilyn's death was a tragedy. I cried all day. There were pill bottles stacked in the shelves of the open cabinet in our kitchen, and my mother now scurried to hide them in my parents' bedroom. I had been in charge of my own prescriptions for a year. My father insisted I was not going to take pills to kill myself. Anyway, the ones I took for my disease wouldn't kill me. They were both right. Marilyn's death had put thoughts in my mind. I might choose to kill myself someday. I found private power in the knowledge there was an immediate exit if suffering got too much—-if one had enough of the correct pills. Like my father, I assumed my prescriptions wouldn't do the job.

Late in the day my father suggested an outing. He and I got in the car and drove to the back of the Lakewood Shopping Mall, where there was an Orange Julius. We had a drink and a hot dog, one of our standard treats. He talked about Marilyn. What had happened, I asked.

We might never know. Perhaps she did it to herself, or it was an accident and maybe someone did it to her. She had a lousy life. Men horsed around with her. Don't ever let men horse around with you.

We left the Orange Julius and returned to our car. The seats were baking hot from the summer sun and the car had no air conditioning. I was wearing shorts. The scorching leatherette burned my bare legs and I screamed. *OK! It will cool down, Sarah Heartburn. Give it a minute.*

As we were pulling out of the parking lot, I noticed a pair of women's high-heel shoes sitting on the roof of the car in front of us. They were red and very high, stiletto style. We tried to get the attention of the driver, a man, but failed. The shoes didn't move and I thought they were glued to the roof. Finally one shoe fell on its side, but not off the car.

What do you think will happen to those shoes? I asked my father.

They won't stop riding on top of that car roof until they get to Marilyn.

And they will. That guy is taking them up to her now. She needs them to go dancing. Her troubles are over.

We laughed and I came home without tears.

My mother was astonished at the change in my mood. She asked where we had been.

Only to the Julius.

What happened there?

We saw a man driving a car that had red high-heel shoes sitting on its roof. He's taking them to Marilyn.

Dallas.

Ninth grade at Herbert Hoover Junior High School began with a minor triumph. I was assigned to be features editor for the school newspaper, *The Scotty Scroll*, a name that complemented our Hoover Highlanders school theme. The Advanced Journalism class produced the paper. I had never taken a journalism class before, but I convinced the teacher to admit me. Her name was Carolyn Muck and she became my first teacher-mentor. I would have taken journalism from her all day. She told me that she believed I might do something that mattered with words. I would visit her classroom at the end of each day. She asked me what I hoped to do as an adult woman. I told her about my love of acting and theatre and weekend drama workshops downtown.

More than anything else, I wanted to be on the stage. She wanted me to consider being a playwright, not an actress. When I told her my high school class schedule would not include journalism, but drama instead, she was sad. She said that writing left a person unless they kept it going. I would lose the possibility of being a writer she said. It would be lost in activities and buried by pursuits that were, frankly, more engaging and not solitary. She warned me it would be a mistake. I didn't listen and went into acting and theatre with my whole being. But writing would come back to claim me, and then it wouldn't let go. I never found her to tell her she had started my life as a writer. If I had I would have edited her remarks. Writing is an even lonelier pursuit than she suggested.

Defining moment has become a tired and over-used phrase. But they happen in history and in our lives. November 22, 1963 was such a moment for Americans and much of the world.

I was sitting in homeroom mid-afternoon. Homeroom was in one of the bungalow classrooms at the back of Hoover's property. Bungalows were supposedly temporary schoolrooms, repurposed from World War II. A girl named Carole announced she heard President Kennedy had been shot in Dallas. Carole was popular and in a junior high school cliquish sort of way socially important: she had long blonde hair styled in a spiral ponytail and wore expensive dresses from a boutique called Judy's. Miss Cunningham, the homeroom teacher as well as my English teacher, called Carole out for spreading frightening and untrue gossip. But Carole was confident, assured, in charge, and beautiful. Nobody intimidated her, not even Miss Cunningham.

A few moments after Miss Cunningham's lecture, the P.A. system went on and we were told to march, in assembly formation, to the front of the auditorium. Vice Principal Whelan, a redheaded Irishman, came out to the front steps. He spoke directly, in short and clear sentences, without bracing us: *Our President John Fitzgerald Kennedy was assassinated in Dallas, Texas.* His face was streaked with tears, his eyes swollen. He looked the way I felt. I wanted to hug him and tell him that somehow we would all be fine, but I didn't think that was true. I was sure we would never be fine again. There were screams and crying. Tough boys looked down at their shoes. School was dismissed and we were told to go home immediately.

Two thoughts preoccupied me as I walked the few blocks home. Foremost was my assumption that the country was now broken, finished. If a president could be killed in his own motorcade, then we were doomed. It was the end of the world.

My other fear was that my parents would not know yet, that I would have to be the messenger. I found them in the backyard, standing, not speaking, holding hands, and weeping. We stood together for a time and my father held us close. Then he said, "They slaughtered our beautiful president." As a war veteran my father knew what it meant to be slaughtered; he had seen the ravages of battle.

It seemed unthinkable that one person could do this, so the pronoun "they" felt appropriate. It must be a plot, a foreign plan to destroy our country. My parents, who were not politically paranoid, became so that afternoon. They were not alone. What would happen next?

My world became grey, subdued, pointless. What could matter now? How could I go on in school, how could any of us go forward now with games, with frivolity? Everything around us would fall apart and I couldn't imagine it would ever be fixed. In the next days, another murder—this time of the assassin.

The day we returned to school after the hiatus, I walked home with a girl I had known for a long time. She and her family were devout fundamentalist Christians. Their lives revolved around their church and its activities and her parents were leaders in the congregation. She wanted to know why I was so sad. *President Kennedy was killed*, I said. She said, yes, but so what? With luck, Republicans would be elected in the next term, her father had told her. I peppered her with questions and with accusations. Hadn't she seen the funeral, the First Lady, the children, the nation in grief? She said they weren't allowed to watch the television coverage because what had happened was God's will. JFK had been an evil force in our country. He had been a Roman Catholic and therefore not a Christian.

Mrs. Muck assigned me to write the feature about the President's murder. I wanted to expose my former friend but I knew it wouldn't be published. I also was fairly certain she wasn't the only classmate who did not see JFK's assassination as the tragedy my parents and I did. I became serious about American history and wanted to know more about politics and how our government worked. I thought action was required, not mere words. I had heard enough words. I had read enough, and seen too many photographs of what became known as JFK's Camelot.

It was a time when I understood at last there were no fairy tales and few happy endings. What became clear was that everything is unknowable and unpredictable: the future, my future, everything in our country and in the world. Being a thirteen-year-old girl felt silly. I wanted to become an adult as quickly as possible.

5
The BOOK

Your Aunt Madeleine will tell you if you have a clean kitchen you will be a happy woman. It's not true.

The housekeeping problem on Arbor Road had overtaken us. Each day Mother grew more resistant to the idea that housework was worth anybody's time. At moments of extreme domestic disarray, Aunt Madeleine would arrive and frenetically have at the place with her cleaning supplies. When Madeleine put up the ironing board and whipped out her professional steam iron, my mother would retreat to the bedroom and her books of poetry. For several days after my aunt's visits, our home glistened. Shiny surfaces emerged, freshly cleared of clutter. I enjoyed the sense of found space and tidiness while it lasted. Mother hated housework so intensely she wasn't humiliated when her sister-in-law came to the rescue. Late in the game I learned that my father would ask Madeleine for help.

My aunt found household chores satisfying in ways my mother never could. A clean house and kitchen did seem to lift her spirits. She didn't talk about the burdens of cleaning house or say it erased her identity—phrases Mother used. My aunt would say: *Ida, you'll feel better if you tackle the house and get your nose out of the books.* For Madeleine there were no shortcuts to a clean and tidy house. Even as the last morsel of her delicious food was still warm in my mouth, my aunt was clearing the table and beginning the evening dishwashing ritual (no electric dishwasher). She mopped the floor each night—never an excuse—and waxed it every Saturday. Given how neat she was, it wasn't necessary but that's what she did. Once a month she stripped the wax from the floor, an involved and smelly procedure. I assumed there existed a reasonable territory of housework somewhere between my mother and my aunt, but I couldn't discover its location.

I was just shy of fourteen when Betty Friedan's *The Feminine Mystique* was published. It was not my book initially; it was my mother's. Holding it aloft in his hands my father pronounced: *If it isn't in The BOOK, I don't have to worry, but if it is, I am in trouble.* *The Feminine Mystique* swept through the country, a rallying cry for women. It brought change to my mother. Friedan's book gave her a new sense of self. She was no longer a failed housewife but a woman, like so many others, shoved into a slot designed by a male culture she wasn't in charge of and in which she had lost her way. Mother quoted Friedan often. At the end of each memorized passage, she would add: *That's me. That's just the way I feel.* All over America women were saying similar things. For Mother *The Feminine Mystique* became a private dialogue with the author. It fed and sustained her. She talked about the book as though Betty Friedan had written her a long, personal letter.

Mother had worked until she unexpectedly became pregnant with me. Her closest friends were women who worked. She had always been employed while my brother was alive, and continued to work after his death; perhaps this need to stay busy may have have prevented her from committing suicide. Mother talked often about her jobs, bosses, and co-workers. She had been a bookkeeper, an executive secretary, a supervisor, and an office manager. Her favorite job was in Detroit as personal secretary (now called executive assistant) to the president of a savings and loan company. Mother kept up a correspondence with his widow until they were both old. She held and kept a good job throughout the Depression. She was competent, personable, organized, efficient, enterprising, intelligent, and of good spirits. All qualities she felt she had lost living inside a planned garden town in a ready-made dream home. When women in the neighborhood boasted they didn't have to work, Mother was silent. Until Friedan's book became my mother's bible, she was too insecure to express her own feelings about women and work.

Change was first apparent in my mother in her choice of clothing. Mostly she used to wear simple housedresses, flat shoes—nothing appropriate for an office setting. But after her conversion to modern feminism, the wardrobe expanded: a tailored skirt, a pair of medium heels and a jacket instead of a sweater. It was the first sign that she saw herself as more than a suburban mother and wife. But she remained frustrated and bored. Mother went to the Helms truck each day, but it was more to talk to Virg than to buy baked goods, although she always purchased something. One morning he had big news. A good friend of his was looking for a full-time employee. Handing Mother the phone number, he said his friend was waiting for a call. Mother walked into the house and called. Then she put on her pencil-straight tweed skirt, her medium high heels, her tailored blouse and jacket, a strand of pearls, a pair of earrings and drove the few blocks to the woman's office. Her name was Della and she was about my mother's age (mid 50's) and, had never married. She had been the right hand man (as she called herself) to Ben Weingart, one of Lakewood's developers. He had seen a need for more modest housing and the opportunity to make a great deal of money.

He had built a large rental community on empty land and called it Lakewood Manor Apartments. In a town that liked to claim it only had one class, the apartments represented a *lower class* of the middle class. These were people who could not afford to buy a home but could still live in Lakewood. The tenants were younger families, newlyweds, newly divorced, single people and those in transition. It was a lively and family-oriented community. The apartments were quite spacious but there were no backyards, no pride of ownership that was necessary to claim any status in Lakewood. Weingart had made Della the manager. There was a small staff that showed the apartments and checked references.

She was looking for someone to assist her, take over when she was away. Della admitted she was lonely in the job, and that she wanted a colleague she could consider a peer. My mother became Della's right hand *man*. (The job lasted for years until my mother took a better position on the next street in an adults-only complex owned by a smaller real estate developer.) Della and my mother respected each other but feminist principles separated them. Della claimed women didn't need Friedan or a woman's movement to do what they wanted with their time and lives. Della was unaware of the reality of her own circumstances or chose not to see. She was never promoted within Weingart's empire to a position of power and a salary that was commensurate with her skills. She felt powerful and important only because the big boss said she was. My mother knew better and Della was too smart not to have known better.

Betty Friedan had brewed a cup of feminist tea just the right strength for my mother's tastes. Friedan's was an intellectual women's liberation, and its fundamental arguments were based on the premise that suburban life was an entrapment for women. Mother was captivated by Friedan's inclusion of men in the book, that they too were suffering under the status quo. *The Feminine Mystique* made the case for reform *within* the system; it was not a manifesto for dismantling the country. Although in some ways that's just what it was as Friedan was arguing for a complete rethinking of domestic relationships and household power. She wasn't angry with men. She spoke of their high rate of heart disease from overwork and bad lifestyle choices. Mother scolded detractors who said that Friedan hated men and that she devalued motherhood. Mother would be quick to inform them that Friedan had dedicated her book to *all the new women and the new men.* It was my mother's ideal feminist conversation. In my mother's view the written word trumped everything else. Mother had read the book and found the woman who proved her right. She would remind everyone that a major social movement began with one woman who wrote a book. My mother especially identified with Friedan as another miserable housewife with a fine mind, though one who had been privileged to receive a good education.

She fantasized they might have been friends under other circumstances. Friedan could have been channeling my mother when she wrote: *A baked potato is not as big as the world, and vacuuming the living room floor — with or without makeup — is not work that takes enough thought or energy to challenge any woman's full capacity.* Mother did not interpret *The Feminine Mystique* as the revolutionary tract that others did. Some neighborhood women thought Friedan was insulting them and that she was as anti-woman as she was anti-man. When Friedan was treated unfairly or harshly by women in conversation or on television or in print, my mother took it as a personal attack. Mother was impressed by the scope of the book, by the range of Friedan's mind, by her keen discussion of economics and politics and by her critical analysis of Freud.

In no time Mother's copy of *FM* was underlined and frayed, and this at the hands of a woman who kept the dust jackets of her books pristine after years of rereading them. No point Friedan made was lost on my mother. What do housewives do with their time when they aren't cleaning and cooking? They buy things for the house, of course. Friedan wrote: *Why is it never said that the really crucial function, the really important role that women serve as housewives is to buy more things for the house?* My mother was not a consumer; she shopped only under coercion. Betty Friedan hit all of my mother's issues and it was if they were having a conversation at the kitchen table (A neighbor once asked my mother how and where she had met Friedan).

While Betty Friedan quickly became a household name across the country, for me she became a member of the family, an invisible but very present guest at the table. I thought Feminism and Friedan were synonymous. With Friedan as my mother's new literary companion, I started to listen more closely, and heard things that appealed to me as well. One of my mother's favorite phrases struck a chord with me even then. Now it's become relevant again for younger women who wrestle with guilt as they attempt to solve the balancing act between career and motherhood. *We can no longer ignore that voice within women that says: I want something more than my husband and my children and my home.*

When I was grown and had become a different kind of feminist than my mother, she would defend *The Feminine Mystique* (by then only one of many feminist books), demanding that I praise it as the sole text needed, or at least the primary one. *Change, not Destruction* was my mother's mantra, which was an implied criticism of my brand of feminism. Undeterred, I shot right back at her: *Revolution, not Reform.* The women's movement was dividing between radical versus reform. Our discussions weren't much different from those being held inside the women's leadership. What was unique was that my Lakewood mother was a self-identified feminist. The majority of the mothers I knew were not.

The legacy of suffrage was inside my mother's core. As a girl she had carried a *Votes for Women* banner in one hand while holding her mother's hand with the other. Returning to home on Lillibridge Avenue in Detroit, her father and all seven brothers howled at the stupidity of thinking women would ever vote. My mother always remembered that one of her brothers tried to grab her banner but she refused to let go of it. Mother was twelve when the 19th Amendment passed. I think the fight for suffrage gave her a deep faith in the power of working within the system. Mother would later characterize *The Feminine Mystique* as an elaboration or an extension of the suffrage movement. *Suffrage at home* was Mother's phrase.

My father was not a *salary man*. The end of each week produced a different pay packet, and money was often short. His quiet elegance belied the reality of our circumstances. Although his early years in Georgia and then briefly in Miami were spent in considerable comfort, the loss of that lifestyle kept him from assuming life would ever again be free of financial worry.

Many things contributed to my mother's unhappiness, but a lack of money did not overwhelm her. My parents shared an understanding that money was a tool, not the way to happiness. Money needed to be watched, saved, and guarded. They felt fortunate to have a home, and there was no expectation of luxury or excess. There was always the awareness of the War and what it had done to the many millions in Europe and to the families in America.

Before the publication of Friedan's book, my father had taken a second job. Business was bad. I wondered how he could work virtually all night and all day, but that is what he did for two years. Madeleine's husband Uncle Bud held a skilled supervisory position at the North American Aircraft factory. He was a respected employee because of his wartime service building bombers, and that enabled him to get my father a job. My father disliked working in the factory but did it without complaint. After closing the nightclub and with only a few hours of sleep, he would get up and work the day shift. At that time it was against company policy to have an outside job; discovery would lead to instant termination. My uncle understood my father couldn't give up his *real* line of work. Nonetheless, he got my father the job. Daddy wore dark trousers to the factory and a casual work shirt. He parked the car in the far reaches of the factory's lot, hoping not to be seen, and at the end of the shift took off the work shirt and slipped into his white-on-white French cuff shirt with cufflinks. He would arrive in the nightclub on time, looking his impeccable self. Apparently, none of his co-workers were customers.

But working two full-time jobs took its toll. He was weary. When he woke up to dress for the factory, I could see how hard it was for him to put his shoes on. His feet hurt and he would admit that they ached. His beautiful hands were worn and raw. It took a long time to restore them on Sunday afternoons for the week ahead at the nightclub.

A few months after she began working, Mother presented him with a new budget based on her earnings and the amount she had saved. She told him to take six months off immediately. He must quit working; he needed to rest and recover. She said he should go from having two jobs to no job.

But men didn't do that. He said it was impossible. What was she thinking? He had worked full-time since he was seventeen years old.

His life did not include time off; there were no vacations. For him there was work and there was looking for work or business opportunities. But my mother was adamant. *Alfred, this is the way it is going to be.* His six-month work hiatus turned into a year and then lasted a few more months. I spent time with my father alone, something I had not experienced before. He taught me how to cook. I became the woman I am in part because I got to spend so much time with him. My mother was right. The work sabbatical dramatically improved his health.

My mother thought she needed Friedan's book to survive a suburban existence. Still much of what was in *The Feminine Mystique* was already part of her thinking. It was the expression of Friedan's own frustration that gave a voice to my mother and to so many others. Friedan did what had not yet been done: she packaged the mistakes of post-war suburban life for women to open and discover themselves, or for them to rediscover whom they had been. Betty Friedan's words awakened millions of other women. Mother viewed the writing of the book as a heroic act.

Mother thrived as a paid employee and held jobs into her late seventies. The power and appeal of Friedan's reasoning might have led Mother to enroll in college, even at a late age. She was not yet in her sixties when it was published, but she had been defined as old for so long she didn't feel able to move into a new world with much younger people. The public colleges in California, community and four-year, were filled with older women. Tuition then was almost negligible and there were special re-entry programs, known in sexist parlance as the *retread track*. Many women did go back to college, or to college for the first time. But Mother insisted it was too late. She was afraid of failure, afraid of sticking out from the crowd even more—fears that could not be overcome by Friedan's call to action. Mother thought she was too old and so she became too old. The women's movement was fighting sexism but a serious awareness of ageism and how to fight would come much later. It was the subject of Friedan's book, *The Fountain of Age*. (Her memoir, *My Life So Far*, was in fact her last published book). *The Fountain of Age* was Friedan's final book about American culture and her last extended piece of critical social commentary.

In *The Feminine Mystique* Friedan wrote: *Fulfillment as a woman had only one definition for American women after 1949 – the housewife-mother. As swiftly as in a dream, the image of the American woman as a changing, growing individual in a changing world was shattered. Her solo flight to find her own identity was forgotten in the rush for the security of togetherness. Her limitless world shrunk to the cozy walls of home.*

Friedan's idea of true and rewarding liberation was based upon women's education and *then* employment. But employment was as much as my mother could envision for herself. To the fear of being ridiculed for her age and her conviction that failure was waiting around every corner, my mother added her refusal to break too many barriers. She believed that work was an entitlement, a gender-irrelevant civil right, but that questioning other boundaries was too dangerous, too radical.

Colleges were places where different forms of female freedom were afoot. The so-called *consciousness raising groups* terrified her. I admired Gloria Steinem, who inspired me. Mother insisted Steinem had bad manners and wasn't interested in *regular* women. The irony in her opinion is that it's hard to identify a major feminist with better sisterly manners than Steinem. Fierce in battle and a warrior for all women and against all barriers, Gloria Steinem was then, and has remained a woman of kindness, generosity, and compassion. When Friedan raised her voice, Mother heard it as a call to action. *It's time to wake up and go to work*, she would say. But when Steinem talked about patriarchy and the need for fundamental change and major shifts in power, my mother cowered. She labeled Steinem a firebrand who was too angry and maybe didn't like men. Steinem was glamorous, unmarried, and most decidedly not anyone's mother. Steinem transfixed me and gave me the opportunity to feel a connection to the feminist movement. Gloria Steinem represented everything my mother feared I might become. Betty Friedan was everything my mother thought she might have been, if only she had been born later and into a family of means and education.

Much has been written about pre-feminist times, before Friedan coined the phrase: *the problem that has no name*. It was she who first spoke for so many, although she wrote primarily from what she knew and understood. *The Feminine Mystique* takes the perspective of its author: a white woman with considerable advantages. But Friedan was especially intellectually curious, and had a history of political involvement and advocacy. Her suburban context was a community in Rockland County, New York—upscale compared to the planned town where my mother was unhappy and underused. But virtually all of what Friedan wrote and observed made sense in Lakewood, and it made particular sense to my mother. Life was far from perfect in "Lakewood: Tomorrow's City Today." Women there did offer one another support, concern, and cooperation. But *feminism* never found favor in Lakewood and that contributed to my mother's ongoing sense of isolation, despite her job.

The Feminine Mystique opens with these words: *The problem lay buried, unspoken, for many years in the minds of American women. It was a strange stirring, a sense of dissatisfaction, a yearning that women suffered in the middle of the twentieth century in the United States. Each suburban wife struggled with it alone. As she made the beds, shopped for groceries, matched slipcover material, ate peanut butter sandwiches with her children, chauffeured Cub Scouts and Brownies, lay beside her husband at night—she was afraid to ask even of herself the silent question—Is this all?'*

My mother said she had a name for the problem. It was just one word: *Boredom.* From where I stood in 1963, I thought it was two words: *boredom* and *housework.* Friedan laid the groundwork for a future that would be very different from the status quo, but would later claim she hadn't counted on the social explosion that occurred following its publication. A woman's revolution was coming. Neither Friedan nor my mother wanted any part of it when it happened. My mother had a fine mind that could have brought her to any number of destinations. But she did not or could not face the challenges of doing more than she did. She was a worker, not a professional. She held jobs, but did not have a career. I wanted more for her and she was certainly capable of more. But going back to work did give her a sense of empowerment and financial independence. When she was very old, Mother confessed to me a desire to have been a professor—she dreamed of a life spent in scholarship in literature or philosophy. This came as such a surprise that I had no response. After her death, I found many notebooks in which she had meticulously recorded her thoughts along with summaries of what she was reading. Her intellectual range and tastes were far ranging. She challenged herself considerably, but only in private.

I inherited the wedding rings of my grandmothers. Two wedding rings, two very different stories. Rosina's is a smooth round gold band, undiminished by wear, the ring of a woman who did not do housework or chores. Inside is engraved ALB to RLM. Martha's ring is wider and made of a thinner gold, its edges rough and worn, the ring of a woman whose life was defined by dreary hard work. What unites my grandmothers and their rings is the story of women's inequality. They both died while still in their sixties, Martha of a rare misdiagnosed breast cancer and Rosina of heart disease and diabetes.

Holding their rings in my hands now, I remember the days when I would argue for *Revolution not Reform*. My grandmothers needed the domestic revolution that was still many decades ahead and impossible for them to imagine. If they had been alive, I suspect Martha would have welcomed Friedan's message, but would have said it was too late for her—but not for her daughter. Likely Rosina would have been repelled. For her to be a lady, to inhabit all things feminine, to be soft and gentle in speech and behavior, and elegant in movement, to conduct oneself always in a graceful fashion, these were the sum total of womanly aspirations. It is what she wanted from and expected of me. But Rosina's femininity had no mystique. It had yielded only dependence and poverty.

6

Kenny, My First Love

When I became a student at Lakewood Senior High School my two selves collided head-on: the bookish girl with dreams and aspirations and the girl too serious for most boys, but who still wanted to be chosen.

I said my hair was strawberry blonde, but it was closer to a dreadful shade of orange. I had a secret desire to become a blonde—Grace Kelly was fighting for attention. But it was more difficult to disguise the progression of the autoimmune inflammatory disease. My illness fueled the intense longing to be accepted as a regular girl. I went to the Sav-On Drugstore, which had served as my Ken doll's delivery room. I bought a hair-coloring kit in a shade warmer than Marilyn Monroe's signature color, but one that I thought was within the rainbow of what a Southern California blonde should look like.

I plotted carefully. There were few times when both my parents were out of the house. My father was working again. My mother was still working, he at night, she during the day. Like all the houses within the grid we had one bathroom. On a Sunday afternoon I excused myself from accompanying them on an outing, citing too much homework. I had read the instruction pamphlet so many times I knew the lines and diagrams by heart. I prepared the glop and applied it meticulously to my Lucille Ball-like locks. I waited exactly forty-five minutes for the process to finish. When the second hand of the clock hit 6:30, I proceeded to the shampoo. I dreaded the wrath of my parents, and I had prepared a defense. But I never imagined an error. When I stepped out of the stall shower to view my transformation in the mirror, I had to rethink my plans. My hair was now an unmistakable dark olive green, the color of military camouflage. From that day to this, I don't understand what happened when the chemicals met my virgin hair.

The rest is a blur, until the moment my parents returned. I walked into the living room in a bathrobe, my head wrapped in a towel. I dropped the towel and provided a minimal explanation. My mother blew up in a rage. My father looked as if he had been hit; I saw tears in his eyes. This time it was he and not my mother who retreated to the bedroom, closing the door. My mother now sprang into action. She didn't scream again nor demand a defense or apology. She called Bernice, a good friend who was a hairdresser. I heard her say, *Alida had an accident with hair dye she bought at the drug store. Her hair is now olive green. I have no idea what to do.* There was a long silence. I didn't expect what she said next: *I think she was trying to fit in with the popular girls.*

She announced in a calm voice that we were going to Bernice's. We came in through the backdoor so that her teenage son wouldn't ridicule me. Bernice looked at the empty box of hair coloring and pronounced it garbage. She understood why it happened, and why hadn't I talked to her if I wanted to become a blonde, she would have done it properly.

This was my introduction to a new realm where women protected each other's beauty secrets and deceptions. I asked my mother if she would have permitted it. Mother indicated perhaps, but she would have asked for Bernice's advice. I doubted that, but I still wanted to be a blonde.

Bernice offered a lengthy explanation of what that would require. I listened attentively as she described all that was involved in maintaining the pretense of being a blonde, and what a root touch-up entailed. I understood that money I had earned from much babysitting would go into the *Dyed Blonde Hair Fund*. When Bernice finished, I asked meekly if she could return my hair to its original color. It took many steps and lots of bottles of foul-smelling liquids poured over my bedraggled locks but I emerged from her home late that Sunday night with my own hair color, more or less. Because the chemicals had singed the ends, Bernice cut it into a short, but popular style. The redeemed color was nicer than my own, but it wasn't a drastic change. At school on Monday I felt special because a beauty professional had spent hours working on my hair. But mostly, I was chastened.

Not long after, I met a boy, Kenny. I was a sophomore; he was a senior. Kenny was shy, tall, lean, had dark hair, eyes that sparkled (or so I insisted) and a warm smile. He wore crisp madras shirts (ironed by his mother) and proper trousers, not Levis. He lived in Lakewood Village, a cut above the tract homes of the grid. He played water polo and belonged to the DeMolay Society, part of the larger Masonic order of organizations. Kenny and his buddies liked to have a good time, but he was anything but bad or dangerous. He was sweet. I now had a toe in the wading pool of high school dating, which felt daring.

Any concerns my parents had about Kenny's presence in my life because he was a senior and I was a sophomore were allayed when they were introduced. He had to meet with their approval before I was permitted to go anywhere with him. Kenny was polite, well mannered, gentle, and they were reassured.

He was not a reader, except for homework assignments. I tried to dazzle him with chatter about books, movies, and plays. Kenny was bound for the Douglas Aircraft factory where many before him and after him found work. His father had larger hopes for his son, but his presumed lack of intellect foreclosed paternal dreams. Kenny's courses were all within the manual skills curriculum. He could do anything with his hands: construct, deconstruct, reconstruct.

Early in our courtship I discovered Kenny was far from stupid. Once he relaxed, he was intellectually curious and really did like to listen to talk about books, poems, and literature.

Years later I realized that Kenny was likely dyslexic, a term we didn't know then, nor did we know any other words for learning disabilities besides slow, stupid or lazy. Students like Kenny were routinely placed into basic skills courses that were non-college prep and made to feel inferior. One day Kenny arrived at my locker during an afternoon break. His sparkling eyes were flat, sad. Tucked under his arm was a thin book, an abbreviated biography of Houdini. *Are you interested in Houdini?* I asked. He said it was for a book report. Almost always accompanied by the Houdini book, he moved through the next weeks with glum resignation. In Kenny's world a book served no purpose; it was something he was obliged to carry around. I hadn't encountered such a thin book since childhood but for Kenny it was a weighty encumbrance, a symbol of personal failure. During those weeks Houdini was anything but invisible or magical.

I was preoccupied calculating how much I would let him "do" to me. Nothing below the waist, but would I permit him to feel my breasts underneath my clothes? Did other girls really like French kissing? I didn't get the point of that. Kenny was calculating how many days were left before Houdini had to make an appearance as a finished and typed book report. Over hamburgers one weekend I finally brought up the subject. Why couldn't he do the report? He said he hadn't begun to read the book. Very late in the term, he came over to my house and I read the book while he helped with dinner. After we ate, sitting at the recently cleared dining room table, I wrote the report. My mother was a willing accomplice.

In grade school she often completed my math homework. She was morally complex, with strong standards about right and wrong, but her mind held flexible definitions. Writing Kenny's book report was not cheating. It was assisting a person in need; people shouldn't have their lives ruined because of something they couldn't master. Mother insisted I would become a writer and so she provided assistance with math assignments to help provide me with enough time to ensure the quality of my term papers. What mattered was that my writing not be compromised in wasting time on arithmetic. Mother appreciated Kenny's many other talents. He must not fail Basic Senior English and denied a diploma because of a missing Houdini book report—that was unthinkable. Of course, I must write his book report.

After I read the book I told Kenny what was in it, explained the major plot lines and historical points. This did not constitute a long portion of the evening. Sitting at the opposite end of the table from him, I wrote the book report and handed it to him. He was furious at me when he finished reading it. Had I lost my mind? The teacher would know he hadn't written it. It couldn't slide through as his work. We enlisted my mother as the judge. She read the report and looked at me in disbelief. *Tone down the metaphors.* I rewrote it. Today's term is *dumbing down*, but I refused to make the report as simple as Kenny insisted. I didn't think he was dumb. He thought he was dumb about books. The Houdini report got past the teacher's radar. Kenny would graduate in June after all; he had passed the required English course. He and I never spoke again about the report, the book, Houdini, or my ghostwriting.

I was convinced my word skills had worked magic. I presumed Kenny was mine and I was his forever and ever. I was rewarded when finally Kenny asked me to go steady. We were now officially a campus couple. We went to Knott's Berry Farm and got hitched in Ghost Town in the re-created Justice of the Peace's office. On Monday we appeared on campus wearing our faux horseshoe nail wedding rings. The pretend event cost two dollars, as I recall. On my 16th birthday I received a going-steady gift purchased at Triangle Jewelers. It was a pendant on a gold chain, with two diamond chips surrounding a modest emerald placed in the center. I never took it off my neck. I had triumphed. I felt that I belonged and that I was normal. But though I was in love with love, my school grades remained high.

It was inconceivable to stop studying.

That year one of my favorite teachers used the phrase the *life of the mind* in class. I thought it was an exciting concept, and it must be a thrilling way to live. I wanted to experience this life as she described it, but wasn't sure how to do that. I did not mention this to Kenny, nor did I share with him much about my classes or other interests. My written work and term papers impressed teachers. Two of them encouraged my creative aspirations. My intellectual concerns and the courses I embraced were in stark contrast to going steady with Kenny. Though he tolerated my drama and theater studies, he made jokes, but not cruel ones. It was a warning to me, nonetheless, to monitor how much I told him about my interests and desires.

Kenny was counting the days before he was to be given full freedom from Lakewood High School. We discussed whether he would enroll part-time in the local junior college. His sister and parents talked to him about it in far sterner terms. He agreed to take a few courses in the daytime and work the night shift at Douglas Aircraft. But the junior college had nothing to do with Kenny's aspirations or desires. I desperately had wanted Kenny to go to college for me but he was smart enough to know it was his life to live. He enjoyed school friendships and would miss hanging out with his fraternity brothers, but not much else. Lakewood High School had inspired me to think and imagine, but to Kenny it only enhanced his sense of inadequacy.

My two selves were in conflict, which I denied because Kenny took up much emotional space. I was numbed by first love. I knew only a few classmates with boyfriends who were seniors. I was going to the Senior Prom. It would be the only prom I attended. In dating Kenny I fulfilled Lakewood's plan for girls. During that year I thought about a wedding, children, perhaps a house in Lakewood Village, or even better, a house in Belmont Shores close enough to walk to the beach. Kenny would work at Douglas and I would be a schoolteacher in the

Long Beach Unified District. I worked out the details in my head. I did not solicit Kenny's views.

In my short stay in the land of adolescence I went from being annoyed by the appearance of the Ken doll to fantasies about spending all my days with a living boy named Kenny. The girl who refused to play house was playing mental house. When new postcards arrived from Tina, they meant little. The worlds of Gigi and Paris, adventures and careers, were still out there, but far away and out of focus. Kenny made me wonder for the first and the last time whether I should stay in Lakewood forever. I had been chosen! But my teacher's words never left me: *The life of the mind.* I didn't know how to combine loving Kenny and the *life of the mind.* I knew there would be a choice, and that I was the one who had to make it, but I still drifted along on my dreamy cloud of romanticism.

With graduation just weeks away Kenny began talking about deepening our intimacy, a step I had no intention of taking. My belief that he was the one was based solely on the fact he had chosen me. Our sexual intimacy, such as it might be described, was conducted fully clothed with the exception of the occasional brief exposure of a breast. Girls talked about *going all the way* with their boyfriends. Some of them did so joyfully; others complied, feeling they had no choice. Kenny and I talked about going all the way but he knew my limits. He respected them but he was unhappy, and extremely horny. I pretended none of this was happening.

He wrote funny and cryptic notes and left them in my locker. (He had the combination.) During class passing period I would find them hidden in a book or hanging on the hook. They were mostly about our way of having sex—called *making out* by everyone. Each time I opened the locker I looked for a new message. Finding no note only intensified my feeling of attachment. Kenny might not have studied psychology, but he knew the power of partial reinforcement. I've since come to believe it may be hardwired into men. They don't need to take Psych 101 to know how to use it effectively. The notes were written in a Swiss cheese of the English language, impossible grammar, misspelled words, but I didn't care.

Our fit was ridiculous, but I clung to the illusion of love. I wrote *Kenny + Alida Forever* on a multitude of paper surfaces. I drew little hearts next to his picture in the school yearbook. I went to dances, Friday night football games, his Senior Prom, and to the school district's all-night graduation dance held in the Long Beach Municipal Auditorium. My parents had said I couldn't go, but relented when the school administration sent around the information sheet: We were to be locked in, and there wouldn't be a drop of liquor anywhere. If you signed up for the dance and didn't show, your parents were called.

Soon after graduation, Kenny went to work at Douglas. He performed exceedingly well on their aptitude test, probably the first test he had taken that he felt good about. He was offered a job not "on the line," but one that required intelligence and skill. Kenny wore the same clothes he had worn to high school. He liked to say he didn't leave work dirty, smelly and sweaty. I'm not sure that any of the men (and few women) on the aerospace lines came out that way; it wasn't a steel mill or a coalmine. Still Kenny was proud of himself. He had been near the bottom of achievement in school and now found himself judged smart and able. And he was more than willing to look down on other workers as his inferiors.

This annoyed me and I complained to my father. My father and Kenny always were pleasant with one another but they shared nothing in common, not one thing of mutual interest they could discuss. But my father was unsympathetic to my negative views about Kenny's newly claimed status. He lectured me about what it was like inside an aerospace factory, something he had learned firsthand from his stint at North American. He knew how hard it was to find your identity, to feel special and that what you did mattered a *rat's tush*. Well into my middle age, in some long-forgotten cardboard box, we discovered pictures of Kenny. I asked my father why he remained so calm while I dated Kenny. He said he knew it wasn't going anywhere and therefore every reason to be kind and welcoming. Kenny also knew it wasn't going anywhere. My mother knew it was a finite moment in my lifetime. I was the only one who didn't know.

My mother was strongly opposed to teenage sex. I was terrified of getting pregnant and wouldn't risk it without birth control. But this would require a visit to the doctor, and prescribing birth control for minors without parental consent was not legal at the time. And I wasn't ready for the whole event. One summer afternoon following his graduation, we came to a turning point. He picked me up from a play rehearsal and asked if I wanted to go to his house. He made clear that his mother wasn't home and I agreed. The family dog greeted us enthusiastically. I didn't like the dog, a wild thing with too much fur, who did little else with his time on the planet but bark and jump.

Kenny and I went into the kitchen to make a sandwich for him to take to work. He opened the package of bologna but before the sandwich was made, we began to kiss. Our encounter quickly became passionate. The sandwich was left unmade. We went to his bedroom and engaged in foreplay, though fully clothed. Kenny was moving too fast for me but I could tell something different was happening. He motioned for me to unzip his trousers. I thought it might be fine as long it was his trousers and not my panties, just then the dog ran into the room and jumped on the bed, the package of bologna in his mouth. Kenny jumped up and chased the dog out of the room. The mood was ruined.

After that Kenny and I had our only serious talk about sex. He didn't like what he felt on his bed that afternoon. He said he was very sorry about his behavior. He confided he was terrified he might have forced me to have sex if we had continued. Kenny said: *When a guy gets to a certain place, it's all you're thinking about. Nothing else matters. For a minute you stopped being Alida. I didn't care about anything except* **it.** I wrote those words in my diary not long after.

But Kenny did stop, dog or no dog. We would have had plenty of time to resume after the dog was punished, but we didn't go back to his bedroom. He didn't take my clothes off or tell me I was nuts not to have sex. He was a good young man with a regular job, ready to have sex with adult women. He dropped me off at home and went to work at Douglas on the night shift.

Late that summer Kenny asked me out for a big date. In Lakewood, most dates consisted of a movie, a burger, the parks, the drive-in theaters (if you lied to your parents), Knott's, or just hanging out with friends. Big dates were rare. Disneyland at night was a big date. Kenny didn't usually plan events or outings, and so I was thrilled. Disneyland was still a homegrown attraction but had become more sophisticated than in its earliest days with Dumbo the Flying Elephant and the spinning teacup rides. At night there were dance bands scattered across the pavilions in the various lands——and a special package admission price: "Disneyland After Dark." The highlight of the evening featured Tinker Bell gliding across the sky on a high wire to usher in the night, with her wand igniting the fireworks spectacular.

I can still replay that big Disneyland date more than forty years later. It would turn out to be the venue Kenny chose to break up with me. I was wearing my nicest dress. It was not made by Aunt Madeleine or purchased in the May Company's bargain basement. I had taken money earned from baby-sitting and bought it in season at full retail price. It was a navy blue sheath with lime green piping around the neck and arms. I wore blue suede and lime trimmed shoes I had found on sale at the Lakewood Shopping Center. When I wore the outfit I felt both special and normal.

Masquerading as a Lakewood Lancer socialite in my coordinated costume I lost my status as a girlfriend. It happened in Disneyland's "Tomorrowland," somewhere between the space ride and the Monsanto Home of the Future. Kenny took my hand and we sat on a bench. He said it was over between us. In retrospect, it was one of the more civilized endings I've experienced. He didn't criticize me or complain or list my faults. I went into the closest women's room and cried so hard I couldn't catch my breath. Women came over and asked if I were all right. Had anyone hurt me? I don't recall what I said.

If I had seen it coming, I never admitted it. I emerged from the women's room feeling I was now *nobody*. I couldn't find Kenny and assumed he had stranded me in Disneyland. I was figuring out how to get home, how to stop crying, how to face friends, when Kenny reappeared. He had taken a few spins around the miniature automobile racetrack. He had assumed I would be crying and all that, so he took the ride several times. The Monsanto Home of the Future loomed in the near distance, the overhead monorail, known as the train of the future, zipped above our heads. He had destroyed me in about three sentences but there he was: he couldn't have been in a better mood. Those cars are so neat or some such popped out of his mouth. He was happy. After all, Disneyland is "The Happiest Place on Earth." He owned a VW Bug not much bigger than the cars in the raceway. I didn't understand why a pre-planned raceway with even smaller (and fake) cars could be so compelling.

I was frightened. I wondered what to do next, how to face the dreaded return of the isolation of illness. In the weeks before Disneyland I had been admitted to the hospital for several days with a sudden flare, but there was not much relief or any useful diagnostic clues. With Kenny I felt less alone in a town where only children were a rarity and where sick and disabled children were not welcomed into the mainstream. I still managed to keep the disease hidden most of the time. But I knew my deception could not succeed much longer. Part of me believed Kenny was entitled to dump me because chronic disease made me an inconvenience. I didn't understand that I had power and rights but I had thrown them away. *I* might have been the one to issue *his* exit-papers.

I had assumed our Disneyland date night was over, but Kenny was ready now to have a great time. While I was in the restroom he checked out the bands playing that night, and he had chosen a sequence for the rest of the evening. Off we went to one fake place after another—"Adventureland," "Fantasyland," and Main Street, where we danced and joked with each other as though nothing had changed. I was the consummate amateur actor, determined that Kenny see me for all I could be, regret his prior speech and retract it.

Kenny had attended to the most important detail of the night: the best place to see Tinker Bell fly across the sky and begin the fireworks. He had another surprise waiting. He announced we had reservations for dinner in the main dining room at the Disneyland Hotel. We took the Monorail there into the land of the recently *unchosen* with a steak and a baked potato. It was the most expensive restaurant we had ever gone to as a couple.

In the end, I was too talky, too intent on living in a wider world and committed to a different way of being to be the right person for Kenny, or he for me. Kenny understood more than I did and more than I credited him with. At the aerospace factory there were women who were available and ready to date, good women who wanted more than rolling around on Kenny's bed with their clothes on. Women who didn't want to correct his grammar or hound him to go to college, or try to turn him into someone other than Kenny. Kenny thought I was fine as I was, but just not right for him. In so many ways Kenny was the smarter one of us. In retrospect, I think he saw the Disneyland date as a generous and gracious good-bye. His parents did not;

they called my parents and apologized for their son's conduct. A year or so later I ran into his older sister. She was still angry with her brother. But by then I had fully recovered from him and was plotting a new life on the stage and as a writer.

On the drive home that night, however, my acting skills left me. I was more openly distraught than Kenny (or I) had anticipated. He had the courage to come into the house and tell my mother what happened. She was polite, quiet. But once Kenny was out the door she took over with a verbal brutality I wasn't ready to hear then. *This is life*, she insisted. I needed to snap out of it immediately and face reality. *Face reality!* was one of her frequent and favorite commands. I resented it because in my view she never had faced the reality of Terry's death. Perhaps this was the reason she wanted me to learn to do it. Or maybe there wasn't enough space in a modest home for more than one person's sorrow.

The Kenny story did not end on the Disneyland date. In a Sarah Heartburn flourish I requested that Kenny and I see each other again at an agreed upon future time. Then we would reevaluate our relationship. Was it a month? Two months? I don't recall. Kenny called before the date to confirm. I prepared for this reunion by writing him a long letter, which I intended to read aloud. I assumed we would be going to a drive-in movie so I tucked a small flashlight into my purse. We did go to the drive-in and once settled into the seats of his cocoon of a car, I read the letter. In it I enunciated all the reasons why we should get back together, as in *Kenny+Alida forever and ever.* (Did I really still believe it?)

Before I could finish reading my manifesto, Kenny put his arms around me. We kissed and kissed. We made out as if nothing had changed. He said I was right; it was a good idea to resume. He nodded and said a few consoling things. I came home victorious. I had won him back using reasoning, polished prose, and persuasiveness.

The next day a dozen roses in a long gold box arrived from Victor's Florist, an upscale shop that didn't do anything on the cheap. (In those days roses weren't found in grocery stores or gas stations.) They constituted a serious investment. These were perfect long stemmed roses, six red and six yellow and I did not know then the language of flowers. Did someone tell Kenny yellow roses were the floral equivalent of goodbye? Did the red symbolize the past and the yellow our non-existent future? The card said: *Love from Kenny*. I never saw or heard from him again.

7
Frothing

By 1967, my senior year in high school, the Vietnam War was going strong and so too were the anti-war protests and the student movement at home. My parents were vehemently opposed to the war, but they would not justify violent protest as a means to end it. Violence was what bad people did, violence was the tactic of Southern racists who burned the homes of black people, lynched them, bombed their churches, and murdered black girls in Sunday school. It was those who hated our country's diversity and who were opposed to equality that used violence in the hope that justice could be stopped. In our home the Reverend Martin Luther King was right and Mahatma Gandhi was right: the only acceptable way for change and revolution was nonviolent resistance.

President Lyndon B. Johnson was taking us further into war. LBJ broke my father's heart. He had been a heroic figure for my father—the Texas civil rights president who persevered until the Voting Rights Act was passed in 1965. Now I hated the president and was no longer interested in his civil rights record. I was concerned by the killing machine LBJ was running, which was sending boys from the Long Beach high schools to Nam, where they would be fodder for his war.

Against this political backdrop, I had to convince my parents why I should go away to college. It was the first time my father was silent to me. It was his way of passive resistance. I was desperate to change his mind, but there was no act of domestic disobedience I could engage in, because I needed his cooperation. If my parents would not pay for college, or fill out the required forms requesting financial need, I wasn't going away to college. He refused and my mother backed him up. For a time they said my health would not withstand dorm life.

After a heated exchange one day, my father confessed he thought my politics had taken a dangerous turn to the far left. He didn't want me arrested, or blown up in some protest, or injured by the police or National Guard. (The killing of the Kent State protesters in 1970 was still ahead of us.) It was clear I wasn't going to win so I gave up, but without any grace. By my sophomore year I was living in a dorm, attending Cal State Long Beach, and the dorm was almost walking distance from the home of my aunt and uncle. My parents had moved from Lakewood to a newly built home in the Fullerton area, about an hour south of Long Beach. My father said going to college in Long Beach was being away from home. We both pretended I had finally convinced him of the merits of dorm life, he but had won: Long Beach State was not on my list of preferred colleges.

During the middle of my senior year my father shocked me and infuriated my mother. He called a truce in our tug-of-war about college choices and suggested I take advantage of a pre-college program in Paris sponsored by George Washington University in D.C. in association with the American University in Paris. One of my favorite high school teachers served on the governing board of the program and would be accompanying the group. She described the program to me and said I would be a good candidate. Dutifully I brought the materials home, thinking my parents wouldn't pay much attention to them. Alida in Paris? A highly unlikely proposition for the girl who wasn't allowed to go on camping trips and who was rarely permitted overnights at my girlfriends' homes. I gave them the information package because my teacher Joanne Weinhoff told me I must.

My father read it carefully. He telephoned Weinhoff and they had a lengthy conversation. He decided I should experience Paris and that this was a good opportunity at the right time.

He thought America was dangerous and college campuses were potential death traps, but that going to live in Paris for a few months at eighteen wasn't alarming. When he first told me I laughed—it had to be one of his jokes. When I realized he was serious about Paris, where I went to college became much less important. I was still angry—it crossed my mind that once in Paris I could stay and become an ex-pat, but I was smart enough not to share that revenge fantasy.

Mother was extremely unhappy and said I had "caught Paris" from my father. That was true—his stories about "The City of Light" after World War II had made a lasting impression on me. I applied for the program, and as Miss Weinhoff predicted, I was accepted, as were two of my classmates, Jan and Tony. I don't know what private negotiations or pleadings my father had with my always-fearful mother, but she stopped badgering me once I was accepted to the program.

Some of the preparations for the program frightened me. We went to a number of meetings in the Los Angeles area with other students in the program and their parents. One was held in a Beverly Hills home, hosted by the parents of a girl whose father was a surgeon. The rest of the Southern California contingent consisted of kids from rich families. They had attended private schools or Beverly Hills High or the flossy public schools on the Westside. The girls wore fancy clothing and talked about their carry-on bags to be filled only with jewelry. At our first meeting one father asked how to arrange to have his daughter's steamer trunks sent over so they would be waiting upon her arrival in Paris. Weinhoff said we were to be housed in the Fondation des États Unis, a modest dorm on the campus of the Cité Universitaire on Boulevard Jourdan in the 14th Arrondissement. She indicated there wasn't much storage space in the rooms and we were there to study and to do things as a group. She emphasized that it wasn't necessary to bring lots of expensive clothing. The father replied: *It is Paris after all, and a girl should have her wardrobe.*

I should have been amused, but I wasn't. These rich girls and their fathers made me anxious. I was an outsider and feared I would be subject to their ridicule. The mothers were friendly, but of a different species from any of the Lakewood moms I had ever met. These students lived less than an hour from Lakewood-Long Beach, but they were as foreign to me as I expected the Parisians would be.

On the drive home my mother said she hoped there would be some nice girls from the Midwest in the program. I recognized that Lakewood wasn't a rich community, but I never thought we were poor or lower class. Meeting the other Southern California participants and their families was my first life lesson in social class—its divisions and cruelties.

I gave Aunt Madeleine a rundown on the Beverly Hills meeting and told her I was apprehensive about going. I told her what worried me the most was I would not have anybody (except Jan and Tony) who would be friends with me in Paris. Aunt Madeleine said Jan and Tony were enough friends and that they would have me as well. But she also said she hoped there would be midwestern girls who would be friendly and kind. I told her I had nothing to wear in comparison to the girls I had met in Beverly Hills. I would be humiliated. I was a typical teenager at that moment, focused more on the clothing than on the experience my working parents were making possible. Money was extremely limited and it was already a stretch for them to come up with airfare and tuition. Spending money was up to me. I booked myself solidly every weekend and after school with babysitting jobs. My aunt promised me a set of luggage for graduation.

Aunt Madeleine said she understood that having proper clothes for Paris was essential. In fact, the dilemma excited Madeleine, and she immediately took it on as her contribution to my Parisian experience. She bought home some high-fashion magazines from the variety store and we looked at them. She selected four pictures of designer dresses that she thought would fit the bill. And one evening dress as well. *I'll whip these up and you'll pass as a Parisian girl.* It seemed impossible to me. The one she selected as my evening dress was a Dior. Madeleine sketched it on a plain piece of paper and tore out the page of the magazine. We made a date to go to downtown Los Angeles to buy fabric; variety store choices wouldn't do.

Unlike my mother, Aunt Madeleine was a skilled freeway driver, though on our ride downtown she lamented the demise of the Red Car, (an electric streetcar) which ran from Long Beach to Los Angeles until the early 1960s. We went to a fabric store that had been recommended to her. She walked into the place as if she owned it, and a clerk stepped up to help her. Madeleine spoke with the authority of a professional seamstress. The woman assisting us treated as if we were important clients. My aunt spoke a language I didn't know or understand. She and the clerk acted as if they had known each other for years. I learned later there is a bond among those who know how to sew at professional levels. We left with four designer patterns for day-dresses and a goodly amount of muslin (for my aunt to make the rip-off Dior evening dress). She chose beautiful fabrics and only consulted me after she had made her initial selections. I agreed with everything the clerk had pulled down for Madeleine. I told my aunt I couldn't pay for the fabric. She said my money wasn't requested and wouldn't be accepted, even if I had any.

The dresses Aunt Madeleine made for me were magnificent designer creations. The Dior knock-off was a body-fitting silk sheath with a flowing chiffon overdress in a matching pattern. The fabric my aunt chose was bold but not gaudy; it looked like it was painted from Gauguin's palette. I wore it for the first time when the group was taken to the L'Opéra to see "Carmen." Marie-Louise, an instructor in the program, asked me if I had bought it in the Dior boutique. I told her my aunt made it. We became friendly and corresponded for a few years. During my time in Paris she took me to lunch several times, and one day asked to come back to my room to look at the dress closely. My Parisian French teacher was impressed by my aunt's fine work, especially the hand tailoring—she exclaimed with appreciation when she saw the French seams. I told her my aunt was French, which gratified but didn't seem to surprise her.

The drive to the Los Angeles airport (a few days after high school graduation) was long and silent. He drove. Mother stared out the window, her face hard and angry. I checked my purse to be sure she had taken not taken out the tickets and passport. I couldn't believe I was really going, and was still worried that something or someone would keep me from getting onto the airplane. But I also knew what they didn't know. A group of high school friends would be waiting at the gate. In those now seemingly ancient pre-terrorist times, there were farewell gate parties where people came to send off friends, bringing flowers and libations. Nobody much noticed as long as you weren't rowdy. I knew my mother wouldn't make a scene in front of others.

The program was probably fairly typical of many like it in that era. But for me it meant an explosion of ideas, sophistication, and culture. I had found a wider world and I immersed myself in all it offered. The courses were held in the morning and sometimes required an evening lecture. The subjects were limited to French literature, philosophy, cultural history and of course, the language. They were general survey courses, and not overly demanding. The point was to experience France and not be buried in schoolwork. It was not the Sorbonne, but some of the professors were borrowed from there.

There were midwestern girls, including two Lauras, and a Louanne, and we became good pals. I roomed with a delightful girl from Texas whose accent was so strong we all nicknamed her Tex; she didn't seem to mind. The midwestern girls and I took the studies more seriously than we probably needed to, but we were determined to do our best schoolwork. Many nights we stayed in and ordered in ham sandwiches from the Café Le Babel across the street and worked late into the night.

In general, I was more interested in the girls than any of the boys, but everyone was congenial and friendly, and there were no sexual dramas among us. However, the young French male assistants and chaperones were ready to offer inexperienced young American girls intimate adventures, and they made that clear. Soon we had conversations about the problem. We included a few of the boys in our program in our discussions and they said the slightly older French guys had to be watched. The American boys acted as chaperones and our protectors. We were all quite unsophisticated.

I was woefully underfunded, even though I kept a Spartan budget. I wasn't going to write back to my family and ask for money. I wasn't sure what to do and became very anxious when I was down to a few francs. I told Laura, from Wisconsin, and she said she didn't have much money either but she had figured out a plan. We had lunch tickets included in our tuition and if you wished you ate in the great hall on the Cité campus with students from all over the world. The food was almost inedible, but the atmosphere was intoxicating at first. Everyday at lunch, when we went right in without standing in line, our prepaid tickets in hand, we noticed there were long lines to buy a daily lunch ticket.

Laura thought we could go to the back of the line where people would have a thirty-minute wait or more ahead of them and sell our tickets for a bit more than they would pay once they got to the ticket cashier. If we stayed at the very back of the line, she assumed, nobody would catch us. I'm still not sure if it would have been frowned upon or if it were flat-out forbidden. We tried it the first day and were successful, and so we continued. Until one day, an older student asked if our entire ticket books might be for sale. We didn't know what to charge. I left the negotiations to Laura, whose French was excellent.

The man and his friend bought our remaining ticket books for what then seemed like a fortune and we were set financially for the rest of our stay. From then on we took our lunch across the street at Café Le Babel, had steak frites and a glass of wine with the other kids who had long abandoned the common dining room, courtesy of their well-heeled parents. Our earnings from the sale of the tickets allowed us some other treats during our stay. Paying for dinners was not a worry; we ate together in a private dining room at the Fondation des Unis, or were taken out to meals and events. Laura and I were both proud and private enough not to have mentioned to anyone else that we were broke, so we didn't have to explain our suddenly fat wallets.

It was inevitable that I had a brief flare of illness. It was in a quiet state when I applied for the program and remained so for the rest of my senior year. My doctor at the time said I was in a real remission, perhaps one that would last for years. I was still taking a small amount of prednisone to control the disease, so I didn't think it qualified as a genuine remission, but was glad he raised no objection to my going abroad. But late one night I had a severe fever-spike, and my roommate went to get Joanne Weinhoff. She called an ambulance and we went to the American Hospital, where the emergency room staff went into high alert. My mother had prepared a carefully typed dossier for Weinhoff along with copies of doctor's records.

I begged Weinhoff not to call my parents, but of course she was obliged to do so. My mother told her she was coming over directly, and then said my father was coming instead. But neither of them had a passport. Weinhoff suggested they wait, and assured them the American Hospital of Paris was superb. Indeed it was. The doctors listened carefully. They talked to my distressed mother on the phone in front of me. And they put me in a lovely room with a great view of the city. I stayed there for a few days. I don't know what drugs they gave me, but they knew enough about autoimmune disease to help me. I was released to Miss Weinhoff and went back to the dorm, where everybody was waiting to give me a welcome back party. Weinhoff had not disclosed the details of what had happened. Most of the students assumed it was food poisoning or flu.

The next week we were to go to the Loire Valley for a few days. I still felt weak from the flare and wasn't enthusiastic about the trip, but assumed I had no choice. Technically, I had recovered and was well enough to go, but Weinhoff knew me well and recognized the apprehension in my eyes. She offered me the possibility of staying in Paris. She would negotiate with the head of the program and assure him I would be fine, that the young women instructors who were Paris-based would look in on me. I was thrilled. Alone in Paris! It was a dream come true. They went off to the Loire, and I went off to the Louvre. No group to contend with, no chatting with my classmates, no listening to boring canned lectures, just the silence and solitude of the Louvre at night.

I had become obsessed with the Venus de Milo and the Winged Victory. I looked at the ancient sculptures, one missing her arms and the other her head, but for me these women comprised the whole story. The world of goddesses and the desire to study them still lay ahead of me, but I already knew that goddesses possessed real power. I remembered the stories of the mythologies well enough to know that goddesses were an essential part of ancient history. The role of goddesses in feminism, beginning in the 19th century, was still unknown to me. Learning about the tradition of Wicca was decades in my future. Mary Daly's book, *Beyond God the Father* wouldn't be published until 1974. But my evenings alone in the Louvre with the Winged Victory and the Venus de Milo became part of my personal discovery of female deities, mystical and spiritual experiences that could be exclusively feminine, not masculine. When I returned from Paris, I taped three things to my bedroom wall—prints of the Venus de Milo and the Winged Victory, and a map of the Paris metro system.

* * *

Paris had ended with tearful goodbyes and promises to stay in touch forever. I did correspond with a few friends I made in the program, but it didn't last long. Back in the States, two of the girls I had cared about quickly became part of the student conservative movement that believed in the mission of the Vietnam War, which left little for me to write them about. All of us were moving onto the next big chapter of our lives; Paris became memory. For me, it was the private moments I experienced there that lingered, and to which I still return. For many years Paris was my dream. But I didn't return for some years after the 1967 college term there.

When I disembarked from the airplane, my parents were at the gate to meet me. They looked younger and were tanned. My mother was playful, not fretful, when she saw me. She announced she was as *brown as a berry* (which was obvious without her comment) and it was clear that they had had a wonderful time together without me. Liberation from parenting suited them. I saw them as a couple, not as parents. It was a revelation—and a lesson.

I agreed to stay home for a semester after Paris and attend the local college, which I detested and cruelly lampooned to my friends who were all at "real" colleges. I felt cheated of a proper college education and was once again angry with my father for his refusal to let me go away. But at the community college in Fullerton I met instructors who took a particular interest in me. Startled by my reports and term papers, they asked to talk with me in private. They wanted to know how or why I had ended up there—a college whose only admissions requirement was a high school diploma. I explained my illness, but only in sketchy terms. I decided to leave out my father's other fear—radical politics—except in one case.

My English professor was a much older man who taught part-time. He was retired from an elite university. His name was Raymond Furlong, and he introduced me to a world I had not known before. He arranged for me to study independently with him. In the English class he gave me different assignments from the other students. From him I learned about the metaphysical poets, his reasons why Rilke mattered in ways he said others didn't understand. I was assigned John Donne as a year-long project, which culminated in a term paper about the length of a short book. His private course list for me included Goethe, Chekhov, Turgenev, Pushkin, Dostoyevsky and Tolstoy. He appreciated Virginia Woolf, but preferred George Eliot. He taught me to read something new every day of my life. After all my commotion and anguish about being cheated out of a proper college education, I had here a tutorial with a man of letters that I probably would not have experienced as a freshman even in a first-rate university.

For me he saw a world of literature and teaching, or a life as a literary critic. When I told him I didn't want a career in the academy but one as a writer, he asked me to write something that was neither scholarly nor based on research. I was to write my impressions about something that mattered a great deal to me and to keep it to five pages or less. I wrote about what Paris looked to me on my first night there. Reading it, he agreed that I knew what I wanted and that it was the right choice. He also said that I should never forget that "real" writers read, and read, and then read some more. *Writing is reading*, was his mantra. He said creative writing courses were worthless, and I was to avoid them, that a writer learns best by reading widely. I was dubious but I didn't challenge him. Years later I heard Saul Bellow utter almost the same words, but with even more emphasis. When my first book was published, I tried to find Dr. Furlong, but couldn't. But he is never far from me. On my shelves are volumes of poetry he had insisted I buy. When I complained I didn't have the money to buy so many books, he said books were food and so I should eat less. I think of those books now as *The Furlong Collection.*

There was a French professor, Ira Dudley, who was movie star handsome, always tan with silver hair, always dressed in bespoke suits, handmade shirts, Hermès ties and exquisite cufflinks. He didn't look like he belonged in a classroom anywhere. The women in my class had crushes on him, and some were so smitten by his looks and elegance that they couldn't concentrate on their work. He frightened me because he was so tough and unforgiving of any mistake of pronunciation in grammar. I wanted to be the star pupil, not a starry-eyed girl. I became his best student by gritty determination, not by my natural language gifts.

He was a formal man and referred to all of us as Mr. or Miss. He is the reason I retain any French at all, though I continued to study for years. He wrote notes of appreciation for my work when he handed back the *dictées* and other papers he assigned. When I fell ill midway through the year and had to miss two weeks of classes, he sent a handwritten letter to my home. His note was filled with concern and the suggestion that I read a bit of French each day. He ended by saying I showed great promise, particularly in my love of reading French literature, and he would catch me up in private sessions once I could return. In closing he said, that he wouldn't let me fall behind.

Finally, there was Phillip Snyder, a crusty and opinionated man who reminded me of an old-style newspaperman from the movies, but who taught politics. Just as Furlong had, Snyder picked me out of the class to learn more about me. One day he treated me to lunch. I told him the rest of the story of why I had ended up there and not somewhere else. He laughed and said I didn't strike him as a dangerous radical, but he understood my father's worries. He thought it was a lousy time to be a college student, but I didn't understand this till years later. From Snyder I learned how to read newspapers critically, how to calculate electoral college votes quickly, and why the electoral college system should be abolished, why he thought women might never get into higher office or the Supreme Court, although he wished otherwise. And why he saw Vietnam was a disaster that would not end soon. He said I belonged in politics, that he saw it as my true calling. He told me not to become a writer but to use my writing skills to write speeches, run for office and win.

But instead of following the advice of these three men and *keep my nose to the grindstone and shoulder to the wheel,* I transferred to a four-year college where I rushed headlong into anti-war activities and an ill-fated love.

* * *

Most of the time when we weren't in classes we talked about the war—over dinner, over bottles of beer and glasses of wine, on walks, while reading the newspapers. My friends and I talked and sometimes raged through the night. I didn't associate with anyone who thought the war was justified. We spent hours debating which of the anti-war protests received the most or the least press attention. We looked for the next protest to attend where frequently I saw draft cards burned, along with an American flag here and there. We were furious when we thought the media underreported the number of protesters.

In the midst of the anti-war fury, a beautiful young man appeared one night at an organizing meeting. His flashing black eyes and his rhetoric electrified me. He was two years ahead of me and was the R.A. (Resident Assistant) for the male wing of our dorm. Here I will call him Gabriel Lewis. We engaged each other immediately. He was from a radical Russian Jewish family. My parents' politics appeared pale, almost conservative, in comparison to Gabe's. (I had met his family almost immediately.)

His grandparents were take-no-prisoners-and-make-no apologies, card-carrying Communists. His grandfather had lost his job at one of the major Hollywood studios because of it, but continued to make a good living doing private tailoring. He and his wife had never married and in this family nobody was embarrassed by it. Gabe's father was as radical an adult as I had then met. I couldn't figure out Gabe's quiet and nervous mother until years after when I realized she likely had been clinically depressed. But she was still involved in activism in radical political circles. Friday night dinner talk was loud, stimulating, and combative even if all their friends were of the same political persuasion. It seemed that almost everybody in their circle had been blacklisted by Hollywood. I fell in love with the family and then pretended I had fallen in love with Gabe.

I made the grievous error of equating left-wing politics with sympathy for, or belief in the rights of women. But I didn't understand that until we had formalized our relationship with vows. From the beginning to the end, the marriage lasted just over two years. I was the one who bolted.

By 1970 feminism was in the atmosphere. For me politics was no longer only about the war. I had become disgusted that all the leaders of the student and anti-war movements were guys. Guys were in charge, as usual, and Gabe surely saw himself as in charge of our life (and that included me). But I heard other voices when we weren't at home together or at protests. Women were powerful. We could revolt at home. We didn't have to cook dinner, shop, or have children. More important, we were going to change the world, turn it upside down. We would shout and scream and march in the streets until we were taken seriously. I was reading and learning and going to consciousness-raising groups. We women could claim our own lives, find our voices, determine our own destiny, and control our bodies.

I couldn't wait to talk to Gabe's grandmother Anya. She identified herself as a Worker's Party Socialist, but she had confided to me she was even more to the left. I went to see her for tea to tell her about what I was doing, reading, learning and thinking. She was appalled. Did I hate men? Did I hate my wonderful father? Did I now hate Gabe? Had I become a lesbian? What was I doing? What had happened to me? Surely I hadn't become *one of those feminists;* she broke the word into at least four syllables, enunciated with revulsion.

I was speechless and felt defenseless. She continued on. She told me I should read real Russian literature, and suggested Pushkin. I said I was quite familiar with Pushkin but that he wasn't going to help women's equality. In that instant she and I had become enemies. Quietly sipping tea and eating her delicious Russian pastries, I waited for Gabe to pick me up. When Gabe arrived it was clear something was wrong. Anya was still furious and told him I was a lunatic. A Communist, a Worker's Party Socialist, a woman I had prized having in my life, who hated feminism and now hated me. I wasn't imagining this: she told me I was no longer welcome in her home.

Gabe calmed and comforted her. He shot daggers at me. Gabe said to his grandmother: *Don't worry about Alida, she gets like this sometimes now. I don't think about what she says. I ignore her. She is just frothing at the mouth.*

It took a few more months and a few more insults, such as Gabe's suggestion that he should have tied me to the sink in the kitchen rather than let me attend women's studies classes and women's meetings. Finally, there was his awkward and half-hearted attempt to strangle me with the cord of our electric blanket. It was late at night. I ran out of our apartment to the nearest phone booth, and called a close friend who drove to where I was standing on the sidewalk and rescued me, providing shelter in her studio apartment until I could figure out what was next.

8

The Way We Almost Were

I wish meeting B could be told differently because it is such a cliché, but it was combustion. And of course it happened at a political event. It qualified as a Hollywood beginning: *An Affair to Remember.* Or better: Nora Ephron's retelling of that classic in her *Sleepless In Seattle,* without the kid or the teddy bear or the Empire State Building. At moments we were Streisand and Redford in *The Way We Were,* but B and I shared the same politics.

B considered himself the more radical. He contemplated actions I wasn't willing to consider, and he was prepared to suffer the consequences, including arrest. Our anti-war sentiments swamped our emotions; we were enraged much of the time. Sometimes I wanted to ditch the whole American enterprise, live abroad, become an ex-pat. B said that was a bad idea and unpatriotic. He wasn't about to let the other side force us to abandon our country. So which one of us was the radical?

The African-American congresswoman Shirley Chisholm announced her decision to run for the presidency in 1972 and I wore her button proudly: Hit The Chisholm Trail. She wasn't hated the way Hillary Clinton was when she ran in 2008, because Chisholm wasn't taken seriously. We put what was left of our hope for the country into George McGovern's campaign. As I look back I wonder if we seriously believed George McGovern could win. B and I interrupted our lives—I took a break from college and he from work—traveling across the country working in swing states for the campaign. It was pretty much a grass roots enterprise, and the ground effort was largely run by people in their twenties like us. Gary Hart was McGovern's campaign manager. Some of us wore green buttons that said I Am A Grass Root.

In the last stretch of the campaign we were sent to upstate New York. The campaign flew us from Los Angeles to JFK, where campaign workers handed us cash and herded us onto buses destined for our assigned locations. B and I were given the Utica-Rome area. Once there I stayed, but B was sent to help run the Cooperstown area. We had to communicate by letter and the occasional phone call from our campaign offices or from the homes of the people hosting us. But by then I was just serving time, disenchanted once again with the male bias of politics and my understanding that finally and fully what McGovern was only really about was ending the war. His position on women's rights was weak or negligible, nor had he supported the abortion plank at the Democratic convention. Gloria Steinem was right when she said that George McGovern didn't understand the goals of the women's movement.

One night some of us went downtown for dinner and drinks. Utica-Rome was already an economically depressed area but people still had jobs. The head of our campaign office said he knew a nightclub that both served excellent and inexpensive steaks and poured the booze generously. He took us to a dark and slightly shabby place. I knew my way around nightclubs since childhood, so when we walked into the lounge I sensed something strange, something sleazy. We were seated at a booth adjacent to a large piano bar area. As we were drinking and eating our steaks and baked potatoes, the piano player came out and banged out a few tunes with little enthusiasm. He asked for requests and looked around to see if anyone there was likely to contribute to his empty tip glass.

A few of the campaign workers were increasingly restless; they wanted to go smoke dope; they could care less about cocktails or steaks. Then a thin platinum blonde dressed in red and black appeared from a back door. I assumed she was the singer, but she was scantily dressed, even for a bar entertainer. She smiled and waved to the customers, many of whom knew her and called her Candy. By now the bar was packed and more dining tables had filled. All the customers were men. Without effort, and most gracefully, Candy climbed onto the bar top and began a kind of dancing I had never seen. Only when she turned directly to face our table did I notice that her vagina was exposed. As she moved and swayed seductively toward the men at the bar, they held out mostly one-dollar bills. These Candy captured with her vagina.

I got up, left the bar, and vomited on the street. Then I went to a phone booth and called my hosts, professors at nearby Hamilton College and asked if they would come get me. They did so immediately.

The wife and I stayed up all night talking about the terrible things that happen to women and the abuses they suffer and what kind of a life the woman at the bar might have endured before she decided to earn her wages with her vagina. We didn't judge her. We saw her as a victim. We began talking about how little McGovern seemed to care about women's rights and needs. Once started, we couldn't stop.

At the campaign office next morning the others made fun of me for not being able to "handle it" at the nightclub. Not one of them saw what we observed as a woman's issue to be concerned about. Not one of my campaign colleagues was a woman.

I soldiered on and still enjoyed, in limited ways, the camaraderie of being on the road working in a national campaign. But I was also learning that I didn't want to spend my life in national politics. I wanted to work with and write about women's political issues. Within the campaign ranks, we recognized McGovern's campaign was doomed. None of us expected the loss to be so overwhelming. (McGovern carried only the state of Massachusetts and the District of Columbia. The Electoral College count was 520 for Nixon and 17 for the senator from South Dakota.) By the time our work was done in upstate New York the campaign was running out of money and optimism. We were sent home on Greyhound buses.

B and I got off the bus in Chicago. We checked ourselves into a rather upscale hotel for a few nights. We slept for many hours before we could face sunlight or reality. Then we ate decently for the first time in months, took in a few Chicago sights, and B found out about a jazz club, primarily for me, but which we both enjoyed. We tried not to talk about politics and avoided mentioning the 600-pound elephant waiting for us—Richard Nixon, the current, and clearly next president. Depressed, depleted, and unwilling to face more Greyhound travel, we bought airplane tickets and flew back to Los Angeles.

* * *

We struggled to find our equilibrium. The election was some months away but few gave McGovern a chance. We were invited to Boulder to stay with friends of B's; it was to be a holiday. Our hosts were close friends of his—James and Nella, Wilson and Charlotte. They were welcoming to me, but I was an outsider and I felt isolated. James, Wilson, and Charlotte had gone to the same small prestigious college together, Pomona College, on the Claremont campus in California.

That was salt in my heart because I had wanted to attend Pitzer, another one of the colleges in the Claremont complex. Nella was from an authentic Mayflower family with a pre-colonial family tree and important pre-colonial silver kept in a vault somewhere in Massachusetts. I had a pre-colonial family tree as well on my father's side, but we were Jews, and didn't have possessions to give evidence to the lineage. Nella wasn't anti-Semitic but Jews were from another galaxy than her own. She used two family last names along with her married name—three surnames. Her father had been headmaster of an elite boys' boarding school. Nella was friendly, but there was an elegant, perhaps regal, reserve about her. Though she was curious to learn something about the daughter of a barkeep who was the product of a public college education and yet appeared well-read (as she allowed in her crisp New England accent). B was part of their world because he had gone to college with the other three, but his world and mine were far more parallel than his to theirs. His mother was a schoolteacher, and his father a battalion chief in the Los Angeles Fire Department, a feat and triumph for a Jewish man in those days.

But it wasn't really social class that separated me from the other women, it was motherhood. They already had their first babies, both girls. I was transfixed watching them as they mothered, but I was also confused. Having a baby appeared to be so natural and easy for them. For me it was fraught with worry and superstition. I watched as they prepared to nurse. In Nella's case this included squirting her breast milk across the room and then laughing with unbridled joy. Nothing had ever made me that happy. Would breasts overflowing with milk do that for me too? There was much laughter between the young mothers. I listened silently as they talked about things I didn't understand and wasn't interested enough to ask.

I knew that being a mother and not being a mother represented a large divide between women, but with them it seemed insurmountable. They wanted to know *when* B and I were going to have our children, not *if*. I didn't express my fears or reservations. I revealed nothing about my illness, which was conveniently quiet at the time. I didn't express my anxiety about health and pregnancy. Instead, I said I didn't absolutely need to have children.

With this sentence out of my mouth, I was sent to social Siberia. They were polite, but now I was officially excluded from their club, not because I wasn't yet a mother but because I might never be a mother. They talked of almost nothing except babies and strollers and baby equipment and feeding habits. I felt as intolerant of them as they were of me, and thought that they had turned into morons rather than the well-educated and well-read women they were. Charlotte did once ask me to take a walk with her one lovely afternoon. I jumped at the chance. They lived in a gorgeous and as yet unspoiled area of Boulder. She put Sara into an infant backpack and we set off. But there was no conversation between us. I asked a few geographical questions and she answered them. The rest was just Charlotte's voice singing a rhyme she had made up for her daughter: *Sara-dara-do-mommy-loves-you.*

That night in bed I told B that the other women had lost their minds. I asked what brilliant women were doing singing silly rhymes to their babies and showing no interest in joining our talk about the war, about the election, about what was going on in our country and the world, about women's rights, or any talk of going to work when the girls were older.

In retrospect, I acted poorly. Reinforcing my presumed indifference to motherhood, I didn't cuddle the adorable little girls. I wrote constantly in my journal and kept my distance as best I could. My journal had a picture of Virginia Woolf on the cover. On the first page of the journal I wrote: "Virginia never did have children did she?"

I wanted to be a mother, but I was scared to death. I didn't know how to say to anyone, not even to B: *I am so afraid to get pregnant. So afraid I will have a dead baby or a miscarriage. But I am most afraid I will produce a baby who will become a child just like me and live inside the prison of disease.*

Not much later I learned that my fear of miscarriages was not a false one. I never found a moment in my marriage where I was brave enough and trusting enough to admit how terrified I was. B's family expected, and his father demanded, that we have children. He was already impatient.

To admit that I thought I might not be able to produce a healthy child felt more disabling to me than hiding behind professional desires and hopes for my writing life. I created a verbal, ideological barricade and behind it I felt safer. During the Boulder trip I pretended that not becoming pregnant was a central part of my feminist identity. James and Nella squabbled a great deal and were already in couples counseling. I predicted to B they wouldn't last another two years. They did, had another child, and as far as I know are still married.

One night the women did engage me and asked me if I owned the first issue of *Ms.* magazine, which had come out in the spring of 1972. I had and they said they were jealous—they hadn't snagged one. Now I thought, at last we could talk about what was happening for women. But within seconds the conversation turned to body hair. They didn't believe in shaving their armpits or their legs. (And they were hairy!) I applauded their decision as a feminist one, but it wasn't one I would ever contemplate. They questioned how strong a feminist I really was—wearing dresses, make-up, and shaving regularly. We had judged each other harshly and there was to be no backpedalling to some mythical land called sisterhood, which in their company seemed as surreal as castles and princesses.

They asked me what I enjoyed reading. I was reading the diaries of Virginia Woolf. They were both reading the diaries of Anaïs Nin, and were enthralled by them, and tried to convert me. They offered to loan me an extra copy so I could read along with them while we were visiting. But I wouldn't play their game, though their invitation was well meant. I thought Nin was a silly narcissist, obsessed with sex and men, navel gazing in her obsessive jottings. They talked of Nin as a fine stylist, a painter of words. *Not for me,* I demurred, likely saying it between my teeth. But I did not attack Nin nor offer my fairly vicious analysis of her work.

I had gone to hear Nin speak in Los Angeles and she and her entourage had turned me off. She had been carried down the aisle on a regal chair with women attending her—handmaidens to the priestess. I was bored and annoyed by her talk, and what I saw as affectation and arrogance. I was not the slightest bit interested in reading more of her writing. (But perhaps the reason she was carried down the aisle was that she was already suffering from the cancer that killed her. She died in 1977.)

In 1995 I read a biography of Nin by Deirdre Bair because I so admire Bair, not because I cared about Nin. Bair saw in Nin what I had not. I had been too stubborn and unaware of Nin's life and lies to appreciate there was a real woman behind her extreme artifice. Bair wrote in her introduction to the book: "I certainly agree that Anaïs Nin will enter posterity as a minor writer, but I insist upon one distinction: that she must be judged a *major* minor writer."

Nin had long been dismissed as a "major minor writer," but that was not the context in which Bair placed her. She was making the case for why Nin deserved a full and scholarly biography. Reading Bair I saw Nin as a tormented woman who wrote to release her demons, even as she was lying to herself and her readers as she went forward. She still appears to me as grandiose, vain, and selfish, but there is in her life a woman's story that suggests to me a feminist tale of caution and perseverance.

I didn't buy the early feminist analysis of Nin as a feminist writer. She was a man's woman, a lover of men—a supporter and handmaiden to them. What I admired then, and still do, is that she made no apologies for her sexual passion and her own enjoyment of eroticism. In Bair's biography I saw a woman engulfed in her own deceptions, living a double life in reality and on the page—flying from Los Angeles to New York when she was sick with cancer to keep *both* her husbands supported and happy—Hugo Guiler, who lived in New York and was her legal husband, and Rupert Pole, with whom she lived in Silver Lake,

Los Angeles in a de facto union—It is a woman's story. I respect that Nin had the discipline to accomplish what she did, to write constantly, and to publish throughout her life.

Bair was right; the women's canon should include a proper biography of Nin. The time has long passed for a conversation with those Boulder women. But I am curious whether they surmised any of Nin's hidden life when they were reading the diaries. I had veiled too much of myself from them to be able to share anything at all, even my feelings about Virginia Woolf.

At the Boulder house, I often retreated alone to the kitchen and looked out at the wooded view. In the afternoon the men went off to hike and harvest edible mushrooms. The mothers stayed in the living room, playing with their baby girls, laughing and singing. I felt I didn't belong anywhere. I remember it as one of the saddest times of my life. I loved B and didn't think anyone could love as much as I loved him. But I couldn't have the dialogue about motherhood with him, or with them, or with anyone. I couldn't share with Nella and Charlotte, whom I barely knew, that my mother had barely held it together during my childhood because of her own grief over her lost son and her worry about a chronically ill daughter.

And I wasn't yet a writer. I scribbled. I was only a hopeful wannabe who had shown some promise as a girl. But that was in my past. I would continue for many years to divert creative writing into research writing. I was publishing dry and precise scholarship, where a turn of phrase was neither desired nor appropriate. Within the particular area of research writing I was in, clarity and accuracy of argument and reliable data reigned. Quantitative scholarship was important necessary work, but it wasn't what I wanted, not what I had intended. I felt stuck and miserable.

In the kitchen in Boulder at the height of the Vietnam War, the only thing I was sure about was that B and I would never be a divorce statistic. We had an equal and a feminist marriage.

I told myself that I was anything but a traditional wife. We divided up the chores, shared money equally, and treated each other with respect and concern.

I was involved in projects that took me even further from literature and theater. I wouldn't take chances. I had stopped dreaming. And I didn't have the guts to have an open conversation with my husband about what would happen to us if I couldn't, or wouldn't, get pregnant.

The dusk of the early evening in the mountains surrounding Boulder that night might have provided a peaceful and surreal landscape, but it only served as a jarring backdrop to my inner turmoil. Where would I fit in?

Charlotte had stenciled these words across one of the kitchen cabinets:

Don't push the river, it flows by itself

I had heard the phrase often but that night it lodged in my brain and I couldn't release it. Eventually I joined the others in the living room. As we drank wine and ate, I asked about the phrase painted on the cabinet. Charlotte said she loved the quote but couldn't remember where she first heard it. There was a lively debate about its origin. Was it an Indian proverb? A Chinese saying? Hebraic wisdom? Some guru's mantra that had become commonplace? There was no Google, of course, and the conversation went around and around and on and on. Eventually I asked what it meant to each of them. Their answers were variations of: things usually turn out the way they are supposed to in the end, so don't sweat it. Then it was my turn: *I think it means we are really fortunate that we don't have any idea what the future holds for any of us.*

* * *

Our future contained one knowable thing. It would include the presence of chronic illness and its effect on any relationship.

Hospitalizations, wrong diagnoses, too much steroid, too little steroid, drug interactions, mean doctors, arrogant doctors, sweet but incompetent doctors, all were a burden. I became a burden to B and a disappointment to his family.

There were other unexpected surprises, as there are in all lives. Out of the blue, B was offered a job in Columbus, Ohio, which he accepted. It was the right move and the right job for him. He was already a part of a national educational program in mathematics that served elementary school children in disadvantaged areas. But now he was asked to direct the midwestern region. He went on ahead and I came later. At first I called life in Ohio the midwestern captivity, but then the state got under my skin. It was a life so different from Southern California that in many ways I felt like an ex-pat. We bought a small house, originally a carriage house, in the quiet suburb of Bexley. It seemed as small as a doll's house but it had ample land, and I planted gardens I had never had the opportunity to do before. My mother was a splendid gardener and so it was natural for me—flowers and ornamental plantings in the front yard, vegetables in the back.

We took road trips to Kentucky and the Blue Ridge Mountains. We drove regularly into Amish country and up to Cleveland and down to Cincinnati. We both became fascinated with the historic Shaker community in Pleasant Hill, Kentucky, and visited often. We followed the festivals. Ohioans love a festival. There was a bratwurst festival, a pumpkin festival, an apple festival, a Greek festival, a Celtic festival, a sweet corn festival, a canal festival, and countless more. We sampled widely. We made friends easily. A group of us formed a dinner commune, where we dined in a different home each day—Monday through Thursday. It took an enormous burden off the women, but also off men like B who cooked and shopped. We had friends who were also in grad school as I was, and in medical school, law school, and were teachers, lawyers, librarians and the like. It was a university town, but one without pretension. Winters were harsh and icy, but we adjusted.

We joined a temple, a new experience, but one that anchored me. It was liberal, reform and activist. The women there were friendly to newcomers, and the rabbi was also a professor of Jewish history. It turned out he was from Los Angeles too and B had known him from earlier times. We celebrated holidays with temple friends and had a large social circle in the neighborhood and elsewhere. Though I missed California and family, I didn't feel lonely in Ohio. One evening at the home of friends from the temple, I felt comfortable enough to tell the women there that I was terrified about having children. These women were probably ten to fifteen years older than I was. They said they would help me every step of the way. And I knew that they meant it and that maybe, with their help, I would be able to conquer my fears.

School was a different story. It wasn't satisfying, and I wasn't as committed as I should have been. I was serving time, having made an unwise choice. I was in the school of social sciences in a quantitative research-intensive department that was a hotbed of petty politics and inter-specialty fighting (which was ironic as it was supposed to be a model interdisciplinary program). Tenured professors and female grad students were having illicit encounters, and there were few women in the program. I was trying to master statistics at a level that I believed would help me professionally, but this did not play to my strengths or skills. B attended my advanced statistics class and took notes and told me to just listen. At night he tutored me, the gifted mathematician with a wife who was a slow learner at anything connected to numbers. It was an act of love.

I was unfulfilled. I knew it was time to take action and take charge of my life. I was leaning again toward politics, having put the McGovern experience behind me. Our next-door neighbor was the assistant state attorney general. He talked to me about applying to the Ohio Senate Fellowship program, which was run just like the White House Senate fellowship program. The competition was stiff and the odds were against me. My neighbor was forbidden to help me in any way. But I completed the application, which included essays. I asked B to read it, after which he said he was stunned by my clarity and sense of purpose.

I made the first cut. There were more hurdles and then the second cut. I made the final cut and was asked to the senate offices for an interview. There was a round of interviews with senators, their aides, and other administrators. Finally there was an interview with Governor John Gilligan. I was intimidated and felt queasy, but I hadn't dreamed I would get this far; at that point, there was nothing to lose. Gilligan was warm, chatty, and anything but intimidating. He was interested in my McGovern campaign experience and in my feminist politics. I remember little of what transpired, but I recall there were numerous aides in the executive office. At the end, he asked me where I saw myself in twenty years. I said, *Governor, I would hope to be sitting in your chair.* He looked at me, with a wide grin and said he hoped I meant it. I replied that I intended to mean it more each and every year. And I did. I saw that in Ohio a woman had a chance to break through at least some political barriers.

I received a fat package from the Senate Fellowship office. I had won one of the few places. My next year would be spent in the Ohio Senate, learning the ropes of state legislation. My parents said that now I was on my way.

One month later B received an offer from University of California, Berkeley. It was a bigger job with more responsibility, money, and prestige. I shouted with anger and horror when he told me. He said that if he accepted the offer I should stay and experience my senate fellowship year. And that was my intention.

In the weeks that followed, our talk was heavy with the

dilemma of decision, but it was clear he was going to accept. B rightly reminded me that I had called Columbus the midwestern captivity. But that was then, and this was now, I thought. I had a long conversation with our neighbor in the state attorney's office. He laid it on the line. The fellowship would help prepare me for a political life in Ohio, but not anywhere else. I believed him, and maybe he was right, and maybe he wasn't. In any event, my calculation was that a political career was always a gamble, especially for a woman, but it was my marriage that was the sure thing.

B prepared to move to Berkeley and I stayed behind to sell the house. By now we talked about the move to the Bay Area as a mutual decision and a dream come true. I wrote a letter to the administrator of the fellowship program declining my appointment and explaining the reason. Then I wept the entire day. B drove across the country. Our dog Bernie and I were left to deal with the transition. Bernie was a quirky animal and high-maintenance, but B's departure sent him over the edge.

The house sold quickly. B bought a home in Oakland that I had not seen, but my in-laws drove up and gave it their stamp of approval. It was an interesting and eccentric house on the top of a hill that appealed to me more than it did to B. Perhaps he had bought it for that reason.

The day of our move was sheer melodrama. The mover got into a fight with the day-worker he had hired. The mover was a white man who was surly to the day-worker, who was black. I had already signed off on the bill of lading and they were closing the van's doors when I heard screams and then police sirens. The two men were brawling in my driveway. The white man had the black man on the ground and was choking him. I came out screaming and crying and quickly turned the garden hose on them, and they stopped. Neither man appeared injured. A neighbor across the street had called the police. Bexley was an all-white community. They sent out four police cars. The mover told his version, which was that the worker had jumped him. He was able to gain control and pin him down. The black man said the exact opposite. There were no witnesses until the two men were seen fighting on the pavement.

I was questioned, and said that I had witnessed the worker being choked. The mover glared at me. The police checked both men and decided they were not injured seriously and didn't require first aid. The black man was handcuffed and taken into custody. I protested, but it was useless. The mover said in a hostile voice: *Well, I'll see you in Oakland.* (But the truck and the driver went missing for months. We didn't ever see him in Oakland. Eventually the moving company located our van and a different driver brought out our stuff.)

It was time to leave. The night before, the neighbors gave me a party. The hosts put a banner in front of their house: *Goodbye Columbus! Goodbye Alida!* It was a loving send-off. Bernie was a crazy dog but he was smart and instinctive. He refused to go into his crate. He fought me and fought my neighbor, who had a good relationship with him. We bribed him with hot dogs. I called our vet, a neighbor and good friend, and he came over with Valium. It had an opposite effect on Bernie, who began to run laps around the backyard. But finally, he was drugged into oblivion, and off we went to the airport.

Not long after we were in the air, the pilot announced an immediate emergency landing in Chicago. The windshield was seriously cracked and it was too dangerous to continue. We would deplane and board another. I was sure that either Bernie would be lost or would die. I fell apart when we got off the airplane. An airplane representative took me to a special area where I could watch Bernie be reloaded into the luggage compartment of the new plane.

I called B from Chicago to tell him all that had happened. In tears, I told him everything was an omen. We would never make it. He calmed me, and said it was an omen that meant that once

I arrived, our time together in Berkeley would be magical. When we arrived in San Francisco, I saw him waiting at the gate. He felt to me like home, like refuge, like safety. When Bernie was delivered to us we both could see the dog was traumatized. He was never completely the same again. Neither were we.

In the beginning in Berkeley I had no job, and the interviews I had at the university didn't result in offers. One afternoon, sitting in Tilden Park, reading the letters of Toulouse Lautrec and wondering how to connect to anything or anyone, I thought how I might be able to get a decent paying job. An older woman, who had been my supervisor when I worked in a maritime law firm in Long Beach as a student, had moved to the firm's main office in San Francisco. Her name was D. J. I think it stood for Dorothy Jane but nobody ever called her anything but D.J. I called and she was delighted to learn I was living in Berkeley and told me to come over to have lunch at the firm and meet the head of personnel. Graham and James was one of the oldest and most respected maritime firms, and I had been an excellent legal secretary in the Long Beach branch. The personnel officer was a smart woman, who said I wasn't a lawyer, they didn't have any research positions, and I didn't have any paralegal training. Surely I didn't want to be a secretary. Surely I did not. We said goodbye.

The next day she called and said she had an interesting proposition. Would I like to come over and meet Mr. Leonard James, the founding partner? That's all she said. I was on the next BART train. Mr. James was then in his 70s and losing his hearing. He was the only living founding partner. He took me into his confidence. He needed someone to be his personal assistant, in his words, *to be his ears*. I understood he feared he might be missing things that were important to his position and to retaining power in the firm. We became an excellent working team. We understood each other. He respected me and always treated me as an equal. He had been married for many years, lost his wife and then remarried a much younger woman with whom he had his only child, a son. They lived in Sausalito overlooking the Bay in a house that was so inviting, so delightful, that even now I wonder if I may have made it up.

I might have stayed at G&J until Mr. James retired or died. The pay was good, the benefits excellent, hours reasonable, and I was writing on weekends. The idea of a career, any career, in politics had died when I left Ohio. But the controlling partners decided Mr. James could not have a full-time and well-paid assistant to himself. I was assigned to work for another partner as well. He and I hated each other instantly. He was sexist, and I could smell it on him. He knew I was a feminist without my uttering a word. And I distrusted him with regard to Mr. James. He demanded I bring his coffee and fetch his lunch. I often had to work through lunch (without a food break) because he was a procrastinator who never had his pleadings or briefs done on time. One day he lipped off to me when I hadn't even had a bathroom break. I walked into Mr. James's office and asked if he could do anything, and he said he couldn't. *They are after both of us I fear, my dear.* I told him I couldn't leave him. He told me I must. Why not go to law school, was his suggestion. It was an echo of my father's wishes, but I didn't want to tell Mr. James that I really didn't want to be a lawyer. Instead, I said I was fed up with post-grad education. I left the firm that very moment—walked off the job. Having never done such a thing, I found it exhilarating. B was furious and shaken by what I did. He thought it was irresponsible and damaging.

(Years later, when my book *Dimensions of Tolerance* was published and Mr. James was a very old man, he read a review of it in *The New York Times*. He wrote me a long and thoughtful letter expressing his pride, and affirmed he always knew I was going to do something "in the law.")

Several months after I'd walked out of the firm, I got a research job at the university. On paper and in the initial interviews, it appeared to be the ideal job for me. But it would turn out to be something else entirely.

* * *

How do you know when a marriage unravels past the point of repair? Was it obvious to everyone but me? When I overheard my husband say to a friend that at least his friend's terminally-ill wife had the good grace to die, I knew. But I wanted to believe I hadn't heard that. I deluded myself. Our eccentric multi-level house on a hill had become a safety hazard for me. I was regularly falling down the stairs. B was increasingly edgy and restless. He wanted to change his life and change houses. One day he announced, after making the decision without including me in any of discussions, that he was going to move to Los Angeles. He intended to leave immediately after the Thanksgiving holiday that year.

Los Angeles was to be the next destination on his hopscotch game of personal achievement. For quite some time he sold his move to me as yet another commuter marriage, something quite common in our circle. We would be together every weekend and on holidays, but this house had to be sold. He was right that I couldn't handle the house alone, stairs or no stairs. We purchased a sweet, small house in the Berkeley hills. It was reasonably priced because it didn't have a view, but was in a redwood stand. It was on one level, with a compact patio and garden in the backyard. I liked it enough to feel content. We moved in as a married couple and took ownership as a married couple, but he had begun his next chapter, a dual life, in L.A. He didn't just want a different house, a different town, and a different career. He wanted to be relieved of me.

In the beginning, he stayed with his brother, but that didn't preclude spontaneous, unannounced weekend visits. When he came to Berkeley we resumed our lives as if nothing had changed. I learned he was in love with someone else, but continued to wear his wedding ring. Playful cards and notes from *the other woman* were scattered across the top of our shared bedroom dresser. I looked at them and then pretended I hadn't noticed. Who was *this other woman?* I didn't demand he choose between us. If we stayed married, eventually the affair would be remembered as a minor disturbance in a long and eventful marriage. It was a childish, perhaps a romantic, calculation.

One night while we were making love he *taught* how me to kiss his neck in a way he found newly erotic. Apparently she had better (or fresher) techniques than I did. Even sex lessons via his new lover didn't dampen my desire to be desirable. I felt pathetic. I wasn't proud. I was embarrassed, humiliated. I pressed on, convincing myself he would end the affair. Wiser and older women friends told me to take action, *any* action. My psychiatrist cautioned me about letting the status quo continue. But I ignored everyone. It was my passage into the land of magical thinking.

There *were* other options. I could have asked him to end the affair and that I move to Los Angeles to join him. If he refused (and I suspect he would have), at least I would have taken control of my destiny. I should have faced the fact that the marriage was irretrievable, and discussed separation and divorce. But I couldn't cut the bonds of love and attachment. I dined out on a smartass remark: *I'm too young to be left for a younger woman*— which was pure melodrama. His new love interest wasn't much younger than I was.

I adopted a new, flamboyant style of dress. More costume than clothing, it was a futile attempt to appear larger than life. Young, pretty, and recently detached, I was now a target for the roaming adulterous male academics. Faculty wives perceived me as a threat. My social life took a speedy detour from being asked to Friday and Saturday night dinner parties to casual Sunday brunches with friends and their young children. Suddenly I saw

Berkeley as a small town where the hot gossip was of news about shifting domestic arrangements. My story became part of the cocktail chatter.

My husband made no serious overtures toward reconciliation, nor did he file for divorce. The front yard of the new house on Olympus Avenue was planted with daisies that seemingly bloomed twelve months a year. An entire property covered with sweet daisy bushes was antithetical to my state of mind. I wanted to return to our old Oakland hill house and to *our* feminist marriage. When I talked to him of earlier, happier times, B didn't respond. I took his silence to mean he was leaning in my favor. Then I began to wonder if the domestic picture I'd painted was based only on my perceptions. It took years for me to accept that the death of our marriage had more to do with chronic disease than with my feminist politics.

In our last act, I blamed myself for everything. B was so reasonable, so brilliant, so handsome and admired. It must have been I who ruined our marriage. When our friends pressed us about our future, B had a stock remark: *Our marriage is just weird enough to have a divorce in the middle of it.* The glib cruelty of the comment eluded me then. When my parents asked him about our marriage, he gave the same "weird enough" answer. Mother viewed the quip as hopeful. My father said it was arrogant bullshit spoken by a coward. B still took no legal action. His much-used remark was the only context in which he ever used the word divorce.

9
A City of Women

I was a fierce champion of women's rights, but my private life belied my public positions. Contrary to the rallying cry—*the personal is political*—my personal life was apolitical. My professional life was also based on a series of compromises. I was a project director at one of the university's research institutions, under the oppressive thumb of a reigning "Great Man." I didn't have the power to choose the topics in the national surveys we were conducting on American attitudes toward tolerance and civil liberties, but I was responsible for the outcome of the project and management of the research budgets. I fought hard to include basic women's issues. My situation wasn't unique at the time—men dominated quantitative academic research.

Far more troubling for me was my relationship to the "Great Man," who had hired me and was my supervisor. He was also the principal investigator. Because the project was funded with grant money from outside foundations (known as soft money), my position was not protected by university regulations. He was considered one of the university's more difficult Great Men and had a reputation for being neurotic. I learned early on that this character trait had been understated.

Once B was living in Los Angeles, I found myself swimming in treacherous waters. Anita Hill's testimony to the Senate Judiciary Committee about Justice Clarence Thomas was a decade and a half in the future. *Hostile workplace* was not yet part of the vernacular of gender discrimination. It would not become so until 1986, when in *Meritor Savings Bank v. Vinson*, 447 U.S. 57 (1986) the Supreme Court held that a *hostile work environment* constituted an actionable form of sex discrimination under Title VII of the Civil Rights Act. Even after laws and protective provisions were put in place that defined hostile workplaces and harassment as actionable offenses, many universities and colleges failed to aggressively enforce them. Although we were on the cusp of a new era, even in progressive Berkeley it was not yet law, nor was it the culture of the workplace.

Women frequently endured sexual harassment and aggression at work (now commonly defined as abuse of power). Coping strategies were of several categories. Some of us resigned quietly or disappeared, leaving our careers in shreds. Others went along to get along to preserve their family's economic stability and their professional viability. The anti-woman remark, S*he slept her way to the top,* was heard often, including the academic environment. But women rarely slept their way to the top. Some of us may have s*lept our way to the middle* and to a precarious form of economic security—or slept our way into staying employed. Many of us were degraded verbally, but avoided unwanted sexual encounters. When status and power reside in one person who can fire or demote you, the resulting sexual liaison is unequal and not completely consensual. It isn't always rape, but all workplace relationships in this category constitute a kind of submission.

Some of us persuaded ourselves that we wanted intimacy with powerful men. We said *yes,* and then regretted it. We weighed the options (if they could be defined as legitimate options) and went forward without recognizing the unfair power dynamics in play. We didn't comprehend that these kinds of entanglements should have been illegal far earlier than they were. Sometimes we did what we did because we were flattered and excited that high-status men wanted us. Often, we were frightened at the same time. We spun romantic fantasies attempting to cheat the truth, pretending our situation was special.

Many years after such an affair, my friend M summarized

what had happened to her in the last of the 1960s and early 1970s:

Was there anything really romantic about the years I spent with Professor S?

No!

What happened between us wasn't love. When he seduced me I was still a virgin. I was his student. By the time I finished graduate school, he was the head of the department. Then I became his employee. My fate was in his hands.

Nobody in power would have listened or cared if I had complained. He was the power.

I refuse to remember it as a beautiful love affair. I paid dearly for it. He took everything from me. Yes, I "let" him, but it wasn't a victimless crime—I was a victim. I felt trapped.

I starved myself, trying to disappear, and ended up in the hospital. Only after that did I find the strength to leave, to start a new life, to launch my own career.

But I lost those years. Nothing can give them back to me.

Workplace affairs and sexual encounters between people of unequal power and status are now recognized as potentially illegal and discriminatory. Without substantial evidence to support claims to the opposite, these liaisons are no longer assumed consensual. But controversies and battles continue to surround women who object. When they pursue legal action, women may have to defend themselves against their predators. Often, men do not go away quietly once they are accused or sued. Only rarely do they confess. They claim it was consensual or insist the woman was the seducer, the *temptress*. Nonetheless, the employment legislation laws and ordinances long fought for are important victories, and they must not be underestimated. The avenues for legal remedy also apply to men who are victims of workplace predation.

This was not the case when I was young and vulnerable. Euphemistically we were called *The Handmaidens to Great Men*.

Infrequently these liaisons led to long-term relationships, sometimes even marriages. I have known women who began that way, but went on to live with professors or bosses in what appeared to be fulfilling relationships. Whether or not the initial choice for these women was made freely, there likely was a feeling of redemption.

With B's obvious absence from Berkeley, I was subject to the increasing advances and demands of the "Great Man." He was in equal measure compelling, controlling, charming, mercurial, and seductive—and he was my employer. Decades later, I look back and am still enraged. It took place over almost a decade and it felt endless then. He was experienced at the game and knew how to play it. When he needed a defense, I was portrayed as a flirtatious predator, and he was but dough in my hands. His spouse dubbed me the Scarlet Harlot. In their joint spinning, he was the innocent victim of a young Circe who drove him to temporary madness. He expected others to believe him and several did.

Perpetrator As Victim is one of the oldest moves in the book, but I didn't yet know there was a playbook. Famous, celebrated, and feared by many, the "Great Man" held professional power over me. He was thirty-four years my senior. And I was yet another young woman in a life punctuated by similar seductions. His wife was also his victim, so no wonder she vilified me. Today he could be accused of creating a hostile workplace and charged with abuse of power. I suspect the university's administration would have negotiated a compromise, even if the legal protections and federal laws had been in place. I am too war-weary from the battles of sexual harassment and abuses of power and status to believe otherwise. He had published distinguished work and was a celebrity-scholar. Most importantly, he had substantial clout because he brought millions of research dollars into the university's coffers.

It took me longer than it should have, but eventually I

stopped wallowing in confusion and bemoaning my entrapment. I ceased being flattered by the "Great Man's" attention or frightened by his demands. I didn't try to change his mind about women and politics. I came not to care what he thought about me, or about anything else. His profound distaste for feminism, women's literature, women's studies, and gender research no longer mattered. I was done with his nonsense. My paralysis was over. I decided to run for my life. It took years for me to accept this action as a victory. Holding onto the slender threads of sanity and hope, I extricated myself. His threats were seasoned with manipulative enticements about all he would do for me—if only I would stay. But I had moved beyond his grasp.

From the vantage point of a professional life nearing completion, my youthful departure from Berkeley appears well planned. The "Great Man" insisted I had plotted against him for months. I was infuriated he believed I had any power. He wasn't wrong. I had a strong survival instinct—a real power that women possess. I didn't have a plan and there was never a nefarious plot. I simply decided to move away from him and forward with my career. From an outsider's view my actions may have looked like sailing, but to me it felt more like lurching.

I decided to take a month of unused vacation leave and bought a cheap air ticket to New York. When I landed at JFK it was a chilly mid-November late afternoon. I found the unaccustomed autumn air invigorating. In the taxi to Manhattan, I convinced myself I could conquer private demons and see life as one to fill with my own experiences. I wanted to live without the control of authoritarian male filters. I could no longer deny that I had married a man whose preferences and career had dictated what we did and did not do, and it had limited my options. And I had permitted it from the beginning.

B and I talked a good feminist game and shared chores and domestic drudgery, but it was and always had been his life that we were living. I was determined to shed male definitions and criteria of what it meant to be a woman, how to compose a daily life, what to do in the future. In the taxi my fantasy became how to live and breathe my own thoughts, ideas, and desires. I vowed to stop waiting for male approval. I envisioned planning destinations and choosing goals. I was no longer a sad and abandoned wife, or another handmaiden to a "Great Man." I wanted to join the group of women (historical and contemporary) who existed within their own spheres.

The words of my high school teacher resonated: A life of the mind. Maybe I could inhabit such a life in New York. These fleeting thoughts represented an essential first step toward becoming a wholly new person—myself. I was unclear what I should do next, but I intended to stay off roads previously traveled. I remembered the shoeboxes filled with Tina's postcards. That November night I sensed personal freedom was possible. I wanted to release the frightened girl of the past and also recapture the sometimes-fearless child I had been. It was a more exciting goal than sailing for Monaco to an awaiting prince and his attendant demands. But it took loss, betrayal, and disappointment to realize that.

As the taxi approached the city, I saw Manhattan as if for the first time. She stood before me. I saw women walking together and alone, getting in and out of taxicabs, waiting for a bus, headed toward the subway. These were working women meeting friends for a drink or dinner, or headed home, or to a meeting or an appointment, an event or…or…or. I saw them more as characters in a play than actual New York women. I saw them as women with options. I imagined them living in a variety of different arrangements. These women had their own realities, but they also filled my fictions. I saw on the streets that there were more women without men than with men—an exciting foretaste of independence. Now I was a woman alone in Manhattan, a woman resolved to enact some of the dreams Kathe and I had at the end of the 1950s, using our Barbie dolls as surrogates.

My previous moves had been dictated by the needs or desires of others. As a child, of course, I moved with my parents. In a checkerboard college career I had transferred in and out of schools because my disease was in charge. At one point I wanted to be closer to B's family and transferred without much thought about the consequences. Graduate school was more default than decision, because B was already established there. The move to Berkeley was occasioned by his job offer. I fooled both of us into believing the Bay Area was a place I had always wanted to live. But all I did was follow my husband to his next career move and then scramble to find acceptable employment. Berkeley never had anything to do with my goals. In that move I lost forever what the future may have held for the once-confident young woman selected to be an Ohio State Senate fellow.

B's family considered me a strident feminist—and sometimes found me provocative and annoying. But they supported and were sympathetic to the movement's mission. They didn't approve of my keeping my maiden name, however. My mother thought it was a pointless offense to my in-laws. Women could never claim their own last names. *Our names remain that of a man's—a father's or a grandfather's. Even if you choose to use your mother's maiden name, all you are doing is taking her father's name. There are no women's names. You need to go back to Eve to accomplish that, and then all you have is a first name.* I refused my husband's surname, but I still felt like a throwback to the traditional women of earlier eras. What my in-laws defined as strident or militant feminism, I feared was nothing more than angry chatter.

The marriage was finished long before B and I divorced. He had retreated from the demands of my assorted physical woes when we were still living together. But his physical move from our home frightened me. I became dangerously depressed after his departure. But when I realized I too could leave Berkeley,

I regained strength. It would take time to learn how to cope with Manhattan. But from that first cab ride into the city, I had glimpsed its possibilities.

Despite the prevailing left-wing political ideology and endless conversations about equality, my primary experience in Berkeley had not been about feminism. I had imprisoned myself within the straight male research community, within parts of the academy that clung to its New Left identity complete with the sexist remnants. Its opinions about women remained somewhat unchanged from the 1960s. It was far more subtle than the old days, when radical men screamed *Free Food, Free Women, Free Acid* and the like, but I didn't encounter much feminist consciousness in the Berkeley men I knew and worked with. Lesbians were established in richly independent lives and had developed a vibrant culture in Berkeley and the Bay Area. I was envious of their orientation and lifestyle—what I observed as superior strength and vision.

Although its institutional core was still sexist, I thought Manhattan was a place for women. But it wasn't easy to navigate the exclusionary rules. The prestigious private clubs had yet to admit us as members. We could become members of the university clubs, but once admitted we were segregated within them. At the Yale Club, men controlled the pool, where they enjoyed swimming nude—a tradition that began in 1915 and didn't end until 1987. There was a sense that things were shifting in our favor throughout the country, and I felt it more palpably in New York than I had elsewhere.

I didn't come to Manhattan Island to replay scenes from the classic romantic film *An Affair to Remember,* starring Deborah Kerr and Cary Grant. I didn't choose the city as a place to become famous or celebrated or powerful. I came to Manhattan to exist as a serious woman in a serious place. I intended to find a place in the ongoing work for women's rights. I viewed much of my past as a refutation of my feminist ideals. Soon enough

I met women who reassured me. Confident women, including those with public feminist credentials, revealed that their private lives didn't always match their ideology and involvement in the struggle. They confided they could also become submerged in hypocrisy. As feminists we were involved in something bigger and stronger than any one of us. Individually and together, we would find our way to private authenticity in addition to our public activism and advocacy. Months passed, and then I celebrated the first full year of living in Manhattan. It mattered less then, and as more years passed it came not to matter at all, that it was difficult relationships with men that brought me to the city. Manhattan had become a city of women.

It was during that first November exploratory trip when confident of my decision to move to New York and start over, I phoned my father. I expected both validation and approval. As a girl I had listened to his stories about life in New York. But now he was concerned and decidedly unconvinced about the wisdom of my plans. My euphoria was not contagious. He pointed out the basic truths of that moment: I was chronically ill with a serious disease and had no New York job offer. I had only a modest amount of money saved. I had neither friends nor a support group in New York. I knew one person in New York, but he lived in the suburbs.

My father didn't say it was a ridiculous idea. He said: *The House is against you.* He claimed to be a gambler at heart, but when it came to making any significant changes to the status quo, he was among the most calculated and cautious people I've ever known. His much-used phrases—*The House is against you*, usually followed by *The House always wins*—were verbal warnings. I understood the cautionary message from girlhood: If you think the deck of cards is stacked, or the dice loaded, whatever the original plan or strategy might have been, change your plans and get out of the game—fast.

My father appreciated there was nothing left for me in

Berkeley, but we went over the negatives point by point. I replied that I might as well become a New Yorker. He insisted it was a bigger gamble than he had ever made, a misinterpretation of his personal history. He left home during the Depression, knowing he had to earn money for his parents and younger siblings. When he came to New York he made his way, first with tremendous struggle and then successfully. But it was this testimony of his that I had held as an important life lesson: If things became impossible, start over, without whining or self-pity. I had him. Silence ensued.

He might have said his life lesson didn't apply because I was a young woman, not a young man. But he had encouraged me to think of Bella Abzug as an appropriate role model. He had cautioned me about men. He was a primary instructor to me on the importance of female independence. He hoisted the feminist flag as often as my mother did. Now I had put him to the test. I reassured him my decision was made with careful consideration of what would be required. He became cautiously supportive. I promised not to make a final decision at least until I had secured a temporary job. We agreed I would try to take a leave of absence from the California research project, but both of us knew it was unlikely given that the "Great Man" was in charge. But I was not to be tested on my promises. Within days I was offered a one-year position at the Russell Sage Foundation, a New York-based social science foundation that was also the primary funder of the civil liberties project in Berkeley. I convinced myself a year was enough time to find a more secure position elsewhere in the city. That also turned out to be unnecessary because the Sage position became *the job* for me for several years.

Prideful about getting a job quickly, I treated myself to a trip to Paris. My dormant adventurous spirit had returned. With more than two weeks of vacation time remaining, I booked myself on a cheap flight and reserved a room in a budget hotel in the 1st Arrondissement, on Rue Sainte Hyacinthe. I was taking enough prednisone to keep my disease quiet, but not enough to make me insane. The steroids made me believe, however, there was little I couldn't conquer. Over the years I came to describe this drug-fueled sensation as *The Twenty Minute-False Sense Of Well-Being*. Traveling alone to Paris in late November was hardly smart. Recalling a particularly dismal and lonely Thanksgiving Day, I now question my sanity at the time. Those first Paris experiences were filled with people, events, and excursions and were exciting because I was only eighteen, and loosely supervised.

But Paris experienced alone was something else entirely. Despite yielding little joy, that trip marked the beginning of a lifelong habit of running away during difficult times. I've repeated it many times to different destinations. It took until 2010 and a disastrous trip to Berlin and Sardinia for me to face reality. I had spent many of my adult years trying to emulate Tina. I'll never know what motivated Tina's travels. Perhaps she was also on the run from sorrows.

I would embark on solo journeys on the brink of a flare—a defiant and dangerous challenge to the disease. After personal loss and in despair, I made numerous such personal trips. Mostly, I chose foreign cities where I knew no one, foolishly tempting fate in many ways. I persuaded myself that these escapades were proof positive of my competence and independence. I would doggedly get to know a place, visiting historical sites, art museums, attending ballets, operas, plays and concerts, going to libraries. I ate alone in restaurants, refusing to give into the further solitude of room service. But dining in interesting small and local restaurants proved among my most pleasurable experiences during these interludes. That aside, these travel expeditions were frantic, and perhaps pointless.

My Paris hotel wasn't low budget—it was sub-budget. In an excellent location, it was nonetheless dreadful. The interior spaces were cramped and dark. I could have moved to another inexpensive but more pleasant hotel, but inertia had set in. My hotel was immaculately clean and there were fine linens and lovely pillows on the bed, which consoled me and justified my laziness. The breakfast room in the basement was charming, even without windows. After a few mornings of taking my *petit dejeuner* surrounded by people who appeared to be staving off desperation less successfully than I was, or worse—tables filled with jolly family groups, I gave up. I ordered my croissant and café au lait served in my room. Having the chambermaid wake me up each morning was also a strategic measure to keep me from spending the day in bed.

The concierge was a man about ten years older than I was. He had a slight build, brown hair, brown eyes, brown suit, brown shoes, and his complexion gave no hint of a life outside the confines of the hotel. He was kind and helpful. Most comforting to me was that he was never enthusiastic about anything. The ease with which I had spoken French in the past had now disappeared. I was lucky to get out three or four sentences anyone could understand, but he was always solicitous. Parisians are many good things, but patience with foreigners who can't speak their language properly is not one of their admirable traits. I found that when I spoke French, the answers frequently came back in English. Refusing to acknowledge this hostility, I continued to speak only in French.

Each night I went out for a walk. I kept to the busy avenues and crowded attractions. I was afraid of getting lost. Primarily I was afraid of men on the prowl or worse (some basic things, about being a woman alone in a city at night haven't changed much). One evening I bought a bag of roasted chestnuts on the Champs-Élysées. When I got back to the hotel, I offered some to the concierge and he invited me to sit down and talk. Because my French was so fractured, I asked him nothing. But he asked me many questions. Even with my halting French, he understood and asked even more. It was the most animated I had seen him in the by then nearly two weeks of my residence, and I was the most fluent I had been.

Hours passed from evening into the late night, and we continued to talk. I became more confident of my proficiency. Finally, he asked if I were married. With a new fearlessness, I answered with a poetic turn of phrase, rather than the simple truth. I thought I said my marriage was dead, but what I had said was that my husband was dead. As the words left my lips, I realized the mistake. Just as quickly I saw the error would not be corrected. His face expressed shock. He took my hand, shook his head sadly and quietly repeated a few times: *Mais vous êtes tels une jeune femme.* It was a deceitful thing to let stand. I wasn't in the mood to wade back into the sentence and work it through so he would understand I was only trying to be clever. He spoke little English other than hello, goodbye, and thank you, along with a few rudimentary map directions. I was only capable of making the simplest correction, which I chose not to do. It was easier and it felt appropriate to take on the role of a sad young widow. I said good night and went upstairs to bed.

When I got to my cell-like room I wanted to laugh, but I was too ashamed. A part of me did think of B as dead. Now the concierge became so attentive that my shame gave way to annoyance—at both of us. The night before my departure, I thought the phone had rung, and grabbed it. But I had been dreaming. B called and said he had decided he would move to New York with me. When I was awake enough to realize it was a dream, I did laugh. B living in New York City wasn't funny—it was hilarious. I laughed imagining how confused the concierge would have been if he had listened into this imaginary call from my most alive husband. It was the only time I laughed at anything during the trip.

I had conceived the trip as an act of celebration and independence. But it wasn't that, nor had it been a vacation, a renewal, or an adventure. Once in Paris I had descended into dread and depression. As the days and nights dragged on without anyone to talk to or dine with, or share anything, the excitement about my upcoming move to New York vanished. I told myself I couldn't leave Paris early because of the penalty on the restricted air ticket. In truth, I stayed because I didn't want to admit defeat or confess the mistake. So I turned Paris into a self-tutorial. I packed the days and went everywhere I could manage. Like an accountant from a different era, I recorded in bed every outing in detail. But the jottings were without much description or color.

I went to Père Lachaise Cemetery several times to visit the graves of my literary heroes. Standing in front of Colette's grave one afternoon (a favorite stopping point), a woman appeared and stood close to me. She was dressed in black, had beautiful thick graying hair, which she had tied back. She wore several strands of long beads around her neck, so heavy the neckline of her dress sagged. She spoke first in French and then in English. Firmly, but not roughly, she pushed me aside. *Please*, she said in a gently accented English: *You must not stand in that spot. Colette's aura appears at exactly this time of day and you will block it.* I nodded and quickly left the cemetery.

Years later I was in Paris with Marilyn, a good friend. One afternoon we decided to go to Pere Lachaise. Arriving at Colette's resting place she said almost the same thing. *What the hell, Marilyn!* I told her of my earlier encounter with the strange woman with the hair and beads. Marilyn, a tough and smart lawyer, looked at me in astonishment. She was startled I didn't know about the afternoon visitations of Colette's aura. Marilyn claimed it was a fact and was well known.

It was Pablo Picasso who salvaged the trip. The Picasso exhibit had opened in the Grand Palais (later renamed the Musée Picasso). I went almost every day. France had permitted the heirs of Picasso's estate to pay the death taxes in artwork. The French government had received an enormous trove. I learned more about Picasso than I thought possible and wanted to know even more. Pablo and I became pals. Roaming from room to room, I traversed his life as an artist. Standing in front of the portraits of the women in his life, I tried to make sense of them—not what he thought of them, but what they had felt about him. Through the rooms that contained his earliest representational pieces, to the galleries that contained the later abstract and Cubist pieces, I couldn't make sense of Picasso, the man or the artist. His earliest work seemed to bear no resemblance to the artist he became. Until one day, I opened my heart and began to understand the trajectory of his immense gift.

Attractive Frenchmen came over and engaged in pleasant conversations. My halting French amused them. Their flirtatious banter was always accompanied by invitations for drinks or snacks. Some suggested dining at a fine restaurant. Presumably these were dates that could have led to awkward negotiations. Several of the men were hard to dismiss, but I politely declined. I decided that having a fling with an unknown Frenchman, however charming, would be emotional suicide. It might have been a grievous judgment error. I can't know. But my refusal to be courted ended any chance of becoming a modern Parisian courtesan. The ghost of *Gigi* and the aura of Colette must have hovered as I repeatedly rejected handsome Parisians.

Each afternoon was given over to finding a pleasant place to take my main meal. If I wanted a quick bar meal, it was easy but not particularly satisfying. I couldn't navigate the restaurant scene with any confidence or competence. In later solitary travels it was always the restaurants that cheered me, but not in Paris, not then. One day I happened upon a small omelet parlor with lace curtains and beautifully appointed tables. The posted menu prices were within my range. Looking in I noted the place was almost empty. I had gotten caught in a brief light rain— my hair was damp but not dripping wet. I was wearing a smart new pearl-gray raincoat (a pre-departure New York splurge). I walked in, and the maître d' inspected me as if I were curbside debris. I asked for a table. He spoke deeply, from down his nose: *Avez-vous une reservation, Madame?* He articulated *Madame* with a derision I can still hear. I said *Non*—and gently gestured toward the empty tables. In perfect English he responded: *There is no table for you here.*

Decades later I still don't know why I was unwelcome in an omelet parlor in a regular street in Paris, but it ended my restaurant bravery. Hungry and humiliated, I wandered around for a long time, finally arriving at the backside of my hotel's neighborhood. I went around one corner, then another and another until I came upon a tiny square that had an inviting small restaurant on one side—*L'Auberge de Chinoise*. The maître d' greeted me warmly in French. When I said I was alone, he seated me at a spacious table. I dined on dim sum more delicate and delicious than the fabled dim sum of San Francisco's Chinatown, where I loved to go with friends. I had found refuge.

I dined there for late lunch for the rest of my stay. They had my table reserved and a glass of wine waiting for me.

I would bring along something to read, but the waiters and owner were so welcoming I didn't need to maintain dignity hiding behind printed material. On the last day, I said goodbye and gave each waiter and the owner a JFK half-dollar. They bowed, smiling, each shook my hand and wished me *bon voyage*. The owner said *à bientôt* and asked my name. He repeated my last name with some difficulty. But without effort he said *Alida* several times and told me it was a beautiful name. I fought back tears. I hadn't heard my name spoken in more than two weeks. Solitude can be a luxury, but isolation is disorienting.

In the room after my evening walks, I worked on improving my French, but in a haphazard way. I read guidebooks written in French, worked through a collection of bilingual phrasebooks and an old college text I had brought. A small phrasebook with inane categories and phrases amused me. Under the heading, *In Emergencies* there was a section: *At The Beach*, with this sentence: *A child has fallen in the water*. The next section: *At The Dentist* and the first phrase: *This tooth can't be saved*. I linked the two phrases and muttered them to myself as I moved around Paris. Nonsensical though they were, they served as mantras of endurance for me.

Decades later, I tried my hand at fiction and wrote a novel, creating a character based closely on the worst of what I can become. I called her Natasha Levy—a feminist writer my age, who went to Paris alone and had a nervous breakdown. After returning to Manhattan and to sanity, Levy wrote a short, slight novel about her experience. In the manuscript Natasha tells her best friend Leah Tepperman, that she wrote the novel for the hell of it, after publishing many serious and well-reviewed (but commercially unsuccessful) books. But the novel is a bestseller, and Natasha is finally both famous and financially secure. At the end (but of course!) Natasha finds true love with a flawed but bravely feminist man. I thought it was a politically correct feminist fairy tale with wide appeal. (The title of Natasha's fictional bestselling novel: *A Child Has Fallen In The Water And This Tooth Can't Be Saved*). Nobody wanted to publish my novel, but not for lack of my attempting to convince editors of their judgment error.

I returned from Paris to Berkeley. I planned my exit from California with surgical precision I didn't think I had. Three months later I had moved to Manhattan. Again I was as excited about my prospects as I had been on that November evening. Today it is harder to visualize the New York City of the late 1970s and early 80s. The doors were being forced open and women were walking through them. We weren't in many of the top jobs (there still aren't enough of us in those) but we were already in positions that would have been unthinkable in prior decades. Hard-fought battles by feminist activists and lawyers were changing institutions. In our communal enthusiasm (and on good days) we believed that once there was a critical mass of women in places of influence, we could attain power and transform everything. Many of the men, who had much to lose, didn't want us inside and did their best to make our jobs a kind of hell. But change was evident—even to the men who opposed us and resented our presence in their companies, foundations, departments, divisions, and boardrooms. At a minimum, those in positions of authority in corporate and nonprofit institutions begrudgingly had to set a few more places at the table for us. If these men were armed with sharpened knives, women now had real forks, not plastic ones.

The feminist presence in New York taught me how important it was for women to have each other's backs. Most weeks a group of us, who were working in foundations, met for breakfast, usually in a hotel dining room, or at the Brasserie on East 53rd Street. We discussed coping strategies and survival techniques, how we could negotiate with male bosses without stepping over the line into insubordination, and employment termination. It reminded me of the consciousness-raising cells from the early days of the women's movement.

Some of us became active in *Women and Foundations/ Corporate Philanthropy,* a newly formed nonprofit membership organization. *WAF/CP* advocated for increased funding of projects and programs for girls and women, as well as for the inclusion of more women in leadership positions in foundations and in corporate philanthropy. At the Russell Sage Foundation I was then the only female member of the staff not serving in a clerical position. But its roster of visiting distinguished scholars did include women.

* * *

I remained legally married. B lived in Los Angeles and I lived in New York. He was the eldest son in a traditional Jewish family and referred to by his father as the *Gold Standard*. His younger brothers joked about it. I doubt it was much fun to follow him in school. He was the tallest, had the most hair, got the best grades, was musical, wrote well, and was particularly gifted in math and science. And he was adept at leaving the scene of a sibling fight before their parents arrived. His well-maintained self-image did not include walking out on a sick wife.

We remained married. I suspect that he hoped I would play the tough cop and initiate our divorce. If I were listed as plaintiff it would have been more consistent with B's reputation as a good man. Why didn't I? Did I want to punish him? Or, did being legally married give me social protection that I didn't want to relinquish?

Periodically, he asked when or if I was going to proceed with divorce. Now I had a standard response: *Why? I don't want to be divorced from you.* If I had initiated the proceeding in New York, a for-fault state, I likely would have ended up with a better settlement. California was long a no-fault state. But New York divorce law was still governed by laws that strictly dictated the grounds and terms of divorce. It was financially self-defeating behavior not to seek a divorce. And, I also ignored the advice of older wiser friends who urged me to file.

A few years into my Manhattan life, B did file for dissolution of marriage. I hired a seasoned Manhattan divorce attorney who proposed that we countersue in New York. I listened when he explained my rights as a legal resident of an equitable distribution state were far greater than they were under California law. But I did not take his advice. Our divorce agreement was speedily finalized, without a murmur from me. But given the status of my health, my earnings compared to his, his assets, as well as his potential life earnings, it was anything but equitable. Three close friends of ours in California asked him to consider giving me the small Berkeley house, or a larger share of the proceeds when it was sold. He was, after all, the recipient of generous gifts from a wealthy grandmother. He was unmoved. I never asked him for anything directly.

There was no demand (or request) for spousal support. There was no consideration for the likely deterioration of my health. My lawyer was horrified by my willingness to conclude the matter. It was the kind of divorce settlement feminist scholars and lawyers were writing about. Women's lifestyles and financial security plummeted after divorce. Most of the time, men's did not. Some feminist friends called me *a poster child* for the divorce reform movement, but I didn't identify with it. I believed it was wrong to demand that an exiting husband support me, a professional working woman, even for a limited time: to do so would be to play the victim card. During the long years of living with chronic disease, I had trained myself not to become ensnared in victim thinking. I couldn't contemplate fighting for the divorce settlement my lawyer suggested, because I was on automatic pilot, cruising in two gears—sick, but never a victim, and always an equality feminist. When it was over, both men and women friends insisted I had cheated myself. They weren't wrong.

Still, there was something more significant at play. In my memories and dreams, B continued to be the spousal gold standard. It is now beyond my ability to comprehend why I felt that, but it was true for a long time. It was as irrational as it was self-destructive. But more than that, it was a big buy into the fairy tale of the *one-true-love*. In matters of the heart, I was a slow learner. B remarried quickly, but not to the woman he had loved during our last days in Berkeley. She had grown impatient with him because he hadn't divorced a wife he no longer lived with and with whom he had no intention of reconciling. She was smart, and never the fool in our triangle.

One afternoon not long after the divorce, I walked into the Barbizon Hotel for a proper cocktail. I don't recall what happened, but I walked through the hotel and went home without having the cocktail. While inside, I thought about what the Barbizon had represented to generations of women. It was a part of the New York fantasy as a woman's place, and not only as a man's kingdom. Even in the bad old days, women came to Manhattan to make their mark. Frequently it was about glamour, becoming a famous Broadway actress, finding the millionaire husband, or the occasional available prince. But living in Manhattan was also about landing one of the fabled jobs in journalism, and other career dreams.

Young women arrived and stayed at the Barbizon Hotel as women with the intention of becoming something bolder and braver than we would have been, had we remained in our original hometowns. Women sometimes failed to reach their goals, usually not for lack of trying, but often because of the dearth of opportunities and the unfairness they experienced. Manhattan was, is, and always will be about romance, but it is not just that. The hugely popular "Sex and The City" was as much "City" as it was "Sex." In 1947 Grace Kelly lived in the Barbizon. She studied acting and worked as a model. She was a young New Yorker like many before and after her. It was a decade before she would become Rainier's consort. For months after my post-divorce walk through the hotel, or whenever I passed by it, I nodded to Grace Kelly. The glory days of the Barbizon were by then far behind it.

Soon she, too, was gone. Princess Grace of Monaco, formerly Miss Grace Kelly, actress, died on the 14th of September, 1982 of a brain hemorrhage following a car accident. She had lost control of her Range Rover as she attempted to navigate a sharp curve. Her Serene Highness and Stephanie, one of her daughters, were on their way from Roc Angel (the family farm above Monaco) to the palace. They were then to proceed to Paris by train where Stephanie (the younger daughter and middle child) would start school. Stephanie was injured in the crash, but recovered fully.

There were no lasting conspiracy theories about Princess Grace's death. She wasn't murdered—the car had not been sabotaged—there were no dark stories of palace intrigue. She was fifty-two, fatigued, overweight, and out of shape. She had a cerebral incident while driving her own car, with her daughter in the passenger seat—without the chauffeur. They had filled the backseat with dresses and belongings, and there wasn't room for three of them in the vehicle. Grace had insisted she could manage on her own. The only conspiracy involved in her death is one of fairy-tale lives or endings, even when women become real princesses. The truth is that they can die in car crashes like *regular* people, as happened again in 1997 to Princess Diana.

But girls and women continue with the myth that it is love and romance above all else that must and can be found. And that once attained, the love will never change. Perhaps contemporary women hang onto the myth because the reality of love in the context of a day-to-day relationship can be anything and everything, but often not at all romantic. Married life is a big job—filled with domestic chores of all sorts—and frequently accompanied by a load of personal disappointment.

I have long believed that the truths of married life are at the root of why marriage ceremonies turn into orchestrated fairy tale events. And perhaps it explains why many brides choose dresses that make them look like virgin princesses. They certainly don't want to look like women about to enter serious and legally binding lives of responsibility and obligation. When women emerge from their wedding ceremonies, some leave behind essential aspects of themselves. Core parts of a woman's identity now become secondary. The right to claim one's separateness vanishes (in most cases). But at least, we are no longer required to abandon our careers.

One Saturday afternoon my good friend Joann Vanek and I went to see George Clooney in the film *The Descendants*, a decidedly unromantic look at married life. Lines snaked around the multiplex theater. I asked a young woman what movie she was waiting to see. She said it was the opening day of *The Vow*—a film about a newlywed couple whose dreams are shattered when a car accident puts the bride into a coma. Upon awakening, she remembers nothing. Her valiant husband fights for their love and her health to return. The film is redeemed somewhat by the fact it is based on a true story and has a less than idyllic ending.

The young woman's face flushed when she told us she was not waiting to see *The Descendants*.

I smiled.

She replied: *I am so embarrassed. Please no judgments.*

I admired her honesty with a stranger and laughed with her.

"You think I would judge you? I'm not going to see *The Vow*. But I can't promise the forever-and-ever craving dies off completely. It diminishes with age and my many years as a feminist keep it under control. But it creeps up on me. I have to curb the impulse," I said.

"That's depressing! But at least you're in line to see the right movie," she replied.

I watched *The Vow* as soon as it hit Netflix—and pretended it was strictly for research purposes.

* * *

In the late 1990s B and I were in Washington, D.C. the same week. He was attending a science education gathering and I was part of a symposium on women's research. When a mutual friend informed me of the coincidence, I didn't see it as reason to take action. I hadn't seen B in at least a decade. But he called and suggested we meet for breakfast the next day at the hotel restaurant where he was staying. After an awkward greeting, we ordered coffee and food. He admitted he was apprehensive about seeing me. Knowing I had been quite ill, he wondered if he would recognize me. But he claimed I looked so good it was hard to believe I still had chronic disease. I didn't reveal that I was wearing my ego-saving wig.

He rattled on amiably about his work, wife, children, siblings, parents, and proudly described their home in a prestigious Southern California neighborhood. He sketched a nearly perfect life. Even discounting for the likelihood he had airbrushed the domestic portrait, I wondered if anyone's life could be painted in such exuberant, *color me happy* tones. But I smiled, nodded and trimmed my responses to affirmations: how great...how lucky...how lovely...how wonderful.

He returned to my disease. Reports from friends about treatments I received had saddened him. Tenderly he added there was something else he needed to say. It was this: He didn't feel guilty that he had left me. This revelation was delivered in the gently modulated tones I remembered.

But this time it wasn't the softness that caught me. It was the bloodless way in which he conveyed his reasoning. He had needed to preserve the quality of his life and ensure his future. He presented the decision as inevitable. He didn't see it as a free choice. *It probably sounds selfish, and I guess it was. But I've never been troubled by what I did.* I waited to respond. He looked at me intensely. I stopped short of saying: *I am going to kill you right now over your plate of eggs and toast.* But I didn't feel that. What he said startled me, but it didn't hurt all that much. Instead, uncontrollable giggling came over me (a response unaided by steroids). He looked uncomfortable, and fidgeted with the silverware. *I didn't know what you would say when I told you, but I didn't expect this. Why is it funny?*

That he imagined after all the years that I was interested in his rationalization wasn't only incomprehensible, it was hilarious. I composed myself. *Not many people could have left the way you did and not feel the slightest guilt. But what I really don't get is why you felt the need to seal the deal now with a late confession?*

He did not defend himself. He didn't respond to what I said. I didn't want his guilt. I had once wanted an expression of concern or an indication of remorse. If not remorse, then some responsibility for the shreds he left behind as he galloped toward the happily-ever-after ending. But not now. Now I wanted nothing from him. We steered the conversation away from personal lives past and present, and toward impersonal topics—politics, California, New York, current work projects. The talk was calm, cordial, and fairly pointless.

I felt relief when we said goodbye. I didn't want to live with or be married to that man—whoever *he* was. If we were still married, who would I have become? Chronic illness notwithstanding, maybe I wouldn't have had the chance to be the woman I had become. A thought crossed my mind. If still married to B, I could be another long-married woman with children who appears to be happy and content (and who is in many ways), but who secretly envies women like me. As we walked in opposite directions, he called out my name. I turned and looked at him, but he just waved goodbye. Whatever he had planned to say, if anything, didn't materialize. But he kept looking at me, shrugged, and then waved goodbye again.

Walking toward the meetings I was about to attend, I thought about the life he had been given and had made—one essentially untouched by undue challenges, tragic events, or serious illnesses. His life had been punctuated by success and professional affirmation, along with financial reward—he lived a graceful life. He expressed self-satisfaction with all of it in confident tones, but he wasn't smug. In his words he had the proverbial charmed life—career, marriage, and two kids who were easy, healthy, and smart. He emphasized my continued bravery and how much it impressed him. Strength and bravery, he repeated more times than necessary. Like most people with chronic illness I've learned to summon courage—we must do that or risk being doomed.

When my book *Dancing At the River's Edge* was published, I went on a promotional tour. On the road, besides encountering women and girls who inspired me, I also met courageous husbands, partners, and companions. I talked with them, men from every socioeconomic level, every faith, and those without a professed faith, who lived in different parts of our country, of all ages and diverse ethnicities. They were compassionate and patient, and had chosen to stay and stand up for the sick women who were their life-mates. I came to recognize a certain look in their eyes when they came up to speak with me after a book-signing or speech. They would ask me how to be more supportive and useful to their partners.

There are men who make calls to potential donors, support the walks, the runs, the fundraisers and the galas, and many work tirelessly to raise awareness about the diseases that afflict their partners. Their fears, fatigue, sorrow, impatience, and at times exasperation have not robbed them of the ability to love and to nurture. These are men who believe in the phrase: *for better or worse, in sickness and in health*. And not *for better or better,* to quote my long-time physician and co-author Dr. Michael Lockshin.

I couldn't erase the love I felt years ago, or the excuses I had made for him for decades. But I could face that what B did was cruel. Or was it? If he had remained my husband he might have resented me because he stuck it out, to stay with me, or worse, feel he had wasted his entire life waiting for me to get well. That would have been more painful than the leave-taking, which he conducted with faux civility, if not generosity. It wasn't only that I was the wrong spouse for him. He was also the wrong partner for me. I asked the Feminist Muses to grant me *the fool's pardon*. The breakfast reunion gave me back something I forgot I possessed—the ability to embrace myself as a woman of worth and substance, in charge of my own fears and dreams.

10

A Woman Across Time

A life spent with a stubborn chronic illness, and yet a sudden flare surprises me. First, I'm confused. Why didn't I see it coming? I chastise myself for not heeding the warning signs. In 2009 I was asked to give the after-dinner talk in San Francisco at the annual conference of the Sjögren's Syndrome Foundation. Before an audience of more than 300 people I said we must not take the blame for being ill, or fault ourselves when we're unable to function as we wish, or when we become incapacitated. Sjögren's, like many of its sister autoimmune diseases, overwhelmingly strikes the female population.

Two months later that's exactly what I did: blame and scold myself. Was I too tired, too fragile to keep such a full schedule? Did I go into denial the instant I suspected the disease was heating up in my body? Did I miscalculate my need for more drug infusions? I was playing hard at a game I knew well: *If only I hadn't done this or that…but had done this or that instead.* It's a miserable game because one never wins. Many chronically ill women I know play it as regularly as I do. We can't win because we bet against ourselves.

May is Lupus Awareness month. In 2009 *Dancing* had just been released and the response to it was gratifying to my co-author of the book Dr. Lockshin and me. May swept me along with it. There were trips in cars, on planes and trains. I made speeches, gave book readings, did signings, and conducted or facilitated panels, discussion groups, and workshops, and gave radio and television interviews on the topic of women and autoimmune disease. By the end of the month I was exhausted and red-hot angry. I was diagnosed with Lupus as a young woman. It was the wrong diagnosis. I don't have a classic version of Lupus, but an atypical form of Wegener's Granulomatosis, a close relative that can present similar symptoms. I've learned a great deal about Lupus—during that initial diagnosis experience, and later when working with Dr. Lockshin. But I wasn't angry that May about my flare. I was furious that in the 21st century I met women and girls taking the same primitive drugs I had taken decades before, and suffering the same horrid side effects. Women in their early 20s stood before me on huge doses of prednisone, their faces distorted, blown up to jack-o-lantern size. They were in pain, depressed, often enraged, experiencing the myriad emotions and impulses we often are unable to control because of steroids. In each of their faces I saw myself. I was all too familiar with the sound and tempo of their steroid-driven manic riffs as they expressed their despair and anger.

My audiences were filled with women and girls who were struggling to regain their emotional stability in addition to their physical stamina. I encouraged them to define themselves as more than drug side effects, diagnosis codes, and symptoms. I told the truth—that I always had to press myself to go forward, fearing that the impulse to give up would one day overtake me, that at some point I might give up, but I hoped it wouldn't be soon. I said that it was hard but worth it to press on as long as possible. More than a few women and girls collapsed in my arms weeping.

Some women asked how they might become more like me. I got to a point where I openly shared how often I felt as they did. The book I had promised myself I was never going to write, the disease I had kept hidden whenever I could, now had become a large and public part of my life. I don't regret embracing full medical disclosure. But I am aware of the dangers if younger women attribute supernatural strength or bravery to me, which is neither true nor helpful to them as they go forward.

In her book *Revolution From Within*, Gloria Steinem wrote about the battles women face against insecurity and self-doubt. She writes honestly and openly about her own fight against self-doubt and negativity. Steinem is here unmasked, and is not only the beautiful symbol of the women's movement. Steinem can feel as vulnerable and as self-deprecating as the rest of us. I loaned the book to Laura, a young woman who lived with me over the course of several summers. She was a curious and vibrant college student in the Pacific Northwest who loved to read from my library of women's literature. One rainy afternoon she disappeared for hours. Coming down the stairs at the end of the day, she tossed Steinem's book on the sofa. Starting to cry and almost to scream, Laura said: *How could she write this? Why did she do this?*

I was baffled. Laura was distraught because she only wanted to know *The Feminist Gloria Steinem*, without flaws and certainly without exposed insecurities. She wanted her Gloria as a living embodiment of Wonder Woman. Steinem's position and popularity in the women's movement had empowered Laura, making her feel more confident and competent. And she didn't think Steinem had the right to confess her own weaknesses or tell the tales of others. Laura's feeling of betrayal stunned me. We talked for a long time. Laura came to understand the power of the book for women like me. But she still wished she hadn't read it. That saddened me. However fierce or famous the individual feminist, not one of us is Wonder Woman.

Later that night I thought about my adulation for the founding mothers—from Abigail Adams through the Suffragists, especially Elizabeth Cady Stanton, Susan B. Anthony, and the Grimke sisters. Laura was too far removed from the living leaders of the contemporary women's movement to think of them as real people. She had never met or seen Gloria speak in person. Steinem was a glittering feminist star—no more real for her than Abigail Adams or Susan B. was for me.

The revelations I made in *Dancing* have worried me from time to time. When I was writing, it, I didn't expect to become a role model. We imagine role models as bigger-than-life almost super-humans—but none of us can be that. It's a misconception that leads to disillusionment and disappointment.

When I was a young feminist I thought men put on a better game face than we did—that they could fake it and not show their insecurities or inadvertently unveil a lack of self-esteem. Their ability to exude confidence was disagreeable to me. I saw it as arrogance. It was easy to make fun of men in private. I did plenty of that with a group of professional women I knew well. It was hard for us to find a place inside the male-dominated worlds; so, it was our humor, some of it vicious, that kept us from throwing in the towel and declaring them the victors. Our sarcasm sharpened our tactics and toughened our hides.

I see men differently now. They age well and not well, they have fears and worries, they lose out in love, face disappointments, and suffer the isolation that comes from failure and from aging. The world isn't universally kind to them either. But I don't forget that men still have the home court advantage, a fact that continues to make me righteously indignant, usually not at individual men, but at an entire system that promotes inequality and tolerates male abuse of women throughout the world. What has changed for me is that I carry words and memories of men who have communicated with me about their wives, lovers, sisters, mothers, daughters, aunts, cousins, and friends who suffer with chronic illness. These men challenge the stereotype that when disease barges into relationships, men leave and women stay. These men softened my jaded view that had grown out of my own negative marital experiences.

I was surprised when Laura expressed unhappiness about Gloria Steinem's disclosures. But I myself am not always comfortable when faced with full disclosure from women I've turned into heroic figures. Years after its publication, I turned to *A Transatlantic Love Affair*, the collected letters of Simone de Beauvoir to Nelson Algren. Theirs had been a passionate affair, and de Beauvoir retained a lingering attachment to Algren. The ending had been hurtful and cruel; Algren had behaved miserably. Still de Beauvoir instructed she be buried wearing a ring he had given her years before. I encountered a de Beauvoir I hadn't expected. I didn't want to know about this aspect of her life. But there she was, revealed on the printed page in her own words, exposing her heart, her desire for love, wanting to be cherished.

In places her letters have a girlish tone. She writes head-over-heels in love, and in the language those emotions produce. It was Nelson Algren, not Jean Paul Sartre, who had opened her to a deeper sensuality with a man. How could *my* de Beauvoir write these letters to a man who would prove so unworthy of her love? How dare she—one of the leading French intellectuals of the last century. I wanted her to be above the romance crap. I had expected of her what Laura had demanded of Steinem.

I've come a long way since then. In the end, exposing one's vulnerability is probably the best policy—whether in love or in illness, or other circumstances. By doing so we join with everyone who has loved, been embarrassed, suffered heartbreak, experienced failure and triumph, become ill but yet fought on. And, sometimes have given up totally but wrote it out until the very end as did the late Dr. Oliver Sacks, a celebrated neurologist and author.

On the road I met women with medical histories similar to mine, women who had not received the level of care I had. In Scranton, Pennsylvania I was introduced to a resilient and powerful woman who had an almost identical medical journey to mine, but had lost parts of herself to Vasculitis. (She had undergone multiple amputations. I had never come close to that.) Everywhere I went that May I met women who had lost family to Lupus at much earlier stages than I had heard about in previous conversations with support groups and doctors. These women lived far enough away from major urban medical centers to make travel impossible for the very ill and the impoverished. The hospitals in their local communities often were not staffed with seasoned rheumatologists—or any for that matter.

I talked with women who had been diagnosed and treated by general practitioners. Who were probably not bad doctors, and they likely did the best they could and may well have reached out for opinions from specialists. But there were no local rheumatology resources available to provide these women with the ongoing care they needed. There are large populations of women who live in urban centers, geographically close to the top doctors in the country, but who do not have the money, or in some cases the language skills, to get the care they need.

In Scranton my activism was reborn. I spoke at an all-day conference on the Mysteries of Autoimmune Disease sponsored by the Northeast Lupus Foundation Resource Center. The strong women who founded that center remain in my thoughts. They began by organizing from their homes before they could begin the Center officially. They wanted to assist and advocate for women with Lupus and related diseases in northeastern Pennsylvania. Over lunch, they told me how they met in living rooms and around their kitchen tables. They knew that Scranton and other former industrial towns in their vicinity had been all but forgotten, but not by them. They believed they could change lives and improve treatment options for those in their area.

Their commitment, their rebellion against injustice and their dedication to the work ahead reminded me of the early days of the women's movement when much was accomplished on the streets and in public, but also in homes—especially in kitchens and around dining tables over meals. Reform for the Scranton women began as it did in the early days of feminism. Florence Howe created the Feminist Press from her home. Betty Friedan let dirty dishes gather in her sink, thought through her life, then sat down and wrote *The Feminine Mystique*. The Scranton women I met that day might not have described themselves as feminists or as part of the women's movement, but they were.

I have always positioned the fight for the American Disabilities Act of 1990 squarely within the goals of feminism. The work of Feminists With Disabilities (FWD) taught me about entrenched prejudices that exist even in the feminist community. The words *Ableist* and *Ableism* should be part of every feminist dictionary and always included in any dialogue about equality. The women in Scranton educated me. I wished I had been part of their earlier conversation and activities. They considered me a celebrity, which embarrassed me. They had done the hard work, the real work. I had arrived late to the discussion about women and chronic illness. I had written about my own life only reluctantly, which it turned out, was about lots of our lives.

I kept quiet about disease because I needed and wanted to work. Even after the passage of the ADA, I did not want to be defined as a Sick Woman. It wasn't that I might not have been covered under the ADA protections—it was that I was determined disease not turn into the main text of my life. I was a whole woman, not just a sick one. I wanted to talk about political issues, not my health problems. I wanted to help change the world. I wanted to be loved as myself without the interference of disease.

Plenty of friends knew about my illness but were kind enough not to spread the news to my less intimate friends. When I was in my early thirties, the disease unexpectedly erupted in my lungs. I underwent lung surgery, which also yielded the Wegener's diagnosis. At that point, it could hardly be kept secret from friends and work colleagues. It was my first serious consideration of life and death. I didn't want to die then. Nor did I want to spend the rest of my life explaining a strange disease with an even stranger name. It occurred to me that if I were dead I wouldn't know anything about the life I might have lived. Dead, I would not mourn everything I missed experiencing. The tragic elements surrounding the death of a *young woman of promise* would have been a snippet of news and part of Manhattan feminist folklore for a season. Such thinking humbled me, got me back to work, and I returned to my favorite status: denial.

There have been numerous crises and episodes since then, but the 21st century came and I'm alive and functioning in it. One pleasant afternoon, Dr. Lockshin and I began to talk about women and health, which we often do. I was particularly interested in his career and that of other doctors who chose to work with girls and women with autoimmune diseases. We talked about public health in our country, its many flaws and gaps. His wife, Jane, joined us in a lively three-way conversation. It was a serious exchange of ideas. She suggested Michael and I write a book together. At the end of that conversation and in subsequent ones, the book neither of us contemplated writing took shape.

The time had come. Michael and I wrote *Dancing at the River's Edge: A Patient and Her Doctor Negotiate Life with Chronic Illness*. It was a true collaboration. Written as a dual memoir, the chapters alternate between his voice and mine. I revealed not only the secret parts of my life, but also the story of my relationship with my physician of three decades. Dr. Lockshin revealed some of his secrets—how it has felt to treat and care for women and girls with autoimmune disease and to experience the deaths of some of them. His chapters put to rest the major gender stereotype that male doctors don't get it and never will.

By the time the book was published, my illness wasn't much of a secret. But my childhood trauma had remained guarded and mostly untold. When the book came out many things changed. The number of women of all ages who told me that

I had spoken for them took me aback. They also had blamed themselves, had been written off as insane by the medical profession, had lost large parts of their lives to illness, and been unable to sustain meaningful relationships.

It was an unexpectedly late addition in my life as an advocate for women. Writing *Dancing* might have been my most radical act as a feminist. I had told the truth about women and these sometimes invisible and always mysterious diseases through the lens of one life—mine. Women who felt alone and abandoned now found their way to our book. Reading Dr. Lockshin's words, they now understood what they should expect and were entitled to receive from their doctors. And when they couldn't, women readers wrote to us about how they were empowered to move on and find doctors who listened and cared.

Readers saw me as a friend, a sister in the same struggle. Some wrote that they realized they might be feminists and asked questions about feminism, not disease. I hadn't needed to keep my illness segregated from my feminist politics. I could have and should have been advocating for decades for the right of women with autoimmune diseases to be taken seriously by the medical establishment. Illness and a feminist consciousness had been with me from the beginning. As a girl before the movement existed, I had invented a primitive form of modern feminism, which got me past at least some of the barriers constructed by medical patriarchy. As an adult feminist, I hadn't connected the earlier dots, and so I didn't see the full picture.

For a time disease became the primary text of my life, so that I could once again move it to the footnotes. After my speaking obligations were over, I thought about the two parts of my life and how they were connected, and had always helped each another. I am a passionate feminist. I speak with personal and tender affection for what the women's movement did for me. But without that all-important disease footnote, my feminism would not have come into focus in the precise way it has. I accepted privately, but did not announce publicly, that as the disease has determined much of the course of my life, so has it shaped the kind of feminist I am. Writing *Dancing*, my two selves merged into one person—flawed, damaged, resilient, and strong.

During public appearances for the book, I was re-radicalized. I met readers who were appreciative but who asked why the word feminist was attached to my name. I was asked this so frequently that it became troubling. Why did I permit that label in my introduction? Confusion linked all these inquiries. From one end of the country to the other, on local and national call-in radio shows, the comments and questions were of this sort:

You are so sweet and gentle, why would you want to be called a feminist?

You seem like you like men and even have men friends? So you don't hate men, right?

You wrote a book with your male doctor, so why the feminist label?

You are still a pretty woman…

You seem reasonable and kind, so…

Feminism was the other F word. I was so distressed that at one point I suspended speaking about illness and did a two-week national radio show tour: *Feminism is NOT the Other F-Word*. But it didn't help. Back on the road, the questions continued just as before. Women working to raise money and awareness for diseases that are overwhelmingly concentrated in the female population (and engaged in what I define as feminist advocacy) asked me these same questions. Women who admitted they and their daughters were beneficiaries of the changes the women's movement had made possible nonetheless wanted to protect me from myself. Women running 21st-century versions of the old consciousness-raising sessions (but this time about women's health) inquired why I had chosen to be known as a feminist author, a feminist social critic, a feminist anything, let alone the introduction I prefer: Alida Brill is a feminist.

These were well-meaning fans of the book and supporters

of my work who desperately wanted me to stop damning myself in public. At a dinner in Los Angeles following a speech I gave, a woman at my table insisted that I understand that by claiming the feminist identity, I could be mistaken for one of those *awful women*. I had lived too long among those who did what I did, thought what I thought, believed what I believed, and worked for the same goals. Once you find your place, there's a natural inclination to remain where you are understood. I had not chosen to engage much with those who don't, or won't, appreciate the value of feminism.

After countless conversations about my hapless self-identity, I wondered whether I would have had a better chance of convincing Americans, even in conservative towns, that Communism (at least as a theory) had some redeeming qualities, than persuading them that feminism was a positive force in society. And that, yes, feminism benefits men. I began to think that contemporary feminism is the most misunderstood social movement of our time.

On a scorching summer Saturday afternoon, I headed back to my hometown. The mothers of the senior class of Lakewood High School had organized a signing at the local Barnes and Noble. I was an original Lakewood kid, a girl who had never been part of the popular or social crowd, but I had come back to them as an author. They viewed me as a homegrown success. I was a girl who had hidden what was wrong with me, but now I had returned to talk about girls and women and what chronic illness does to us. The store manager made a fuss over me. There were posters with my picture; the store had run advertisements in the *Long Beach Press Telegram*. There was a large crowd waiting when I arrived. This audience mattered more to me than all my other signings and engagements.

The last person to come up to the signing table was a man about my age. He told me about his wife of many years who was severely disabled from Rheumatoid Arthritis. He wanted me to sign a book for her. A friend had bought a copy of the book for them and they had both read it. But he bought a second one and asked me to write a personal inscription to his wife. He told me that she had urged him time and again to leave her, to find someone else, a well woman, and make a new life. She believed, he said, that she had ruined his life and there was no convincing her otherwise. He told me all that had changed when she read my chapter in the book: *Love and Loss*. Near tears, he confided she had not suggested again that he leave her. I was moved. I hadn't considered that the chapter about the loss of my own marriage could speak to married women. As he talked I considered him. I liked this man—his strength, his integrity, his compassion, and his vulnerability, which he did not try to hide. Toward the end of our conversation he asked:

Why do you call yourself a feminist? You are lovely. You shouldn't be associated with that word. It spoils everything. You're not one of those angry women.

I looked at this good man, a husband who was living his life as a true feminist man, by any definition. I took a new approach:

Feminists aren't always angry. We do have time and space for lots of other emotions.

He looked at me and smiled warmly. He then gave me a gentle and appreciative hug and said goodbye. As he turned to leave the store, I saw his wheelchair-bound wife waiting for him at the front door with another woman. I will never know what he thought. Was I lying and wasn't really a feminist? Or, was I really angry and just good at hiding it in public?

Jennifer Karinen, the child of lifelong friends, was with me that day. She had heard the entire exchange. We left the store and headed to the parking lot. We were silent until we were in the car. Jenny said: *You should start writing the next book now. It should be about what feminism means to you personally, what it means to my mother, and what it has meant to me.* Jenny was about to enter her senior year of college; she was already a woman. I knew that not everyone in her generation agreed with her about the importance of feminism. Not all of her generation wanted to be associated with the word, any more than the older women I had met on the road. It was hard to brush aside her advice. After each signing I took count of how many said the feminist label was a liability. I had begun wondering if I should tell the story of one girl's life and what feminism did for that girl and still does for this woman.

Throughout time women have told their stories in ways both hidden and open. We have sewn meaning into the hems of our existence—what is disclosed, what is not, what is covered over, or what is omitted from fear of humiliation or punishment. In the past, women censored themselves or were censored. Our experiences were not openly expressed because it was considered inappropriate for women to tell the truth of our lives. Women writers changed my life. I could speak and write volumes of nothing except the influence of women's words on me. Words matter. Stories matter.

It matters when women tell and write where we came from, where we have gone, and where we end up at the end. Women's stories illuminate and encourage discovery in our own lives. And what we write leaves a historical record of what women have gone through. In the 1970s, Elaine Hodges, a feminist scholar brought "The Yellow Wallpaper," a long forgotten short story by Charlotte Perkins Gilman, to light. It became a classic women's studies title, and is in print more than forty years later.

My young friend Emma Claire, read "The Yellow Wallpaper" as a teenager, which I had given to her mother years before. Emma thought the most fascinating part of the book was my inscription to her mother, a young woman at the time I had given it to her. Emma said she couldn't imagine a woman being locked away by a husband, treated badly by doctors, and then descending into madness, *listening to the wallpaper*, as it were. Emma couldn't imagine why the woman hadn't left, hadn't divorced, hadn't hired a lawyer immediately. Susan, her mother, took the opportunity to talk about women's lives present and past. When I read the book as a young woman in the 1970s it made perfect sense to me.

"The Yellow Wallpaper" exists today for different reasons. It testifies to the time when women had no rights and today can serve to remind us that women in the world still suffer in ways similar to those in "Wallpaper," and far worse. "The Yellow Wallpaper" stands the test of time. That is the point of writing women's lives throughout time. It is critical also that we record our mistakes, along with the smart decisions. The title of one of Robin Morgan's books, *The Word of A Woman,* sums it up for me. No other phrase says so much as economically and accurately.

We leave our imprints because when taken together the words of women, in all forms, help us understand that the arc of human history—public and private—includes women as primary actors. This is one of the significant things the rebirth of the women's movement brought with it into the mid-20th century. Women's groups large and small, in schools and in homes, at meetings and in libraries, read each other, and to each other, learned from each other and heard one another. We read, taught, and recalled the words of the feminist foremothers who left a blueprint for more work still to be done.

We are not the original Suffragists, but we live in houses built from their ideas and shelter under their actions and accomplishments, crafted by their tenacity and their vision. We need to continue to speak, tell, and write in as many ways as possible. For all of its faults and dangers, the Internet has made possible the expansion of feminist ideals and their continuation and evolution into the next generations.

* * *

My mother taught me the life-affirming habit of reading. Reading kept her from descending further into grief. And reading also buffered me from the isolation of illness. The C.S. Lewis quote, *We read to know we are not alone*, reminds me of Mother and her books, shelves of books, stacks of books, piles of books—as a girl they appeared to me as mountains of books.

From my mother the women authors entered my life in childhood: Willa Cather, Jane Austen, Emily Dickinson, The Brontë sisters, Pearl S. Buck, and of course Laura Ingalls Wilder. Later there would be George Elliot, George Sand, Colette, Anne Frank, Isak Dinesen, Iris Murdoch, Flannery O'Connor, Eudora Welty, and countless others. My mother used Anne Frank and Flannery O'Connor as examples to me that words can trump just about everything. Anne Frank established the discipline of writing while in hiding during the Holocaust. Even as the world was collapsing for Jews in Europe and all that Anne knew and loved was being destroyed, she kept writing in her diary. Mother saw to it that I focused on that part of Anne's story as well, that she not been seen exclusively as a victim of the Nazis. My mother's lesson was that if Anne had lived, she surely would have become a published writer. When I became depressed and angry that the disease had sidelined me, making me miss out on activities with friends, Mother would wave a notebook and pen. In a scolding voice she would say: *Stop whining and write. Write for Anne.*

Flannery O'Connor was an even more frightening and personal source of inspiration. Lupus hadn't yet been introduced as a possible diagnosis, but I sensed that something in O'Connor's illness was familiar and unsettling to me. Again, my mother's invocation was that I must write, no matter the betrayals of my body. Throughout her long life she believed the best avenue for survival was creative expression, and not dreaded drugs. Even when very old, her first words when I called or saw her never varied: *Alida, are you writing?* There was little point in lying. If I said yes she demanded pages. Her next inquiry was about my health, but it was never the other way around.

When I was hospitalized she asked if I had a journal or a notebook with me. *Write it down or you will forget.* She didn't necessarily mean that I should chronicle my disease, but that I should be thinking of writing projects. *Living above and beyond the disease,* the phrase I wrote in *Dancing* and frequently used in speeches is based upon her advice. When I was young, she repeated: *Writing is your only sure way to live above and beyond what has happened to you.*

As the feminist movement discovered lost voices and published women long out of print and those never published, I collected them in my head as a personal woman's album. In a short time, there was a crowded auditorium of women's voices in my brain. In 1970 Florence Howe began collecting the writings of women and founded the Feminist Press. I was living in Los Angeles when I read the "The Yellow Wallpaper," shortly after the Press first published it, and was stunned by its power. When I read the words on the spine, The Feminist Press, I was excited but confused. I asked the instructor of the summer women's literature class I was attending what this new publishing house was. She said a woman on the east coast had started it. And if we wanted it to survive we had better support it. I took the advice seriously and became a regular buyer. In New York, the press and Florence would become an essential part of my life. Long before, I had worked my way through their list, adding, among others, Tillie Olsen and Zora Neal Hurston to my album.

In Manhattan the books I had read now had faces attached to them. Women writers I admired became real and became friends as well. Among them, Elizabeth Janeway, feminist author and social critic, who invited me into her gracious home often and took a critical interest in my work. Marilyn French, whose novel *The Women's Room* called me to action in ways as significant as Friedan's Mystique had for my mother. Marilyn was a fearless writer, remained fearless when she became ill (and wrote a book about it), and maintained a ruthless writing schedule. Marilyn came to the book launch for *Dancing* in a wheelchair (it was the last time I saw her). Before she left the party, she called out: *What is your next book, Alida?*

Robin Morgan's *Goodbye to All That* had served as kindling for my own rage when I was disgusted with left-wing men who had put themselves in charge of the anti-war movement. I met Robin soon after I moved to Manhattan. From that first encounter it was as if we had always been sitting across a table, sharing a meal, and talking, talking, talking, something we continue to do almost four decades later. When the *Sisterhood Is Global* project was in its initial stages, Robin asked advice about funding sources. She has written that once when she came to see me at the Russell Sage Foundation, she felt like Alice-in-Foundation-Land. But in the early days of living in New York, as I tried to find my feminist equilibrium and my voice, it was I who felt like an Alice. For me it was the strangeness of New-York-Feminist-Land. The sisterhood I longed for seemed less powerful in person than when I used to chant Robin's words: *Sisterhood is Powerful,* and wear a button with the woman's symbol and a raised fist.

It was Robin, poet, author, and activist, who immediately accepted me as an equal. Without a trace of condescension, she cautioned, advised, and pointed me in the right directions as I navigated feminist terrain as an apprehensive newcomer. I still managed to step on any number of landmines, but I never blew myself up, largely because of her wise counsel. She has been unflagging in her work (domestic and global) to make a better world for women and girls.

We disagreed on the fundamental issues of pornography. As a feminist, but also a first amendment civil libertarian, I did not support the work of WAP (Women Against Pornography). But I thought it less than sisterly that there were feminists on the anti-censorship side of the battle who excoriated Catherine MacKinnon and Andrea Dworkin (leaders of the anti-pornography movement) without bothering to read what they had written. Robin took my writing seriously on the pornography fight within the movement. She was my first reader for a long monograph I published about the division inside the movement (*Freedom, Fantasy, Foes and Feminism: The Debate Around Pornography*). We didn't try to convert one another, and we respected the validity of the other's point of view.

We have seen each other through serious personal traumas, and even in the worst passages there is still laughter and a dark and quirky off-the-wall humor, which always sustains us. My 60th birthday present from her was the "Wicked Witch of the West" Barbie Doll, issued in commemoration of the 70th anniversary of *The Wizard of Oz*. The gift is an inside acknowledgement of my "Barbie" past and Robin's connection to the traditions of Wicca. I took a picture of the two Barbie dolls standing side by side, my original and the Wicked Witch, and posted it on Facebook with the caption: *Together At Last.*

And there is also our most sacred bond—the unshakable belief in the importance of women's words. At twenty books and counting, the writing part of Robin's feminist life is a testament to that conviction.

As the women's movement discovered and rediscovered more new and lost women's voices, my personal women's album grew. At first I was overjoyed at all the *new* (lost voices) I was reading and learning about, but then fury swept over me. Where had all these women been? Why had history ignored them? Why hadn't they been taught in college and lower school literature classes? In many cases, they were hiding in plain sight, and in others, had been buried and forgotten. Without the work of feminist scholars inside the academy and those working independently, we would not have learned how large a part of the conversation we have been.

I read Jean-Paul Sartre before I read Simone de Beauvoir. I read F. Scott Fitzgerald before I knew anything about Zelda as a woman in full, as something other than F. Scott's *nutty wife*, as described to me by an older male friend of our family. It was years before I knew the story of what had happened to Vivian Eliot, T.S. Eliot's much-maligned wife. I read the poetry of William Wordsworth before I knew the influence his sister Dorothy had on it: she kept journals that served as notes (and in some cases more) for his poems.

I did know Virginia Woolf through her writing before I cared much (if at all) about Leonard. I, like so many women of my generation, can quote the last lines of *A Room Of One's Own* where Woolf talks about Shakespeare's mythical sister who disappeared without leaving a trace of her existence. The increase of women publishing books as well as the discovery of women writers previously underestimated or overlooked makes Woolf's metaphor seem less a fiction. May Sarton, the poet, novelist, and memoirist is another good example: she was given a much larger readership and considerable late-life fame because of the attention of the scholar Carolyn Heilbrun. Shakespeare's sister was living among us all along in writings past and present.

I have kept Virginia Woolf close to me since I first began to read her. But I don't consider myself part of the Bloomsbury Group fan club in the way others are—those who like to study and comment upon the group's comings and goings and overlapping relationships, artistic, sexual and emotional. My concern with Woolf centers on her work and on her chronic mental illness. It is hard to read *Mrs. Dalloway* and not marvel at her creation of a new fictional clock. To read Woolf's essays, journals, and letters is to be invited to keep company with a literary mind of unparalled bravery. (But I don't sugar coat what she thought about minorities, social class, and her fairly common upper class British discomfort with Jews, in spite of Leonard.)

It is in her writing, joining a unique woman's voice to the invention of a narrative form solely her own, which brings me to her again and again. And there is, for me, the illness that shadowed her. I don't obsess about her suicide by drowning when she was fifty-nine. I think of the years of despair when she maneuvered through the depression and mental anguish to continue writing. She wrote against the terrors of internal demons. And there was Leonard, who did not leave. Later, I read about Leonard Woolf and came to appreciate him as a husband, friend, caregiver, publisher, writer, and thinker. He has been given a bad grade by those critics who insisted he didn't behave as well as he should have to a wife who suffered severe depression. Maybe he was not all he could or should have been, nor did he lock her in a room with yellow wallpaper. What he did was rather remarkable for a man of his time. He made it possible for Virginia to function and to write whenever she could. I am grateful for Leonard's contribution to her oeuvre. Without him, I am not sure we would have a full shelf of the collected writings, fiction and non-fiction, of Virginia Woolf.

And here I confess, I've been searching for Leonard Woolf my whole adult life.

* * *

Aunt Madeleine was always employed outside the home, but I thought of her primarily as a housewife, which was the description she herself preferred. But she worked long hours at her outside job, at a small independent chain of variety stores. Ordering the yardage, patterns, and sewing notions. Her salary was meager, but she always said the owner appreciated her. An accomplished seamstress, Madeleine was a valuable resource at the store where customers asked her advice about patterns and fabric choices. She could eye a pattern for a few moments and calculate the most efficient and economical way to cut the yardage. Women bought less fabric but they came back more often for her skill and her honesty.

Madeleine didn't seem frustrated or unhappy as a married woman, cook, baker, and housekeeper extraordinaire. All her hobbies and leisure-time activities involved crafts within women's arts—crochet, knitting, tatting and other delicate needlework. She was convinced that if my mother and I had paid attention and become proficient in the creative arts, we would not have been so unhappy as we must have been to pursue the cause of women's rights. Madeline attempted to teach me to crochet, but it was a lost cause; I was neither patient nor interested.

My aunt frequently asked me why women were suddenly making such a fuss about all the *women's lib stuff*. We could vote, drive, own automobiles, choose to divorce (although she admitted its difficulties), work for pay, and keep our earnings. Why wasn't that enough? What did I want in life? What would become of my generation of women who wanted so much independence? Were we really willing to alienate men? She understood that men were in charge. In her view, they always would be, so why waste so much energy and effort trying to change something that had existed from before recorded history? She also voiced an all-too-truthful caution: men weren't going to give up their power and let women take over.

Madeleine insisted she was the one in charge at home and this was sufficient control and power for her. But I saw that my uncle controlled everything, except her work at the variety stores. I thought he was a dictator, and neither of my parents disagreed with me. Uncle Bud (as he was called) determined all of Madeleine's domestic rhythms—when meals were served, what was served, the television shows they watched, when they went to bed, and what days she did the laundry and ironing.

Madeleine and my mother had completely different styles

and routines, but they loved one another unconditionally and supported each other until the end of my aunt's life. When she fell off a stepstool at work, severely injuring her leg, my mother was a tireless caregiver. Neither had a natural sister, but they were as fiercely loyal to one another as any two sisters (they had been raised almost as that).

In my early twenties my aunt took the time to explain to me what happened with doctors and at hospitals the day that Terry died. She helped me put my mother's grief into a context about Terry I had not understood before. It brought me closer to my mother. I don't think that Uncle Bud, my mother, or I fully appreciated Madeleine. I underestimated her though I appreciated her presence in my life. I didn't take her work outside the home and in, or her life experiences, seriously enough. When I was about ten years old, Madeleine went through a crisis. For some weeks the adults talked behind closed doors in their house and ours. My uncle was angry, but I couldn't make out the words. My father, always the peacemaker, was calm. My aunt was distraught; it was the only time I saw her express any great emotion. My mother was in a state, not wanting to take sides, but ultimately she decided to risk her brother's wrath rather than be disloyal to Madeleine.

The problem turned out to be Madeleine's long-lost mother, who wanted to be reunited with her only daughter and move to Long Beach—with her lover. His name was Herman. Her name was Marcelle. Once they arrived, the hushed conversations ended. My aunt asked my parents to pass Herman off as her mother's second husband. That could have worked, but Marcelle, in heavily accented French and Parisian to the core, immediately introduced him to me as her lover.

For me it was love at first sight. I thought Marcelle was exquisite. By then she was grandmotherly, but still seemed an exotic creature. One day she took me into her bedroom in the classic California bungalow close to the ocean she and Herman had purchased. She closed the door and said what she was going to teach me might be the most important thing I would ever learn and that I must remember it and follow her advice. What followed was a lengthy discourse about the importance of lingerie in a woman's life. She opened drawer after drawer and asked that I inspect and feel her silk underwear, nightgown, slips, panties, and stockings. I had never seen that kind of underwear before. It certainly didn't exist in my mother or my aunt's dressers.

And so our own love affair began, Alida and Marcelle. There were French lessons, and conversations about manners, food, perfume, makeup, clothes, and men. Much of what she said was inappropriate for my age. Still, I eagerly waited for her to impart wisdom, and I took everything she said as essential to my development. I might as well have been enacting scenes from *Gigi*.

My father wanted me to be a professional woman—a lawyer, if he had his way. My mother wanted me to be a writer. My aunt wanted me to keep a proper house and learn some basic needlework skills. I wanted to be an actress or a dancer, if the princess fantasy didn't end up working out for me.

But Marcelle was something else entirely. She was French and womanly in a way I had not encountered before. She had no interest in anything domestic—that was for other people to do for her. My aunt, of course, ended up cleaning her mother's house too, as she did for my mother.

Marcelle's tastes were those of a fine *Parisienne* from an era long past, but her funds were far more modest. But all that mattered to me was that I finally had a grandmother, something I had not had before, except the brief time with my father's mother. I loved Marcelle.

In time, Herman died. Marcelle lost a leg to diabetes, which she refused to control adequately once he had gone. In some awful way it was a replay of my grandmother's last years. But it wasn't because Marcelle didn't stop living. Though wheelchair-bound, her lively conversations in French about topics that interested her didn't stop.

Uncle Bud showed no emotion when she died, and continued to refer to her as *the old lady*. As a young teenager I thought his reaction was more relief than grief. But my aunt was filled with sorrow and spent time alone with my mother, who seemed to understand just what to do. Aunt Madeleine had never spoken an ill word about Marcelle in front of me. After my aunt's death, Mother told me the truth about Marcelle. She had abandoned her husband, Hector, and her daughter, Madeleine, to run away to France with a lover (apparently there were many before Herman).

Madeleine and her family lived across the street from my mother's family. Hector crossed the street and told my grandmother what had happened. He said he didn't know what to do with his little girl. Immediately my grandmother said Madeleine would come and live with them as another child. As the only girl in a family with eight brothers, my mother was delighted to have her childhood friend from across the street move in with them, and they lived as sisters. It wasn't a surprise that Madeleine married Bud, one of mother's younger brothers. Madeleine didn't tell me the truth about her mother because she didn't want to be the person who spoiled my time with a grandmother I had chosen for myself. And she forbade Bud to tell me, but I learned he often threatened to.

I sensed as a girl in Lakewood that housework and chores dominated conversations, and it was also a source of family squabbles. Neighborhood women groused together about how much they hated to clean and scrub and do laundry, but they did it anyway and without household help. Aunt Madeleine spent most of the time when she wasn't at the store doing either housework or her crafts. She described all the work in her home as personal accomplishments, and that was not something I heard other women say. Before my mother got a job, she did as little housework as possible and when she went to work, she did even less. As a girl I understood housework was something that had feelings attached to it—in particular, anger and resentment.

But not Aunt Madeleine. She took on all home chores with a zeal and skill I haven't often observed even in professionals. Did she feel undermined or unappreciated by my uncle? I will never know. Or, did her paid job outside the home give her a sense of fulfillment she wouldn't have had otherwise? Becoming a political feminist, I suggested to my mother that it was Madeleine's job at the store that kept her sane. My mother replied: *No. A clean kitchen and a well-ironed shirt make your aunt satisfied and happy.*

Mother was a bad housekeeper and she hated it so much that in turn it bedeviled her. The only person at home (other than my aunt) that I ever saw with a mop in hand was my father. I was enlisted for mopping duty when I was a bit older. My father taught me. He was used to wielding a mop in nightclubs when they were short on janitorial services. My mother wasn't embarrassed that my father washed the floor or ran the vacuum. From time to time she took an interest in dusting. Our house was not dirty, but it surely was cluttered.

When company was expected, my mother developed a system she called the *One Minute Cleaning Miracle.* She would walk through our small house, and its circular plan made this simple to do. As she went she opened drawers and closets. As she came around again she would shove whatever clutter was around into the open drawer and closet spaces. She had a collection of canvas bags for what was left. She would stuff the overflow into the bags, which were retired to the garage until the company had left.

My aunt remains a mystery to me. I don't know what Madeleine really felt about her life, because she kept her own counsel. Her death, which came a full decade before my mother's, crushed me. I didn't understand why she chose to compose her life as she did, but she was a reservoir of affection, kindness and love. I think she understood me. At the end of her life, Aunt Madeleine told me she was proud of my achievements, and of my determination to live a different life from the one she and my mother had lived. But Aunt Madeleine couldn't or wouldn't say the words feminism or feminist, or ever admit that I was one.

Feminism has become part of the conversation of what being a woman means, even for those who do not recognize it as such. Years ago my mother told me I shouldn't worry so much about whether we would succeed. She said:

Eventually feminism will become like fluoride in the water. You can't see it or smell it, but it's there and it helps prevent cavities. Feminism will not prevent inequality but it serves as an inoculation against it.

We are all women across time.

II

The Girl from Peoria Who Changed the World

It's another late night at Betty Friedan's Glover Street house in Sag Harbor, which she purchased with the earnings from the book that gave my mother renewed life. Betty drinks icy Pepper Absolut. I drink wine. We talk about writing, politics, sex, love, divorce, and domestic abuse. The conversation moves around, hovers and then lands on respiratory illness, which is our continuing bond. I am congested and coughing. Betty shakes her head and pushes the tissue box on the table across to me. Eventually we choose books from her shelves to take to our bedrooms, I usually bring books to share. Sometimes I hit on one she hasn't read that interests her, novels or short story collections.

This night our conversation takes a sharp turn. Carolyn Heilbrun, a distinguished scholar and Barnard professor, has signed a contract to write Gloria's Steinem's biography. Betty is grouchy with disappointment that Heilbrun isn't writing *her* biography instead. An unstated question lurks. *Why did Heilbrun choose Steinem?* Betty views the news as part of the ongoing competition—Gloria Steinem again trumps Betty Friedan. As we continue talking, Betty's expression becomes wistful, forlorn. Will the Heilbrun-authored Steinem biography eclipse Friedan's place in history?

Abruptly she changes the subject to Peoria. I've heard plenty of stories about Betty's childhood in Peoria—its people, her father's jewelry store, her mother's personality, and the isolation she felt as a girl. Tonight she tells a story I've not heard. Betty was a voracious reader as a girl (something I do know). As a student at Smith College, Betty discovered that words she had known intimately only from reading were pronounced differently than she had assumed. She recounts an embarrassing moment from her first year at Smith. Betty thought *posthumous* was pronounced *post*humous like a post in the ground or the post office. I confess to the same error, and tell her how a professor once humiliated me at a new student orientation reception. Betty laughs and then shares a story:

So that I wouldn't make mistakes in public, I started keeping track of these words. I kept them in my head and I wrote them down. Whenever I heard one I said to myself—Oh! there's another Peoria word.

After I am gone, once the commotion settles down, you should write my biography. You would do a great job.

Here's the title: The Girl From Peoria Who Changed the World

I remind her I've not published enough to be taken seriously as her biographer, and am not a leader in the women's movement. She will have none of it. Betty refers to my research on civil liberties, the political opinions we share, and our bond of friendship. I stop her.

I don't want to talk about a time when you're not around and when we're not here in Sag Harbor.

Betty doesn't like thinking about death, hers or that of friends. The subject is dropped.

On her way up to bed, she turns and says again I must write her biography, at the right time.

If you write my story, it might make you famous.

I don't want to be famous, Betty. I want to be healthy and happy.

Betty makes a familiar sound, half growling-half-laughing signifying impatience and amusement.

What exactly is being happy going to do for you? And your health is going to be what it is whether you write my biography or not.

Many people lay claim to the same Betty Friedan—the

temper tantrums, the desire to be loved and appreciated by men, the fights with other feminists, the initial suspicion of lesbians, the arrogance, the jealousies, the hyper-socializing.

I knew a different Betty.

We met shortly after I'd moved to Manhattan. Betty's outbursts reminded me of my mother's own struggle with anger. But Betty didn't frighten me. Usually I could overlook what others disliked. I've been described as "Betty's younger girlfriend." That remark pleased her, though she referred to us as buddies. I was 28 years her junior, but she didn't categorize friends by their ages. Friedan was fighting the stigma of ageism long before the word was used, and decades before she wrote *The Fountain of Age*. For more than three decades Betty and I were many things to one another. Friedan was an international figure, but I knew her as a private woman. I observed her navigate dual spheres— a personal one of her own choosing— and the one thrust upon her by the success and notoriety of *The Feminine Mystique*.

By the time we became close, my disease had taken a serious turn. My respiratory system was now involved. I had undergone lung surgery and the first of several chemotherapy protocols. Betty had episodic debilitating attacks of asthma. We were both on steroids, which produce many side effects, among them the inability to adequately control emotions and impulses. I was ever eager to blame any lapse of temper on the drugs. Betty was less interested in excusing herself. I never heard her say that steroid use influenced her reactions. She might confess to imbibing one too many cocktails: *Shouldn't have had that last vodka*, she said as I drove back to Glover after a summer garden party where she had made a scene. When I brought up steroids, Betty would wave her hands and shake her head—the Friedan signal of dismissal.

Betty was rarely humiliated by her behavior. She owned rage in a frustrating yet endearing way. After she blew up or stormed out of someone's home, she offered apologies (sometimes frequently). Most of the time, most of us forgave her. And when we were unable to forgive a particular incident, we tried to forget. Preserving the relationship usually trumped hurt feelings and irritation. Though I had no desire to act out the way she did, I saw in Betty the power of a woman's anger. I compared it to my mother's anger, a byproduct of grief that to me symbolized powerlessness.

Heilbrun was still writing the Steinem biography when Judith Hennessee signed a contract with Random House to write Friedan's biography (not authorized, as was Steinem's). Hennessee, a journalist and published author, was a friend of the broadcast journalist Marlene Sanders, who had suggested that Hennessee take on the project. Sanders was also an old friend of Betty's. Betty sent out an edict: We must not speak to Hennessee. She used the word *forbidden* with me. However, Mary Jean Tully, Barbara Seaman, Marlene (and undoubtedly others) persuaded her to cooperate: the book would come out whether or not friends talked to Hennessee. Grudgingly, Betty relented. Mary Jean gave Hennessee my number.

I would agree to talk about our friendship if Betty were comfortable with it. By now she understood there was no way to stall Hennessee's project. Betty repeated what others had warned her: if friends did not give interviews to Hennessee interviews, the book would be published anyway, with only the tales of enemies. At the end of our conversation, Friedan raised her voice and spoke emphatically:

For God's sake, don't deny I have a bad temper, or you won't have any credibility. You must have credibility.

At the appointed time Hennessee appeared at my apartment. Before she opened her notebook, I said:

Judith, if you're here to witness a Bonfire of the Mothers, you've come to the wrong person and to the wrong place.

After she assured me that her goal was to write a balanced

biography, we proceeded. But the questions she asked made me wonder about her motives.

Later I related to Betty my admonition to Hennessee. It was overly dramatic (even for me), but it made Betty laugh and she appropriated it over the next few weeks. *I don't want my biography to turn into the Bonfire of the Mothers.* Friedan was enduring the consequences of an unauthorized biography undertaken by a woman she didn't think a worthy guardian of her life's story. In her view, Hennessee was *an inappropriate scribe.* She wasn't known as a celebrity biographer, nor did she pretend she was. Whatever Hennessee's skills as a writer, Betty couldn't give her the benefit of the doubt. After all, Judith Hennessee was not Carolyn Heilbrun. Friedan was sorely disappointed, but wasn't a fool and decided to take advantage of the only available biography opportunity. She hoped the biography would burnish her historical legacy; so she released her grip on all of us. Eventually Friedan granted Hennessee a personal interview.

Friedan's temper storms did not serve her well inside the leadership circles of the women's movement. Ill-considered words and impulsive flares compromised her position. Sometimes she was punished by exclusion. At the NOW March for Women's Lives on March 6th, 1986, Betty was not invited by the organizers to speak. When she found me standing close to the front with our group, she was near tears. She said it was unfair; it was a national Pro-Choice march and she was a major leader of the movement. In the end, Congresswoman Bella Abzug told Betty to take part of *her* allotted speaking time. A few weeks after the march, Betty became emotional when she spoke about Bella's gesture. I asked if she had written or called Bella. There was no response. For all of her insights and intelligence, Betty was unable to connect the dots from her behavior to the attacks and criticisms made against her. She couldn't own what she had done to others, and often felt victimized, when in fact others felt the same, or worse.

I've been asked how I maintained a close friendship with Betty. I say what I've written: *I knew a different Betty.* That's true. But there are also other truths. We shared chronic illness. We had some similar childhood issues. We had been disappointed in love. We were both frustrated and energized by the writing life. We believed in the elasticity of our democratic institutions to accommodate fundamental change. We both worked within the system—she enthusiastically, and I more reluctantly.

But what overshadowed everything in my relationship with Betty was *The Book*, the text that freed my mother. *The Feminine Mystique* resonated with millions of frustrated women. It has profound personal significance for me. It is an essential part of my autobiography. Friedan's thoughts and words eased my mother's suffering, and so I, too, was liberated.

Friedan and I survived serious differences of opinion. I didn't sacrifice our friendship when she didn't *get it*, or when Friedan didn't hold a number of feminists in the same esteem and respect I did. I didn't cram *revolution* down her throat, any more than I did with my mother. I saw little point in insisting to either of them that the worst traits of individual men could be generalized to the larger male population. If I said to Betty or to my mother: "All men are some part of a system that represses women. Therefore patriarchy is always in the boardrooms and in our bedrooms," they would have heard my anger only and not the meaning of those words.

I observed the radicals and read what they wrote and listened carefully to what was being said. I questioned myself—why did I remain inside the reform/equality camp? Why wasn't I a public militant feminist? I understood why their strategies were effective. I thought the movement would be lost without them. But I held onto the conviction the system could be transformed, and believed a more equal society would result. After all these decades, I am still unable to offer an adequate answer. I've come to accept that my reasons remain unknowable, albeit perplexing.

I advocated for change, and held radical private views, but wrote as a *feminist social critic.*

* * *

Betty's cars were ridiculous. Nelson Algren did indeed fall out of one of them.

The vehicles Betty procured (purchased is too dignified a term) were genuine heaps. The one I knew intimately was a shambling mess and I decided the only hope for the car's survival was to name it; so I christened it Herman. I have no idea why I chose that name. Betty was so pleased, she mentioned the name Herman at one of her birthday parties. After that, other people would insist that *they* had named him.

Herman and I had an intimate relationship. I was his passenger, driver, and part-time caretaker.

When Betty would let him fall further to bits, I would step in and plead to take Herman to the garage on the back road. But she ruled out as unnecessary and too expensive any repair they suggested. Still, the kindly mechanics would negotiate with her, and usually she would agree to a minor repair. So Herman stayed on the road and was marginally safe.

One day I had a Betty-style tantrum myself when she refused to replace tires that had gone completely bald. I was done with her, and done with Herman. I was going to walk back to Glover Street, pack my things, and take the bus back to New York. Under this threat, Betty caved. It didn't hurt that on this particular weekend, she needed me for some project or another.

Betty purchased the tires. She bought two instead of four.

Then she grumbled for hours about the money she had wasted all because of me. She pouted. She shouted. She sulked. I knew nothing about cars, she said. I suggested to her in a chilly voice that she reconsider that remark in light of my years of driving the Southern California freeways.

And then the kerfuffle was over. Betty's temper-storm vanished, leaving no trace. She went on planning the weekend, trying to figure out how to go to a scattering of cocktail parties, attend two formal dinners, as well as showing up at some art openings.

Betty wasn't trying to be difficult about Herman. To her, cars were a necessary evil, and only modest funds should be spent on them. Money was better spent on good food, wine and liquor, interesting clothing, and shoes. Money was also required to dine in her favorite restaurants.

During the season, Betty loved to go to the American Hotel in Sag Harbor. We would drink and socialize at the bar and in the front room, and then take our lunches, dinners, and Sunday brunches in the dining rooms.

One Sunday afternoon we joined Shana Alexander and Gloria Jones for brunch. When Betty left the table to go to the women's room, both women warned me to be careful. Betty could be cruel, they told me. By then, Betty and I had been friends for more than a decade. I said it wasn't an issue. Shana and Gloria kept scolding me. Eventually, I grew tired of the conversation. And I told them, "My mother can be impossible. It doesn't negate her intelligence, or diminish her influence and importance in my life. I love my mother. And I love Betty."

Silence.

After Betty returned, Gloria Jones became overly attentive, and Shana Alexander feigned a sudden interest in my work. The bill arrived. Shana announced it would be her treat.

As I piloted Herman back to Glover Street, Betty wondered aloud why Shana had picked up the check. Then she asked if they had misbehaved when she was away from the table. I answered, "They told me to watch out for you because you are a real pain in the ass."

Perhaps I had the best of Friedan because she had taken

the time to be my friend. Her long relationship with David Manning White, a great love, was in its final stage. Her complex and sometimes embattled relationship with the National Organization for Women had simmered down somewhat. The days of the infamous Long Island commune and its dramas were behind her. Betty's daughter, Emily, and her niece, Laurie Goldstein, generously understood my connection to their mother and aunt. When Betty purchased a home in Sag Harbor, it was a dream come true. Glover Street gave Betty the opportunity to be a socially prominent figure on her own terms in a town she defined as a literary village rather than a society compound. Betty was proud to live in Sag Harbor and quick to criticize the wealthier enclaves in East Hampton, Southampton, Sagaponack, and Watermill.

When Martha Stewart took up residence in East Hampton, Betty claimed Stewart's lifestyle advice was an example of what was wrong with the rest of the East End. One afternoon at lunch she said: *It took me and everyone else in the women's movement a long time to get women out of the kitchen. Now she's sending women back there with her elaborate ideas. Women will again waste their time.*

In my own East Hampton freezer at that moment I had a bottle of vodka sitting in a torn milk carton filled with water that had wildflowers tossed into it. As per Martha Stewart's instructions, once the water had frozen, you ripped away the carton. And, *Abracadabra!* A bottle of vodka standing in a decorative wildflower chunk of ice appeared. I was preparing this kitchen magic trick for Betty, but when I got back to my house I thawed it out, and put the vodka bottle back into the freezer, naked and neat.

Betty and I were easy around each other, expressing political and personal opinions without restraint. We didn't censor what we shared about our fears and disappointments. She was simply Betty—not *The Betty Friedan*. As another mother, she behaved as mothers sometimes do: she could be impossible, tyrannical, controlling, larger than life, enraged, and enraging. Betty excited, inspired, and exhausted me. And sometimes she broke my heart.

She was an enthusiastic booster of friends, showing loyalty and compassion. After a friend's book was savaged in *The New York Times*, Betty decided to give her a garden party. I was startled. This woman seemed to thrive on cruel gossip about other writers. I drilled Friedan, who insisted the writer wasn't as confident as she pretended to be, and was more fragile than people realized. Betty said of this author that she had spent too much time writing a book that would now fail. In the face of a terrible review, our job as friends was to offer support to one another.

Betty often saw matters in fairly primitive (or childlike) terms. Friends should help each other to survive defeats. Because Betty commanded us, there was a large attendance for the book party. She toasted the author and mentioned the bad review, finishing with the remark: *After all, it's a selling review.* Betty had picked out a phrase that suggested readers could be persuaded to buy the book. She didn't interpret her words or actions as inauthentic. She didn't go behind the author's back and say it really was a crappy piece of work. The book tanked, but the writer survived without going into a major depression, which it turned out, had been what Betty had feared might happen.

Friedan engaged life with ferocious intensity. She devoured social invitations as if they were gourmet chocolates. Betty made friends quite easily, and greedily collected scores of them. Her circle was crowded with celebrities, journalists, other writers, well-known members of the intelligentsia, and an assortment of successful male friends she called *my tycoons.* And she was generous of spirit, sadly not a trait usually mentioned.

Strangers pursued her, mostly women who said: *Thank you for changing my life.* Or: *Thank you for changing my mother's life.* Depending on Betty's mood, these encounters could be moving or dreadful. One evening as we were waiting to go into the old Sag Harbor cinema on Main Street, a young woman holding a baby girl came toward us. I thought: *Oh no! Here we go.* But Betty rose to it. She took the tiny child's hand and said: *We're all expecting great things from you.* The mother was thrilled, which pleased Betty. As we walked into the theater I commented: *When she is older than I am or than you are, she will be able to say: When I was a tiny child, Betty Friedan took my hand and said....* She gruffly cut me off, saying she couldn't act like that every time she was approached.

I'm not Gloria, you know.

Friedan experienced Gloria Steinem as the most painful thorn in her feminist side. There are the obvious and much cited reasons. Gloria was glamorous and thin and didn't lose her temper at inopportune moments. Steinem photographed well, interviewed brilliantly and, as the saying goes, the camera loved her. The media preferred Gloria, although they could be as unfair and vicious to her as they could be to Betty. On the occasion of *Ms.* magazine's launch, Harry Reasoner, the CBS broadcaster, barely contained his on-air derision and hostility.

In public settings Betty didn't acknowledge the hurts and insults Steinem suffered, nor offer Gloria due credit for her work and leadership. Instead, Betty insulted her and accused her of things both petty and damaging. There was a rumor that Steinem had been an FBI agent; Betty tried to use that slur against her. But at the strong insistence of friends, she stopped. There was a much-quoted reference to Gloria as "The Hair." Perhaps recognizing it unworthy for a feminist foremother to behave like a petulant junior high school girl, she stopped the attacks. In later years Betty vehemently denied she was the source of *The Hair* remark. Still Friedan couldn't ever forgive Gloria Steinem for becoming the iconic feminist leader, the glamorous poster woman for the movement.

One late night on Glover Street, I upbraided Betty for her hostility toward Gloria. She blew up, walked to the front door and opened it widely. It was a significant gesture because close friends used the side door.

How can you be my friend? How can you defend her? I don't ever want to see you again. Get out!

It was 3 a.m. and I had no intention of leaving. She stood at the door fuming. I remained silent and motionless. Finally, I said:

Do you suppose Elizabeth Cady Stanton and Susan B. Anthony spoke of one another the way you do about Gloria? Maybe all those things we read about their relationship are lies.

She laughed, slammed the door shut, and walked back to the living room. She poured another pepper vodka. I changed the subject to Alice Munro, the Canadian writer. I had brought along Munro's newest book of short stories with me for the weekend. I handed the volume to Betty, suggesting she read it in bed and let the women's movement solve its own personality problems for a few hours. Betty shook her head slowly, her large and hooded eyes now distant. She wouldn't look at me directly as she insisted everyone loved Gloria and had forgotten about her. Now I saw pain, and not the previous hostility.

I then imagined a Jewish girl in Peoria, Betty Naomi Goldstein, daughter of the town's jeweler, waiting to be selected, waiting to be chosen. And maybe waiting to turn into a truly beautiful woman. Gloria Steinem's very existence created a gushing well of rejection inside Betty. The animosity Friedan felt for Steinem was beyond anything similar in the women's movement. Ironically, Gloria, a girl from East Toledo, Ohio (who also made it to Smith) understands and has written about not belonging, about wanting to be accepted. Both were defined (or at the least categorized) by the way they looked. Gloria has long claimed she had to fight against the prevailing stereotypes about how beautiful women are supposed to behave, and has talked about the struggle to be taken seriously in spite of being attractive.

Betty endured different prejudices—she was obviously

Jewish, behaved assertively, and was not pretty in the traditional definition of the word. Being beautiful and not being beautiful are equally heavy burdens for women. Having once been beautiful, I can sympathize with Steinem: looks can get in the way. When Betty and I became friends I was still pretty. She was not threatened by my looks, nor did I observe her showing jealousy toward other friends who were beautiful. Betty did not tell me she was concerned about her appearance, though she was frustrated by weight gain. She never considered cosmetic surgery, which she spoke against often and loudly. Once at a festive gathering in Los Angeles, she whispered I should observe the faces of the women around us. She noted the majority of them had been surgically improved, some drastically. Friedan believed our faces told the stories of our lives and that facelifts were *a scourge* because *the knife erases the chronology of one's life*.

At an interval when I was quite disfigured from drug therapies, she asked how that felt. Betty also asked if beauty had harmed me professionally. What had hampered me most, professionally, were recurring bouts of illness. We talked about that.

"You mean how does it feel to lose my looks? It's not any fun. But some obstacles have been removed. Men listen to me more carefully now in meetings and at conferences. I don't have to repeat myself so often."

She was quiet. Then in a soft voice, she said I was still attractive and was young enough for my appearance to straighten out again. As my father had also cautioned, Betty warned that being pretty could be dangerous and should never be used as a weapon. And that ultimately all beauty faded. Betty talked about beauty comfortably but it seemed a remote topic for her, not one that invoked the same passion that so much else did.

During a visit to California, I told my mother about the night Betty ordered me out of her house. Mother's response was immediate and volatile:

How could you reprimand her about Steinem? How could you betray her that way? I agree with Betty, YOU of all people!

From a pile of saved newspaper clippings, my mother pulled out a picture of Gloria Steinem at a gathering shaking hands with a group of women. Beneath the photograph my mother had written: *I am sure MS. Steinem wouldn't shake my hand.* It angered me. I corrected my mother. Gloria certainly would shake her hand. Gloria Steinem tried to shake everyone's hand. I said once again that Gloria was one of the most gracious of feminists, that if they met, my mother would like Gloria Steinem.

Mother wasn't interested. Her viewpoint was that Gloria Steinem had crashed the party Betty Friedan had planned and organized—the one my mother felt that she was invited to attend. Mother said the *new feminism* didn't welcome women like her. She said Steinem had ruined it with her "radicalism" and "aviator glasses. You should be ashamed of yourself," she kept telling me.

I replied it would help if Betty stopped saying the fight for women's equality was "her movement." I might as well have thrown kerosene onto a fire. I entered my mother's response in my journal. I didn't need to re-read the entry because what she said has stayed with me all these years:

"Suppose you had a mother who was a gifted seamstress and made beautifully crafted clothing for you. Suppose whenever you wore these outfits people complimented you on the way you looked and asked who had made them. Suppose you decided the beautiful clothes weren't quite right any longer, or not in style, or not interesting, or not daring enough, or didn't fit your new sense of yourself. And suppose you went to your mother and said that although you were grateful for all the work of making your wardrobe year after year—you needed to move on—and you closed the door on all the clothes your mother had made.

"You stopped wearing them, gave or threw them away, or destroyed them.

"That's what it's like for Betty when all of you—the daughters of HER movement reject the mother and everything she created. Why don't you ever think about how that would feel? What do you think it's like for Betty to be rejected for a flaming radical in designer blue jeans who has never bothered to get married and have children?

Betty is last season's fashions—discarded, marked down and thrown into the bargain basement. But somehow Gloria is always in season. It's lousy. Shame on Gloria for not caring enough to try to understand how Betty feels.

And you call this sisterhood?"

* * *

Betty wanted to be recognized as "The Original Mother" and pointed to evidence that supported her claim as the single foremother of the second wave of feminism. Friends worried that Friedan's recorded place in history would focus more on her personality than on her contributions. She was haunted by her earlier hostility to lesbians assuming leadership positions. She could never outrun the fact that *The Feminine Mystique* was a book about liberating suburban *white* women. She felt steamrolled by the more aggressive acts of younger and more radical feminists.

Although Betty was still in the big tent of women's rights, she wasn't running the show, and that she didn't like. It was in her DNA to be a leader—*the* leader. Women were on the move. As we evolved and defined ourselves as feminists, we didn't want to only read smart books about housewives stepping away from the kitchen sink and launching into careers. For many Betty became the symbol of our mother's brand of feminism. The diverging visions were illustrated simply and most dramatically in the icons of the time. Betty wore, and gave as gifts (including to the Pope) the biological symbol for woman with an equal sign in the open *head*. Robin Morgan designed and made popular the insignia that would stand (and still does) for a younger feminism—that same gender sign with an upraised fist in place of the equal sign. It is on the cover of her influential book, *Sisterhood is Global*.

Betty viewed much of what came after *Mystique* as personal rejection and political repudiation. She retaliated publically in defense of the vision and plan for women's equality she had laid out so carefully in *The Feminine Mystique*. Unfortunately, many saw her actions and comments as a mission to restore lost status and to feed her ego. Sometimes it was hard for other feminists to see that Friedan was hoping to realize the dream of men and women working together for women's equality and liberation. The new men and new women to whom she dedicated *The Feminine Mystique* were not part of a revolutionary feminist agenda.

Friedan was possibly the most widely read and yet most misunderstood of the major "second wave feminists." She is now posthumously being understood and appreciated once again as young women struggle to balance their careers with marriage and motherhood. A young friend of mine—a smart entrepreneur, married, and mother of two boys—told me she liked what Friedan had written many years before she was born. *The Feminine Mystique*, she said, encapsulated the dilemmas of her own life.

"My husband wants a clean house and delicious meals I prepare, and well-planned dinner parties with friends and colleagues. He doesn't offer assistance around the house, and when I ask him to take on a few chores regularly he becomes irritated. He works hard too and I understand he's exhausted, but I'm left with all the domestic duties. My husband wants sex, but I'm too tired to care. I still want to please him, but I'm trying to figure out car pools, homework assignments, and all the rest of what it takes to raise two kids, maintain a demanding career, and make a disgruntled husband happy. I'm concerned about the kids and my husband's growing discontent. I'm up all night with anxiety. I worry about the marriage, and whether my board of directors is going to approve my marketing plan for the new product line. I think Motherhood is the new feminism."

At first I cringed when I heard her last words, but then smiled. Betty would have loved to have engaged this young woman of the 21st century who understood that mothering wasn't enough of a life for most women, but that it had to be supported and aided by actions, policies and personal domestic politics.

In 1981 Betty's opportunity to articulate a new vision for women's rights was compromised with the publication of her book, *The Second Stage*. Unfortunately, Betty did not attempt to reach across the feminist aisle to form alliances with the leaders of the movement who had competing ideologies, and the radicals and militants saw little point in extending the olive branch or trying to compromise either. Although younger feminists had made overtures toward reconciliation, it was never enough. Graciousness wasn't Betty's strongest suit. Feminist disharmony wasn't specific to Betty nor was it her sole responsibility to find a remedy.

But the message of *The Second Stage* was far afield from the direction feminism had taken. It had become harder to trust her. She wanted to be respected as a ferocious force (and source) of feminism, to maintain her status as a player in established organizations, and to be celebrated at social and political events. Many feminists did not share Friedan's vision of a new world in which men were included as equal participants. Betty cared about men, and had as many close friendships with men as she did with women. She was too willing to accept (or at least to excuse) the persistence of male power to be comfortable in radical company. Increasingly she found herself misunderstood in what was becoming mainstream feminism.

The 2011 HBO documentary *Gloria: In Her Own Words*

clearly depicts the sharp divide between Betty and her followers' goals and those of the rest of the women's movement. These were the leaders Betty was prone to label *feminists with a capital F.* This "other feminism" demanded complete liberation, not only an extension of legal and social rights for women. The more progressive and militant women called for a revolt outside the system:the marshalling of forces to do whatever was required to dismantle patriarchy. Enraged by what they saw and experienced, these feminists used their anger and mobilized it into activism while Betty continued to engage with "the Establishment," an entrenched system many feminists viewed as the ultimate enemy. Betty didn't choose to participate in a *Women's Liberation Movement* that exposed and called out the worst of male opinions and attitudes. Betty could not say—*I do not take my enemy to my bedroom.* She would not have found herself at a conference with the theme "The Penis as Weapon."

And she refused to embrace a certain kind of feminist humor. She found nothing funny about slogans such as: *If we could send one man to the moon…why not all of them?* I had this emblazoned on a tee shirt, and once when I wore it in her presence, Betty was not amused. Although men made jokes at women's expense, Betty didn't believe that hitting back was the solution. She envisioned a new order where name-calling and insults from both sexes would be eradicated.

If Betty feared lesbian power and influence in feminist leadership, what she feared more was the polarization of the sexes. She equated this to lesbian leadership, and opposed lesbians as a visible and powerful force within the movement. She was convinced lesbian leaders would give the enemies of women's rights more ammunition to fire away at the entire movement as a bunch of man-haters. Betty seemed unable to separate sexual orientation from her personally held opinion that lesbians hated men. For too long a time, it was impossible to move Friedan away from this misconceived proposition. She did finally recant and call for the rights of all lesbian sisters, but by then it was too late for most to forgive her fully, or at all. Through it all, Betty adamantly insisted she was not homophobic or prejudiced, but she maintained that since most of the country was, the existence of lesbian leaders could harm the progress of the women's movement as a whole.

During our friendship I never heard her refer to men as *them* or as *other*. She might refer to feminists she disagreed with as *them*, but never men. When I would riff about how men were essentially the same, she would stop me, anger rising in her voice. Feminist boasts that we were the better or more moral sex didn't cut it in Betty's world. When men behaved badly, she acknowledged their errors, but faulted the culture, not individual men (with the exception of domestic violence). She didn't jump on the "abolish patriarchy" bandwagon. If she had a bandwagon it was "abolish inequality," something she was able to distinguish as different from patriarchy.

Becoming a feminist doesn't demand a complete conversion experience. It doesn't require women to abandon everything they once thought and did in order to begin again. Most of us brought our past *stuff* into the kind of feminists we became. Betty surely did. She was an *equality feminist* who was a community activist and an advocate for civil rights. She saw the fight for women's rights as an obvious extension of the civil rights agenda.

She believed in the elasticity of the U.S. Constitution. Along with many others, she fought long and hard for the passage of the Equal Rights Amendment. She believed deeply in our democracy's inherent capacity to transform and reform itself. I think of Friedan as a late-20th-century National Suffragist—a different kind of Susan B. Anthony—one who wore leopard prints and red high heel sandals and hoped to fall in love—but a version of Susan B. Anthony nonetheless. They both held the opinion that giving up on the system was always a mistake. While the quote "Failure is impossible" belongs to Anthony, the words could well have been Friedan's.

Radical and militant feminists also worked for systemic changes, but did not view remaining within the establishment as the most effective strategy. *Reform vs. Revolution* remains a dilemma in all struggles for justice. In this regard, the contemporary women's movement has a similar history to other social movements. In some ways, the split between suffrage and abolition and later between suffrage and temperance contain these conflicting elements. What was stunning in the second wave of the women's movement was how personal the battles became. Fights between feminists of differing ideologies played into two sexist stereotypes: women never get along with each other, ie. *cat fights*, and that women must always get along with each other as loyal sisters.

Betty's reform agenda served as a lightning rod from which radicals advanced in different directions. Their actions fueled her personal antagonisms. Betty had a righteous indignation against restricting women to traditional roles, which she combined with powerful rhetorical pronouncements, but it did not alter the essence of who she was. Throughout her life, Betty Friedan was a politically savvy woman and activist who wanted to transform, rather than dismantle, our existing institutions including workplace, marriage, family, government, the courts, and education.

* * *

Betty was united with other feminists in the fight for family-leave policies and reproductive choice, although she was troubled that the women's movement was increasingly identified as *The Abortion Movement.* I was more concerned we would be remembered as the *Failed ERA Movement.* Failure was possible and it occurred on the 30th of June 1982, the ratification deadline. We were three states short of the required 38. I stood with those who felt it best to declare a victory because 35 states *did* ratify. And I agreed with the notion that we would have reached 38 eventually if a deadline clock had not been running. I joined the view that we should move on and not solidify defeat with relentless talk about it. (It is a position I've rethought in the last decades and no longer share.)

The loss of the ERA was a bitter blow for Betty, who took it as personally as she took a bad review or a personal rejection. She had based much of her persona and spent so much of her time on the ratification fight. I was not as sympathetic or as compassionate as I might have been, because I was caught up with the struggle to keep the rights we had gained in the areas of reproductive choice.

Betty told me that I was too intensely focused on the fight for choice, too involved with keeping *Roe's* guarantees safe. She warned me I was throwing away opportunities to become known for something other than choice. I received threatening and disagreeable letters and experienced heckling when I spoke. But it wasn't as bad compared with what was happening to the women who played central roles in the Pro-Choice movement and who had national media visibility. Having an abortion is not an appealing option; I've never met a woman who feels otherwise. The fight to keep reproductive rights legal and to provide equal access for all women continues into this century. Our opponents still define the struggle as everybody's business—except the woman and her conscience.

Betty was perplexed that I didn't share her concerns about women delaying pregnancy. When reminded of my mother's age at my birth, she argued I was unplanned. Betty believed that corporations, businesses and government agencies should be made to develop infrastructures so women could choose both career and motherhood at reasonable ages. The dream articulated in *The Feminine Mystique* would never come to full fruition without systems in place (both governmental and private) to support policies and programs for working parents. She argued that if feminists of childbearing age (like myself) always put abortion rights before the need for mandated national family policies, it would open the door for the New Right to shape the dialogue on family policy and enable them to set the agenda. Betty understood that reproductive rights were crucial. Our disagreement was about defining the terms of the discourse. She wanted to ensure that the public face of the women's movement was not only about the right to choose.

One summer afternoon when I had her full attention, I told her what I had witnessed as a teenager and then as a young woman. I remained a virgin longer than almost anybody I knew, but that didn't keep me from knowing what was happening in the 1960s and in the first years of the 1970s. Lakewood girls, like girls everywhere, got pregnant. Some were sent off to the ubiquitous "homes for unwed mothers"to deliver babies and give them up for adoption. Some had tolerant families who kept their daughters home and welcomed the infants into the fold. Some girls vanished, or they moved to new places where they either placed their babies or kept them—sometimes with members of an extended family. Plenty of girls got married. In the best circumstances, education and careers were delayed. In many instances these were the girls who became the women who didn't finish their educations or fulfill their plans and dreams.

Although it was still illegal until the January 1973 *Roe vs. Wade* decision, some women chose abortion. In San Diego there was a hotel named the El Cortez, constructed in the 1920s in the then-popular Spanish Colonial Revival style. For decades it was the tallest building in downtown. (San Diego is about 100 miles from the Long Beach/Lakewood area.) In those years, San Diego was known for its zoo, a scenic coastline, and the newly opened SeaWorld and naval port. It was also the place where one went for a Tijuana abortion, and the drop-off point was the El Cortez.

Doctors with guts and compassion made the arrangements. It was the only sane way to terminate a pregnancy, but it required financial resources as well as a willing physician. Some women and girls received excellent care in abortion clinics across the border, but it was risky. Frightening stories circulated in Southern California about mangled procedures, permanent injuries and deaths in the Tijuana abortion clinics.

The girls I knew were among the lucky ones. One friend related her experience in detail. At a prearranged hour a car with blackened windows pulled up at the side of the landmark hotel. Girls and women got in and the car sped away. There were no telephone numbers given, or location specifics, and of course this was long before the era of car phones, cell phones, smart phones, texting, GPS tracking systems. Boyfriends, family members, and friends who hoped for a good outcome could only wait for their return, clueless as to their whereabouts.

The outline of the El Cortez loomed large in the mental skyline of my emerging feminist-girl's thinking. I understood clearly that I must not get pregnant unless I wanted to have a baby, and from an early age I held the conviction that a woman should own her womb.

In fairness to Betty, like my mother, she never compromised on abortion as a woman's absolute choice. My mother likely thought abortion a mortal sin, but she never wavered on the point that it must be a woman's sole right to choose. This stemmed from my grandmother's generation, when women died from too many pregnancies and inadequate birth control. It was also rooted in Mother's own terror at finding herself pregnant in her 40s, with no options. Another aspect of my mother's support came from her knowledge of the infamous "back-alley" or "coat hanger abortions" performed by butchers of that era, who left women to die when things went wrong.

Betty worried about the intensity of the fight for reproductive rights. We were routinely called "baby-killers" (this was even before the murders of doctors). She feared that being identified as a one-issue movement diminished our ability to be heard on other crucial ones. Though we always had a much larger agenda, in the heat of the battle it could be difficult to remember. I have been engaged in the struggle to preserve the right to choose for more than four decades. When I raised my voice for reproductive freedom I could not shut up, and still haven't. *Roe v. Wade* is an essential component of what full equality and justice for women means: the freedom to choose abortion legally together with the access to medical help comprise core civil liberties. Reproductive rights without available medical services for women renders those rights all but meaningless.

In 1989 Bella Abzug asked me to speak at the East End Women's Alliance Forum in East Hampton on August 26th, National Women's Day. She suggested I talk about reproductive liberty, based on arguments that would become part of my book *Nobody's Business*. I had lots to say but decided to put my remarks into a concise format. I called it a manifesto—"Ten Pro-Choice Commandments." Bella was pleased. Later, Phyllis Kriegel, the publisher of *New Directions for Women,* printed it in one of the issues. It was a short document that had a fleeting moment of feminist fame.

"The Commandments," and a subsequent article I wrote for *Dissent* on fetal neglect, "Womb vs. Woman," convinced Betty that I wasn't wasting my time. We had arrived at a new place together. She saw that the larger legal issues of privacy rights (not only abortion) were at the foundation of my work on the meaning of the Constitutional entitlements to personal privacy. She told me it was important for women of childbearing age to keep true to the cause of keeping "Roe" safe from further restrictions.

I too conceded. Betty had been correct. The New Right had encroached significantly on the turf of family policy.

Sag Harbor gave Betty an opportunity to return to her community activist roots. In the late 1980s she met the novelist William Demby and they became quite close. Demby was African-American, and through their friendship, Betty became more aware of the segregated way that middle and upper class African-Americans lived in Sag Harbor. She couldn't digest the fact that their waterfront communities (Azurest, Ninevah Beach, and Sag Harbor Hills) long established and historically important, were by then self-segregated communities. Nonetheless, Betty's impulse was pure if naïve.

Once she was onto the situation, her mantra was: *Blacks and whites are living in social and political apartheid where there is no chance for dialogue.* Demby and Friedan brought a few people together to discuss what a dialogue might look like, what venue would be most effective, and what could be accomplished. For Betty a primary goal was press coverage and general media attention. We were in the middle of the Reagan years and many of us were in the doldrums. Apathy had set in, yet at the same time there was a communal desire among liberals to rekindle efforts toward achieving a more equal America. Whatever Betty's queasiness about lesbians in the women's movement, she did not share the same misgivings about blacks and civil rights. She had a grand vision that a televised town hall meeting in Sag Harbor with African-Americans and whites could start a national dialogue about public policy and the Reagan presidency.

I was too cynical to have such expectations, but nonetheless found it oddly reassuring that she could suspend disbelief long enough to organize with such enthusiasm. On a summer weekend in 1987, we held a public seminar or town meeting at the high school. The program was called "Retreat From Equality." It was an elite gathering of experts, distinguished writers, political people, and celebrities. The panels focused on issues of social justice, economic inequality, women's rights, and cultural segregation. Critics of the Initiative viewed it as less about race, inequality, and Reagan's policies and more a grandstanding of personal achievement and social status. Betty couldn't see that the Initiative might be viewed that way, and was angered and surprised when the media levied a litany of criticisms against her personally and the event. For good measure some critics added the old slur that it was one more example of radical chic liberalism. The Sag Harbor Initiative (as it was called) limped along for a couple of years following that summer.

Friedan's dream of bringing blacks and whites into the same tent of liberalism was ill considered. The African-American communities of Sag Harbor didn't need Betty Friedan. These were well-established, well-placed, and influential people who were already overbooked with professional, political, and social activities. But those who participated in leadership roles, notably Bill and Pat Pickens and Doug and Clem Pugh, were generous of spirit and respectful to Betty. In some part, the Sag Harbor Initiative was one of Betty's attempts to resurrect her role as a leading public figure, similar to what she experienced after the publication of *The Feminine Mystique*.

The social connections made during the Initiative continued for some period of time, but there was never a whisper of a chance that a new and fully integrated Sag Harbor summer social season would emerge. Betty didn't re-examine the first and heady days of the Initiative; it was not part of her make-up to dwell on dreams that fizzled. I came away from that experience feeling that little was accomplished, that what we did together had no lasting impact. But that wasn't something I shared with Betty.

Yet for a fleeting time the Sag Harbor Initiative did recapture a few frames of the mental movie that still plays in some of our brains. It's the one inspired by Martin Luther King's August 28th, 1963 "I Have A Dream" speech at the March

On Washington for Jobs and Freedom when he articulated his dream of a socially equal, legally responsible, fair, just, and integrated America. It's the same mental movie that ran in the heads of many who, decades later, celebrated the victory of Barack Obama. That 1987 summer weekend in Sag Harbor was captured on film by C-Span, and portions of it can be accessed on the Internet. I see the Sag Harbor Initiative as a valentine to a simpler and perhaps a more hopeful time. What I did carry away is a quiet private conversation with Doug Pugh, who served in both the Hugh Carey and Mario Cuomo administrations on the New York State Unemployment Insurance Appeal Board. Governor Cuomo named Pugh chairman of the agency. And he was the first African-American to hold the position. He was an impressive and imposing man. After the weekend event ended, late one night, he put this question to me and said in a matter-of-fact tone that he believed I would tell him the truth.

If you ran into me late at night and there was nobody else around, and we were in a subway station or on the street in Manhattan somewhere, I think you would be afraid of me.

I replied: *Yes, I would.*

He thanked me for my honesty. I had confirmed what he had been thinking throughout the weekend. In his view, holding biracial town hall meetings from now until the end of time would never change the reality I had confessed. I was sad, but grateful that in the middle of much arrogant public puffery and self-congratulation, two people had exchanged their feelings. I doubt our fleeting friendship or that interaction changed much about Doug Pugh, but the memory of him lingers and what he said haunts me.

* * *

Betty wasn't an institutional person, but she was an institution of feminism. She would express a desire for a permanent affiliation and then just as often reverse the opinion, fearing a formal appointment would be constricting. But without a perch to call her professional home, she was sometimes adrift. Her life in Sag Harbor was an anchor that gave her an identity in addition to that of famous feminist. She had many friendships, and became involved in community activities, not only the Initiative. Life on Glover Street grounded her. But it wasn't the same as belonging to a research center, with colleagues and a support staff.

Throughout her life, Betty had appointments at prestigious places, though not always with positive outcomes for her or the host organizations. There was no obvious match. When Cynthia Fuchs Epstein became a resident scholar at the Russell Sage Foundation, we began to talk about Betty's needs. Epstein was a distinguished feminist sociologist and a vocal advocate of Betty's place in women's history. We discussed ways to convince the foundation's president to appoint Betty as visiting scholar for a one-year term. Cynthia was a gentle face of feminism; we were friends and colleagues. Together we devised a plan. Betty would come and have lunch with us and the foundation's president, Marshall Robinson, and the vice-president, Peter de Janosi.

First, Cynthia explored the topic with them. They were willing to talk about the possibility with Friedan. I was the program officer of the Gender program and Cynthia and I saw that as an obvious fit for Betty. A woman, Margaret Olivia Sage, created the Foundation in 1907, and its earliest programs centered on women and work. Cynthia handled the details. I thought it would be a good idea to brief Betty about the men, but I didn't act on my instinct. After all, she liked men. These two were handsome, elegant, former Ford Foundation executives. It would be fine. It wasn't. Betty came unprepared and appeared anxious. They were cordial. She was pleasant and polite, but nothing she said sparked their interest. It was painful to observe her obvious sense of vulnerability that afternoon. Was she intimated by the academic nature of the place? That was hard to imagine, because several of her friends were well-known and distinguished intellectuals and scholars. Or did she feel these men should court her?

Robinson didn't exclude the option of an appointment, but indicated he didn't see a clear way to approach the trustees. It seemed a dubious claim—the board had a scattering of feminists, including the University of California Berkeley law professor Herman Hill Kay. When Robinson presented his visiting scholar choices at board meetings, the vote for approval was always a formality. Robinson went on in a fairly dismissive tone. My mind wandered. In an act of mental defiance, I considered going behind the backs of male power and speaking to the women board members I knew well. It was a fleeting fantasy. Although Margaret Olivia Sage had founded the institution, it remained entrenched in a male model of operation. The patriarchy that ruled the early 20th century in which the Foundation began was still operating in the late part of the century. The women on the board did not challenge the norms; they did not voice their feminist values or convictions at board meetings in any meaningful way.

As we drained our coffee cups at lunch, the talk turned to mutual social connections and to Manhattan life. I realized our plan was doomed. Cynthia rarely made strategic errors when dealing with men in power; she handled men in ways that usually resulted in successful outcomes. Cynthia was a public feminist with a feminine-feminist mystique that was palatable to men. She did not threaten their power directly. Betty *behaved* during our lunch, but perhaps the striking contrast between these two women was in the men's minds. Seated at the same dining table were the ultra-feminine distinguished feminist resident scholar who was pleasing in all ways, and the ultra-famous feminist mother. Friedan decried the feminine mystique in her writings and speeches, and even in her quieter moods did not manifest those traits. Betty was powerful and outspoken, quick to announce her point of view in any conversation or setting. But this day her tone was flat and she exhibited little affect. Betty had keen instincts. Perhaps she intuited from the outset that the luncheon was only a favor from these men to Cynthia and me.

As we were about to get up from the table, Robinson spoke directly to Betty. He said he wanted to speak candidly, and described the intimacy of the foundation, the small number of staff and scholars. He related the foundation's history and legacy, including its revered place in women's history. Then he delivered the kill-line. The issue (he was careful not to say problem) with Betty coming as a visiting scholar was that she would bring an entourage. He elaborated. People from all over would learn of her residency and would come to talk to her, and dine where we were. The foundation would be inundated or overwhelmed, which would present challenges to the support staff and eclipse the other scholars.

He kept up this bullshit for some minutes. Then somewhat cleverly, he worked his way around to her importance. With conversational artistry he trapped Betty into a quick acknowledgment of her international renown. He had tossed the noose and she quickly slipped it around her own neck. It was too easy. The conclusion was simple: she couldn't come because she was too important and too famous. Clearly, even she understood that.

Betty should have come prepared with notes or a written statement about what she would work on while in residence. But it wouldn't have helped her chances. They had no intention of letting her take up space—they saw Friedan as one of those feminists with a capital "F." Maybe they saw her as *The Feminist* in flashing red neon letters ten feet high. I was unhappy that Betty hadn't defended herself when Robinson dismissed (or was it politely denounced?) her for being famous and important.

I wanted Betty Friedan to rise to full stature (she was short, but could appear mighty tall when challenged) and ask them if they would dare say such a thing to a famous man who had changed the world—who had put in motion a social movement? If I had said anything to these men (my bosses) they certainly would have seen to my dismissal. I was already on their "watch list" for being too feminist. I was frustrated by my powerlessness to do anything that might have secured "a place at the table" for Betty.

After lunch we got into the elevator together (the staff dining room was on the garden level of the building). Cynthia and Marshall got off on the ground floor to escort Betty into the lobby and out the door. De Janosi and I rode up to our offices. He shook his head slowly, and in an old-world European style with the slightest of accents, wondered aloud: "Has anyone ever noticed that Betty Friedan looks a great deal like Yasser Arafat?" I stared straight ahead. When the door opened I walked into my office and shut the door. I buzzed my secretary and told him not to interrupt me for any reason. During the elevator ride from the dining café to my office, I burned with silent rage. The Arafat remark fueled this rage, but it also cleared my brain. Betty didn't only need a perch. She needed to get out of the East Coast's winter weather systems. Her asthma was terrible. She needed sunshine. She needed appreciation. She belonged in an environment where celebrity was in fact celebrated.

I phoned Los Angeles. I had contacts at the University of Southern California, especially with Judith Stiehm, founding director of the SWMS (Study of Women and Men In Society) program and then serving as Vice Provost. I got through to her immediately and laid out the reason for my call, after relating what had just transpired. Judy laughed. She was a fearless warrior in ways I envied and wished to emulate. When she had to do battle with the university powers who could derail her projects, she slipped into her bright red cowboy boots and marched over to attend the meetings, or she demanded one, on her own terms.

We talked about what Betty would need besides an academic appointment—a place to live and a driver were essential. From that conversation, Judy went to work, exhibiting her energy and forceful competence. Things fell into place rather quickly. Once in Southern California it didn't take Betty long to find her own way. She couldn't drive in Los Angeles but that didn't curtail her socially or stop her from honoring professional obligations. She found drivers and rides. Betty had many old friends in L.A. and she reconnected with them, and a few pals from the East Coast who had moved to Los Angeles. Soon she was talking about Los Angeles as the obvious part-time living solution. In her customary and infuriating habit, she forgot my role in initiating that move. It was a standard part of the Friedan package—gratitude muffled by a sense of entitlement. I was accustomed to it. I didn't expect her to grovel. In fact, I preferred the entitled "La Grande Betty" to the small Betty of that infamous Sage lunch.

In Los Angeles, Betty had a place set for her at any number of tables. She worked full-tilt on her project on aging, and pushed forward on the manuscript that would become *The Fountain of Age*. She also ran a think tank that met monthly, precisely the sort of activity that sustained her. My parents and childhood friends lived in Southern California, so I was out there often and saw Betty regularly during her Los Angeles seasons. Eventually, I took a small house in the Silver Lake area and she came to dinners. I would pick her up and we would sit in the back garden, designed and planted by a serious woman gardener. Silver Lake is a strangely bucolic neighborhood of Los Angeles, at a remove from the incessant freeway noise (but at that time not from gang violence).

Silver Lake had long played a role in my mythic dream of life in Los Angeles—the Los Angeles I had trouble releasing myself from. That city and I engaged in an emotional tug-of-war. I was torn between the two coasts—should I make a decision for one and against the other? I could not sustain a bicoastal existence in any serious way. It was impossible, financially and medically. The pull of Manhattan remained strong. Sometimes I felt a traitor to my roots and friends, but Manhattan had become *home*. In Los Angeles I never knew who I was (or should have become). Manhattan had given me an identity and a sense of place. Or was it the case that Manhattan had permitted me to construct an existence that made me sane despite illness—sane enough?

New Yorkers talked to me about how odd it was for Betty to live in Los Angeles. Their assumptions about her life were far from what she was experiencing. And I was hardly the person to suggest Los Angeles wasn't a good choice. Betty thrived in the atmosphere of Southern California, with its easier winter weather and a generally more relaxed lifestyle. I found her mood lighter and there was an obvious exuberance when she took a swim in heated outdoor pools.

During the last years of her life, Friedan told a different story about Los Angeles. Once she returned east, she talked of Los Angeles with sarcastic renunciation. The picture of Los Angeles depicted in her memoir was not the whole story of Friedan and L.A. For more than a moment, Betty was part of Southern California and its feminist culture—and it provided her with a satisfying and productive interlude.

In 1987 *The Los Angeles Times Magazine* ran a cover story about Friedan's Los Angeles residency. In the cover picture (taken by Rosemary Kaul) Betty appears as a woman of stature, relaxed and present, with an open expression and a lovely smile. The article, *A Feminist in the Late '80's,* by Betty-Ann Kevles, captured the essence of Friedan's life in Los Angeles. Kevles wrote a nuanced and fair description of Betty, though she was perhaps not dissected and laid out for inspection in Los Angeles the way she was inside the eastern establishment's feminist leadership circles. Although there were bountiful celebrities in L.A., at the time Betty was a feminist star. Barbra Streisand attended Betty's seminars, something Friedan related with pride. Betty's advancing age, and finally severe health problems, combined with having to find a new place to rent each year grew tiring for her. Ultimately it was impossible to continue a bicoastal life. There had been the usual intra-university fights and troubles with some academics; Betty's tempestuous style and demands could rankle. But she did leave her mark on West Coast feminism. Los Angeles was a place comfortable enough with itself to be flexible and tolerant in allowing Betty to be Betty.

The city was socially gratifying. As well as the many old friends from the movement, there were other writers as well, some of them younger women. As on Glover Street, Betty had a reserved place on center stage, not a folding chair on the side aisle. Norman Lear, one of the bigger names in Hollywood, welcomed her arrival. After her near-death experiences from two heart-valve replacement surgeries, Lear, and his wife Lyn, hosted a book party for *The Fountain of Age*.

Betty's last season in Los Angeles had been life threatening. What had begun as a much-anticipated trip to Yosemite with friends ended up with her near death at Good Samaritan Hospital. She initially thought it was a severe asthma attack. But her heart was failing—the valve was no longer working. Medical theories about what had happened were many. One was that years of inhaled steroid therapy to control her asthma had damaged the heart-valve.

My place in Silver Lake was a short drive to Good Samaritan. I spent time with her, arriving in the morning with a cappuccino. The first surgery replaced her own valve with one created from a pig's bladder and seemed successful. But it was a premature assumption and Betty went into crisis. I was in her room the afternoon the decision was made to do a second surgery. She was failing. Emily Friedan, her daughter-doctor was there, of course. There were other people in the room as well.

It was a dramatic and anguished episode. I followed as they wheeled Betty down the corridor for surgery. Emily had on surgical scrubs. It seemed everyone around Betty was running. I didn't expect to see her again. Emily looked at me and said: "I'm so sorry, Alida." In that moment, I was consumed by guilt. I should have been the one to comfort Emily. Sharing a mother with the world was something Emily probably got used to early on in her life.

Betty came through her surgery, and the pig's bladder valve was replaced with a human cadaver valve, at first thought to be that of a woman, but later it turned out to be from a young man. Betty was back in form, although weakened. She made lots of jokes about the "replacement part," but the one she seemed to enjoy telling most was that of course, being a Jewish woman, she couldn't tolerate a pig's parts inside of her.

The Fountain of Age was finished and being prepared for publication while Betty was still ailing in Good Samaritan. On days when I visited and we were alone, she said she would not live long enough to enjoy the book's release. It reached an emotional crescendo the day a lavish bouquet of flowers arrived from Gloria Steinem and Barbara Seamen. Uncharacteristically, Betty burst into tears. I could barely understand what she was trying to say to me. I hugged her and told her that Steinem and Seamen meant the loving words on the enclosed card. Betty regained her composure and said it was proof she was dying because otherwise they would not have sent the flowers or the note. I teased her relentlessly until she laughed.

Betty had so anticipated the pleasure of the release of *Fountain* that she feared a vengeful God or other mystical force would punish her—even if she didn't really believe such existed. She worried that the joy she desired would be denied her, and on bad days it was hard to convince her otherwise. She knew that Fountain was her best work since *Mystique*. It mattered to her more than anything—even more than having a man she could count on as a companion.

Barely out of the hospital, she insisted (against Emily's advice) on going to Miami for the American Booksellers Association convention, where *Fountain* was among the featured books. She went in a wheelchair, and Emily accompanied her. She returned to New York in bad shape. A nasty infection had gone to her spinal column leaving her in intense pain. Admitted to New York Hospital, she was under the care of an excellent cardiologist (he was also my husband's doctor). Betty's feisty determination was now flagging. She was fed-up with the medical dramas and possibly chagrined about her reckless trip to Miami.

On a Friday night I walked into her room and found her without enough blankets, shivering and clammy. Was she in distress? I didn't know and couldn't get a nurse to help me. Betty was not Betty. She was like any other patient unable to advocate for herself because of illness and weakness. I knew this vulnerability from my own bouts of illness. I did what she had once done for me when I was in the hospital and what others friends often had done for me through the years. I became Betty's advocate and spoke to the head nurse on the floor. When I got home I phoned the cardiologist. This time I needed to be braver than she was.

Betty rallied. She recovered and went on as if nothing had happened to her—she certainly didn't act like someone who had come so close to the end. She had begun a new life in Washington D.C. and it renewed her. As a Visiting Distinguished Professor, she first taught at George Mason University and later at Mount Vernon College. In typical Betty style she now said that she didn't miss Manhattan at all. It annoyed many of her friends, but I found it amusing. Coping with my own disappointment at her decision to move away, I concluded that she did miss Manhattan and all of us. But there was still Sag Harbor and Betty reigned supreme there, as before, at least for a time.

* * *

Anxiety and frustration fed Betty's feelings of insecurity and made her appear more competitive than I suspect she was. Betty employed jealous rhetoric to mitigate feeling irrelevant. When in deep self-doubt, she questioned whether she still had influence and clout. She was as aware of the accomplishments of others as she was of her own place in history. At times she compared her qualities and skills to those of Bella Abzug. Their rivalry was such that their fights could be titanic. At one point they were barely speaking to each other and seemed content to live in separate spheres.

I invited both of them to an annual East Hampton Bastille Day fireworks party. It was a casual and large gathering held on the lawn of the house I had then, on Three Mile Harbor Road. Across the water from the house was the historic Boys Harbor Camp. My front lawn offered a perfect view of their extravagant annual fireworks display. I brought my parents (who were visiting) in on my scheme, but nobody else. We placed two large wooden Adirondack chairs next to each other. My father was pleased to find himself in a fairly intimate setting with Bella, the woman he had so hoped I would emulate. My mother coveted Betty's "rule of the women's world" (as she saw it), but never the loneliness that accompanied her fame and notoriety.

By my design, Betty arrived early and we sat her down with a drink. My mother sat next to her and chatted amiably, reserving the seat. When Bella arrived with friends, I escorted her to the other chair, which Mother had just vacated. And that was that. I left Bella and Betty to each other, and so did everyone else. People watched and observed in wonder and perhaps with worry. But there the two sat together—neither moved throughout the long evening. They were enjoying the fireworks, the drinks, and the food, and conversing privately, heads bent toward one another, confiding, probably gossiping, and often laughing.

A Bastille Fireworks Rapprochement or not, there were reasons their bond could not be severed completely. Bella, like Betty, was also the daughter of a merchant, a kosher butcher. They were both mothers. Both advocated for the rights of the state of Israel. At international women's conferences they held off the various attempts to pass resolutions that would have equated Zionism with racism. Bella was comfortable in radical circles and counted close friends in their ranks. But she was also a civil rights/equality feminist. And, of course, Abzug first gained national recognition as a civil rights lawyer. Betty envied Bella's congressional experience, convinced she would have been just as good a legislator and with similar style. Betty had not completely let go of her earlier dream to be in Congress. She believed she could have been elected to the U.S. Senate— which would have required defeating the popular Jacob Javits.

When verbally disabused of the romance of the political life, Betty would say: *Well, Bella was a congresswoman, but she is not a writer.*

* * *

Betty was ill-suited to the solitude that writing demanded. Much of the time she wrote reluctantly, seemingly annoyed by the imposition of the task. But when inspired by the prospects of the future for women, or angry over an injustice, she could write rapidly and enthusiastically. She spoke of the era of writing *The Feminine Mystique* as if she had been on fire. Often when I observed Betty's writing routine, the act appeared to be one of contrition—not one of gift or grace.

Betty used to say she loved the way she felt after a full day of writing, but how hard it was to get to that point, never acknowledging it as a variation on Dorothy Parker's famous dictum: *I hate writing. I love having written.* Betty was frustrated when she didn't write, but it didn't seem to help with the procrastinating and the missed deadlines. After *The Feminine Mystique*, she signed a contract to do a second book, but it never materialized. Eventually, she wrote *It Changed My Life*. It was almost uniformly decried, and cost her dearly in public respect. It was the subject of extreme feminist outrage, which was not surprising, because it contained factual errors and slammed other leading feminists.

Betty continued to define herself as a writer and wanted to be known (and remembered) as much for this as for anything else she did. In high school she had enjoyed theater and appeared in plays, but even then her classmates expected her to become a writer. Later on in her life, when she was under contract for the book on aging, she grew increasingly depressed about not being able to finish. It was way overdue. One afternoon, I suggested she give up social events and find a place to be alone and write nonstop until she had produced a complete draft. I told her what the Russian poet Anna Akhmatova believed: *The only luxury a writer can't live without is the ability to be absolutely alone.* She looked at me as if I had spoken to her in the original Russian. To her it was an incomprehensible suggestion and she dismissed it. What was required to finish the book—being alone and taking the risk of being lonely—was not in the cards. She continued to sandwich writing between the more enjoyable parts of her "real life." Betty would keep one eye on a manuscript, the other one on the cocktail party clock. Anguished as her writing process could be, I think she conquered some personal demons as she pressed (or lurched) forward. In Sag Harbor, she often wrote at the end of her long dining table. She would seat herself next to the side door that everyone used, perhaps in the hope that someone would arrive to interrupt her—which, people often did.

I was one of those such interrupters. She was always eager to stop writing, even when I protested and tried to leave. After the public failure of *It Changed My Life* and the problematic reception to *The Second Stage*, she was determined to write another *big* book. She wanted to make one last, important statement in the hope she would once again be regarded with the same gravitas that had followed *Mystique*.

Haunted by her earlier reputation, Betty confessed at times to feelings of defeat. She was irritated and sometimes baffled by her inability to concentrate fully on her writing. Even after she focused seriously on her work on aging—and placed it in the context in which it belonged, as an extension of the thinking in *Mystique*—completing the manuscript was still onerous. But when she shared her project on aging as a work-in-progress, she invariably struck a chord with audiences. Instead of propelling her to finish though, it seemed to paralyze her. She preferred the term "writer's paralysis" to the more familiar "writer's block," a subject she and I spoke about frequently. This paralysis was an intimate friend of mine as well, so Betty knew I was an understanding ally. I was tougher on her than I was on myself, and she was tougher on me than she was on herself. We may have fooled ourselves into believing we weren't writing for some defensible reason, but we never let the other one get away with bullshit.

In the 1990s, I was researching a sex scandal involving a gang rape at my hometown high school (covered in the media as the "Spur Posse" story). Two brothers were the ringleaders of the Posse group; their mother and I had graduated in the same class. I had a contract to write a book about this horrific incident, and was on a tight schedule. Conducting interviews in Lakewood, I learned about one of the girls who had been gang-raped, and who had then committed suicide. Her death had been kept out of the press and wasn't widely known in town. The girl's grandfather agreed to meet me at the back of a local coffee shop, at an off-hour. I was shattered by the details he related to me, and I didn't know where to put my emotions.

I called my mother, who said she wished I would stop working on that "damned book." I called Betty, who listened to what I said without interrupting and then told me to write it down immediately and stop talking about it. Before we hung up she said: *Don't let this story paralyze you!*

It failed in one of the worst ways a book can fail for a writer. I turned in the draft manuscript on time, and my editor, in a phone call, said it was unacceptable and that she would not extend to me the courtesy to do a revision. I had never felt as miserable and humiliated about my work as I did then. When I asked the editor for her specific criticisms, she said I had been "unfair to the boys." But, I argued, I had been quite fair to the boys, and I pointed to those sections where I wrote about the economic dislocation that had diminished the town's status and the effects this had on its fathers and their sons. I had looked for and found explanations for what the boys had done to the girls, but I offered no excuses for their criminal behavior. The editor left that topic for a moment and said she was disappointed and had expected more specific depictions of sex. "More sex?" I inquired. Yes, she wanted "a bestseller, and sex sells." Realizing she had gone too far with me, she back-pedaled and repeated her objection: I hadn't presented both sides of the story. Then, she added that because I was such a vocal feminist, she sincerely doubted I could; thus no opportunity to revise.

Talking to this editor was like falling into a black hole. Had she read the original proposal or my bio carefully before she'd acquired the book? But nothing would change her attitude. With nothing to lose, I ended the conversation on my terms: "Fair to the boys? When they gang-raped one eleven-year old girl, the excuse they gave was that she was wearing false pink fingernails. Fair to the boys? Well, I guess I could have tried harder to do that—after all, Hitler was a vegetarian and was good to his dogs!"

I hung up without saying good-bye, burning my bridges with

that publishing house. Later, I received a letter from their legal department: they would not ask for a return of the first half of the advance, despite the fact that the contract required that I do so. It was a relief but not a comfort.

It was summer. I called Betty and drove over to see her. She was the first person I told. I cried and raged, and she fumed along with me. When I had calmed down she told me it wasn't my failure (and in time I came to accept that to some extent that was true). Betty also made me face the fact that the book had been sold to the wrong publisher. She was right. The book proposal had gone to the wrong publisher. I was foolish not to insist on another house who had bid on the book (but had offered less) and whom I had liked more. That had been my right—it was my book. But my new agent had persuaded me to choose this particular house and the editor, who was a lifelong friend of hers. I was trusting when I should have been wary. Instead, I convinced myself that three women working together was the best bet for my book. This was flawed thinking, and not feminist. Neither the agent nor the editor had a feminist mindset, something I didn't perceive at the time, or more likely, didn't want to admit. I had hoped, and others believed, that the Lakewood story I had to tell was compelling and it would be a commercial success, and a breakthrough book for me. The disappointment was a sharp one.

Betty's best books, *The Feminine Mystique* and *The Foundation of Age*, were research-driven. In these books she used personal experiences to flesh out important truths about women's lives at the time, and then about the ageism embedded in our culture. Her weakest books were those in which she tried to settle scores, as she did in *It Changed My Life* and in many unfortunate passages in *The Second Stage* (the book that Simone de Beauvoir famously threw across a room in a rage). Positive reviews of *The Second Stage* from the popular essayist Mary Cantwell and the novelist Erica Jong did not assuage her sorrow that the book was a failed attempt to regain public stature.

The Fountain of Age did help resurrect Betty's image as a writer of importance and a cultural visionary. The reviews were somewhat mixed but it became another best-seller. And it gave her financial security when she needed it most as a single, aging woman. Nancy Mairs reviewed it for *The New York Times* and was respectful and positive, although she pointed out that Friedan had again mostly analyzed and interviewed middle-class Caucasians—oldsters of both genders, this time around.

Nonetheless, Mairs ended her review by proclaiming that *The Fountain of Age* would make for an excellent gift for "a woman of any age, certain or otherwise. Or a man, for that matter." She found it an inspirational work, concluding, "with Ms. Friedan for a guide, I intend, like her, to find new adventures for my third age; and if I'm lucky, I'll die on the move, in the air, on the road."

I am one of those who felt that Betty should have ended her writing career as the woman who wrote two substantial books—*Mystique* and *Fountain*. By the time *Fountain* was published, she was older, and frail from illness. It wasn't necessary for Betty to write another book to secure her legacy. But she was resolute that she had to write her memoir. I sensed she wanted to get the microphone back to have the last word, and I feared it would be a tit-for-tat volume. As she began writing the new book and started talking about it, my worries eased. It appeared it would be an illuminating look at her life, and not at all petty. Maybe she was driven to pen a memoir because she had never captured the imagination of a distinguished biographer. There was never a Heilbrun waiting in the wings, nor would there be until the publication of Daniel Horowitz's biography *Betty Friedan and the Making of The Feminine Mystique: The American Left, the Cold War, and Modern Feminism.* Betty chose to ignore it, laughed it off when asked about it in 2000.

I began to hear rumors, followed by first-person reports,

that Betty was losing her place in speeches and arriving at engagements unprepared, or disorganized. At one event, she couldn't complete her remarks satisfactorily. The organizers didn't want to pay her fee, but others intervened, and she was compensated. By then, she was living in Washington, D.C. most of the year, no longer in Manhattan. She was still on Glover Street in Sag Harbor during the summer season. She had held a position at George Mason University, and purchased a rather grand apartment in the building named *The Wyoming*. She enjoyed life there and told everyone that owning an apartment of that scale would never have been possible in Manhattan. When I visited her, I didn't think she was significantly compromised, but I did notice she was slower to put her ideas and thoughts together. The familiar Friedan intensity and passion was now not always present. She was nearing 80, and had been through a grueling passage of cardiac malfunction and repeated surgeries. Most of us who talked about what was (or wasn't) happening to Betty concluded it was the natural course of aging.

But it was more than that. She couldn't finish the memoir without help. Linda Bird Francke, an old feminist friend and successful writer, rescued her. Calling herself an editorial advisor, Francke pieced together what had been written, and taped Betty as she reminisced. From the tapes Francke wrote the remaining sections of the memoir. Betty lived a compartmentalized existence, as many famous people do. Francke knew several of those compartments well, but not all of them. And she didn't sign on as biographer of record, even though she is a distinguished one, having written several political celebrity autobiographies during her long career. Betty was drifting and Linda Bird Francke pulled from Betty what she could. The early chapters in the memoir about childhood, high school, and college years are compelling. But as the book moves forward, it becomes an extended rebuttal of her critics and those she wanted to punish. Betty's fascination and frustration with men and romance are mostly honest and vulnerable accounts.

There are glaring and embarrassing omissions and mistakes in the book. Cynthia Fuchs Epstein, the feminist sociologist, who was supportive of Betty in professional matters and a close friend for decades, is barely mentioned. I am not mentioned. Our long and intimate friendship having apparently been erased. Nor was I the only close friend or colleague who didn't make it into the record of her life. I was furious and heartbroken, as were others, and we talked among ourselves. For the first time I thought I should move Betty out of my life. Initially I didn't confront her because I assumed what she did was intentional, as did others on the roster of invisible friends. A few months after its release, I ran into a mutual friend of ours. After he informed me that Betty was extremely upset that I wasn't speaking to her, and I told him the reason, he urged me to see her and talk about it, and provided more details about the Friedan-Francke collaboration. He told me Betty had admitted she was embarrassed to have left important people out of the memoir. In a bad mood, I said I suspected she didn't leave any important people out, just important friends.

I wasn't convinced Betty cared all that much, other than fearing she might be called out on her omissions. But I did go see her. As we talked about the memoir I realized she had not been fully in charge, not because she was too busy with her social life, but because she couldn't pull it off as planned. Betty asked me to forgive her. That was a first for her. I suggested she speak to Cynthia, and not wait for Cynthia to raise the subject. Maybe Betty did; I never asked either of them. The Epsteins were among those who maintained their friendship with Betty until the end of her life.

Betty was sometimes the Bad Mother. Just as maddeningly, she could turn on a dime into the Good Mother. Many of us stayed (or were unable to leave) because we were grateful to her. But it was also our acknowledgment that we wouldn't abandon "our Betty"—she connected to friendship so intensely. Her need to be loved and cherished was its own seduction, and her vulnerability was obvious to those who cared about her.

At an event some years after the publication of the memoir, I found myself sitting next to Linda Bird Francke. I greeted her icily, thinking about what to say to her, and when during the evening I might have the opportunity to flay her. We were tentative with one another and polite. Undoubtedly she had heard criticisms and complaints from a number of the disappeared friends of Betty. We began to talk about women's issues and our lives as feminists. I asked myself: "If had I been hauled in for the largely thankless job of helping to finish the memoir, would I have done a better job of reconstructing Betty's life?" I doubted it. It might have been different, but would it have been any better? I couldn't continue to be angry with another woman writer who did her best under almost impossible circumstances. The urge to give Francke a piece of mind evaporated before our dinners were served.

Life So Far is not representative of the goodness in Betty. Parts of the book illustrate some of the worst of what she could be. The way she described her notorious temper is illustrative: *I've always been a bad-tempered bitch*. It is a memoir of limited introspection, and it does not grapple honestly with crucial themes in her life—which, had she done so, might have spoken to yet another generation of women.

Most critics of Betty's personality acknowledge nonetheless that *The Feminine Mystique* played a crucial role in the liberation of women. But there are those feminists who point to its limited scope—a book about and for white, middle-class, and well-educated women—and who insist it wasn't that significant of a book. My mother, while white and middle class, was not well-educated (although very smart) and was not living in an upscale suburb. *Mystique's* reach went much farther than the confines of the suburbs, and was also felt by the generation of women who had worked during WWII and then returned to home and housework. And even though much is made about *Mystique* not being about or for working class women, that also is an overstatement. Clerical workers, factory workers, and those who worked for wages found wisdom in Friedan's words.

When *Mystique* was published, Friedan became an instant celebrity, but it wasn't all wine and roses. Many men (unlike my father), who saw the book as a destructive force or as a communist manifesto, reviled her. Many women also felt threatened by Friedan's message. Not all of them wanted to leave home and hearth and head out to the workforce. They didn't buy Friedan's rallying cry that women were suffering from the problem without a name. They insisted they had no problems with names or without names. After re-reading the book, I regretted Betty hadn't included more of the foremothers or contemporary women working on similar issues. Betty is often pilloried for the short shrift she gave to the French philosopher Simone de Beauvoir. While she credited de Beauvoir for inspiration, she said little about her extensive work inside the pages of *Mystique*.

Simone de Beauvoir was far to the left of Friedan in thinking and in lifestyle. She was truly radical and had little patience for anything that represented bourgeois values. She viewed raising children and marriage as pointless and destructive for women. She made enormous contributions to the women's movement worldwide—as did Betty—but they inhabited different universes. Each contributed to the enlightenment of girls and women in important and distinct ways. American women who lived in towns and suburbs (mostly housewives) were far more likely to read the book of a disgruntled housewife named Betty than the writings of a French philosopher named Simone. Betty's readers, mostly mothers, were influenced by what she wrote and said in speeches and on television, and came to raise their daughters differently than their own mothers had.

Betty wasn't awed or humbled by other women. I often am. Perhaps that is the reason I grew annoyed with Betty's criticisms of Simone de Beauvoir, whose intellectual arguments caught my attention and inspired me. Betty was ever competitive with de Beauvoir and saw only hypocrisy in de Beauvoir's relationship with Jean Paul Sartre. And, Betty found the sexually open lifestyle of de Beauvoir and Sartre somewhat distasteful and unappealing. Prone as I was to become intertwined with "Great Men" myself, I felt compassion for de Beauvoir when I thought about her relationship with the brilliant and impossible Sartre. His arrogant style trumped my appreciation of his intellect (most of the time). However, I felt sad reading that, as he lost his eyesight, he found writing difficult because he couldn't see the letters. De Beauvoir stepped in and tried to help him. And as he grew increasingly physically fragile and more dependent, it was de Beauvoir who orchestrated his care and comfort. It was strangely reassuring to me that the formidable de Beauvoir would play handmaiden to a Great Man. Even she wasn't a perfect feminist. Some insisted Betty's friendship with the writer Nelson Algren was to spite de Beauvoir, who had loved him and was then jilted by him. In retrospect, I too think there is about Friedan's liaison with Algren a whiff of competition with de Beauvoir. But neither woman won that round. Soon after Algren moved across the street from Betty's Glover Street house, he died.

Although Betty knew she wasn't alone in her domestic frustration, she was unprepared for *Mystique's* impact. She had heard murmurs of unhappiness among her classmates at a Smith reunion, which confirmed her own misery, and from those personal opinions she had researched and then written the book that ignited stirrings of discontent in American wives and mothers. *Mystique* not only overwhelmed Friedan's life and schedule, it would come to define her. Only with the publication of *Fountain* did she assert herself as a thinker beyond the boundaries that she articulated in her first book. She was 72 when *Fountain* was finally published.

Much has been said, argued, and written about *The Feminine Mystique*. Five decades after its publication, merely the mention of the title alone can fuel debates and disrupt dinner parties. The shibboleths are ever present—it is class-based, myopically white, elitist, male-centered. I've had feminists scream at me about my loyalty to the book. And I've been informed it's an anti-woman book, not worthy to be in the feminist canon.

Here's what I have to say about all the negative descriptions of *Mystique*: Betty began where she was and with what she knew of women's dissatisfaction and their feeling of domestic entrapment. And, then she researched the hell out those issues. She had a vision of a better and more meaningful life for white women in the suburbs in the 1960s who were still bound by 1950s rules for women and for men. That was her starting model, and she took it as far as she could. That focus did not make her a racist. She didn't pretend to understand the lives of African-American women who have always worked and knew the names for their problems. Betty should have included at the least some caveats about the scope of her work. But to apply 21st century, post-civil rights and multi-cultural values to the ethos of the time in which she wrote is unfair. Later in life she defended her choices, saying it would have been presumptuous for her to write and speak for African-American women.

There will always be those who believe, as an article of faith, that Betty Friedan's work was meaningless. The anti-Friedan wing of the women's movement has parked her for eternity in a suburban home with a manicured lawn and backyard, deciding that she and all the women she wrote for didn't do anything terribly important for women's liberation.

Mystique was bigger and bolder than even the big and bold Betty. She drew a map to help women escape—not all women—but a large population of post-war American women. It was an early map—so it wasn't definitive. As a pioneering cartographer for women, Friedan drew new territories and left plenty of room on the map for future women to draw new continents, and they did. But Friedan would never escape in life or in death the label of "that housewife" who started a revolution. The new social order she envisioned was frightening, and at the time revolutionary, based as it was on the idea that men and women were equal. She upended the prevailing cultural norms.

Throughout life she was asked to explain and justify what she had meant in the book. In 1963, early on in the book's fame, she said to *LIFE* Magazine:

Some people think I'm saying: Women of the world unite—you have nothing to lose but your men. It's not true. You have nothing to lose but your vacuum cleaners.

* * *

I now think of the summer of 2005 as the summer of endings. My husband and I had rented a cottage in Sag Harbor. It was a last-ditch effort to see if I could re-create the happy and peaceful times I had enjoyed on the East End when I was younger. But by 2005 too much had changed even in this quiet historic whaling village of Sag Harbor. Now Sag too, like the rest of the Hamptons, was enveloped in the culture of wealth and power. By summer's end, I had decided that it was over. There was no point in continuing with rentals. I was sad and bitter. I had spent much time and some money making the cottage welcoming and hospitable, and had planned on staying there for some years. But now it all came apart. For a long time I had found refuge in the East End of Long Island. It eased my mourning of the loss of space and natural beauty I had when I lived in California. As summer came to an end, I felt almost only loss. But beyond the loss of place, I had to face the real absence in my life.

Betty was faltering mentally. I tried to deny it. I told others that she was really just lonely. Friends talked to each other often to make sure she was covered for transportation to social events. And when I wasn't going to be around, I made calls to a few friends who could check in on her. Her kids and grandchildren were around plenty, especially on the weekends. But I knew better than to believe she was only lonely and bored. Age and fragility were eclipsing her personality. When I knew that Betty was alone, usually during the week, while on my walks, I would make a loop past her house and stop in to visit. She was happy to see me, and eager for company in the way of the elderly. Her anger and much-feared venom now seemed to have dissipated.

Betty had become an old woman. That summer, going out to lunch was our major activity together. She was sometimes frustrated with the menu choices and would just order whatever I did. Betty brightened one afternoon as we drove into the heart of town. She remembered a restaurant she wanted to go to, and said we hadn't been there for too long a time. But she couldn't remember the name or where it was. I suspected it was a restaurant no longer in business. She was angry that her mind was not cooperating but couldn't fight it. She knuckled her forehead and said, *Alida, I've lost my map.* I don't know if she recalled in that moment that I had long called her my mapmaker.

I pulled into a vacant parking spot and we talked over options. We settled on The Dockside Bar and Grill, a small place she enjoyed on the waterfront. It was housed inside the American Legion building, was cozy and served good food. A number of old friends were dining there and came over to greet her. She was pleased with the interruptions. Ted Conklin, owner of the American Hotel, came and sat with us for a bit. She happily chatted with him and when he walked away Betty remarked that Ted was still handsome. It was the old Betty, who reappeared for an instant as if nothing had changed. Then the spark went out and she was suddenly tired. I took her home. We sat together in the living room quietly reading the newspaper.

One autumn afternoon I came to take her out and found her sitting, looking into the distance. She barely greeted me. When I leaned down to kiss her, she exploded that she had been waiting for me for some time. (But for once I hadn't been late). She needed to talk to me. *Just look at the mess this man has gotten us into now.* Betty was pointing to an article on the front page of *The New York Times* about President George W. Bush and his opposition to women's rights. Expectantly I waited for her verbal barrage and political insights. She was angry and defiant but it was a different rage. And that difference, of course, was everything. She jabbed her finger at the newspaper and then pointed to me and shook her finger saying—*What are YOU going to do about this?* It was the first time she had ever said *you* instead of *we* about any women's issue.

I hadn't seen Betty since the end of the summer season but I was aware she was not doing well. In a telephone conversation she had trouble connecting thoughts and ideas, but she knew who I was. On February 3rd, 2006 I was standing in line at JFK to depart for California. My mother was in another crisis, but this time it appeared serious. The doctors warned it was life-threatening. My cell phone rang. It was from other friends, the writer Linda Wolfe and her husband Max Pollack, a neuropsychologist; they informed me that Betty was gravely ill. Betty had introduced me to Max and Linda decades before and we had shared many life events together. Within a few moments, the cell rang with more calls, all conveying the same news.

In a mad moment, I asked an airline employee if he could get my luggage back. I said it was a personal emergency. He kindly made speedy inquiries. But my luggage had been loaded and it was too late to retrieve it. By now I had less than ten minutes to decide if I should go back to Manhattan and wait for news about Betty, letting my luggage go on to San Diego without me. If I chose that option, I was betting that my mother was once again playing what my father had come to call *possum-Ida*. Or if I got on the airplane, it would be with the knowledge that Betty might be dead when I arrived on the other coast.

I boarded the plane. It was a lose-lose choice.

When I arrived in San Diego there was a message from Robin Morgan, but not from anyone else. I returned the call immediately and she asked if I knew Betty was dying. She said that she and the other two founders of the Women's Media Center (Gloria Steinem and Jane Fonda) would like me to write Betty's obituary for the WMC site. I accepted. The next day Betty was dead. The WMC wanted to post the piece the next day. I wrote all night, pages of handwritten notes, far more than I could use. I longed for my mother's advice and her astute editorial wisdom, but she was in an undefined medical limbo. Before daybreak I emailed a finished obituary to Robin and asked her to edit as she saw fit. She called and we went over the changes, Robin gently suggesting some rephrasing here and there.

The obituary had a theme—Betty as mapmaker—something I had felt about her for years. The memory of the past summer when she had referred to her *mental map* remained a poignant one. I included my memory of Betty, jabbing her finger at the picture of George Bush and asking me what I was going to do about it. I had known Betty more than half my life, and she was always part of my New York life. Because of *The Book* and its influence on my mother, it seemed I had always known Betty Friedan—indeed, she was my other mother.

I went to sleep for a few hours. When I woke up I turned on my computer and read the final version of the obituary. Then I walked to the Cove and down the stairs to the sand where the harbor seals congregated. It was February, but La Jolla has no seasons, only the surreal perfection of continuous seventy-degree weather. Betty was dead. My parents were living a few blocks away in an assisted living community. The doctors warned my father that Mother could die at any moment. She was one month shy of 98. The doctors didn't offer a specific medical diagnosis, and he didn't ask. I was stuck. I could not fly back to New York. I would not be able to attend Betty's funeral.

I watched the fabled harbor seals of the La Jolla Cove squabble over the available spots on the sand. I sat in a half-lotus position and concentrated only on the seals, observing their complex status relationships with each other.

In New York I would have been with friends, sharing memories of Betty. Seated on the sand, I was silent, alone in my grief, and in my memories…

* * *

For many years Kurt Vonnegut would organize an annual fishing trip for his friends. Betty looked forward to the event. I was her houseguest in Sag Harbor one year on the weekend of the trip, and had the responsibility of awakening her at a ghastly early hour for the group pick-up (the boat left from Montauk). She left grumpy and groggy. Hours later the car pulled up to the house and I went to the side door to greet her. She bounded across the yard toward me. Vonnegut stayed a few steps behind. He looked bemused.

Betty caught two fish on her own, he said.

Swinging the two fish from side to side, she gleefully corrected him: *NO! I caught two really big fish! S*he was bursting to relate the gossip she had gleaned on the fishing trip. Relaxed, smiling and exuberant—she was again the girl from Peoria. I cooked the fish for our dinner.

* * *

Betty was a strong swimmer; in the water she was

unhampered by asthma and extra pounds. She would chide me about my reluctance to swim farther out in what she defined as *gentle* waters. She was fearless and swam in places where boats would zip past her.

Autumn was my favorite season on the East End. Betty invited me often during the fall before I had a residence of my own. And one Columbus Day in the early 1980s we decided to go to Shelter Island for a final swim. It was as warm as a summer day. We threw cotton dresses over our swimsuits and headed to the ferry to Shelter Island. We drove to a beach on Ram Island and took an autumn swim in solitude. After we were reasonably dry, we headed over to the Ram's Head Inn and had lunch on the porch overlooking the bay.

Friends scolded us, said we were foolish to take such a late-season swim, given our mutual health problems. Betty was outraged: *What's the matter? It was a perfect day for a swim. And it's the last swim for this year, why shouldn't we have taken advantage of the weather?*

But in private Betty warned me: *You better not get sick because everyone will blame me and I'll never hear the end of it.*

* * *

Twenty years earlier at her 65th birthday party, Betty had been delighted at the show of support and friendship. It was a memorable event. Reports on attendance ranged from 250 to 300 people in a funky space owned by Rubell and Schrager of Studio 54 fame. This one was called the Palladium, and at the time it was considered a hot venue. Mary Jean Tully was the driving force behind the party. There were skits, song, and much merriment, and appropriately lots of food, drink, and dancing. I still loved to dance whenever and wherever I could. Daniel, Betty's oldest child, was then still single and my age, and he asked me for a dance. As we danced, I looked over and saw Betty, the hopeless romantic, giving me the eyeball. Before resuming my seat I walked over and whispered in her ear: "No, Betty! It was only a dance." There was something sweetly old-fashioned in that moment when Betty had a fleeting notion she might play matchmaker for me with her son, a brilliant physicist.

Now as I sat on the beach, the memory of the party took me to Betty's dress. Finding the right one wasn't an easy task. Her fashion eyes were almost always larger than her budget, nor did her size afford her all the options she desired. For the party she wanted a spectacular dress, unique but also in keeping with her eccentric style—which I thought of as "formal bohemian." I had become friends with Annie Walwyn Jones, a British designer living in New York. It was during a passage in my life when I wore only her clothing. Her designs are fashionable, chic, interesting, and absolutely original. Betty admired and envied my wardrobe, so I suggested that perhaps Annie could design something for the birthday party. Annie could design forgivingly for those not model-thin. She and Betty got along famously. The one requirement that Betty would not compromise about was color—the dress had to be red. Annie designed a party frock that suited Betty perfectly. It was a daring design that made a statement, yet concealed imperfections. It was a triumph. Betty was so pleased she invited Annie and her husband, Murdoch, to the party.

But Betty hadn't calculated that in a last-ditch effort to reduce (she dropped some pounds before the party, but after the final fitting) there might be a problem. She had neglected to try the dress on again before the party. When I arrived, Betty grabbed me and said it was falling off: where was Annie? The frock wasn't falling off but it was surely looser than it was supposed to be. I nabbed Annie the minute she arrived, and she and Betty went into a private space somewhere in the cavernous club. Betty emerged smiling, calm and radiant, while Annie looked stressed. She had found a way to put the dress in order, with safety pins and whatever else was on hand. More than three decades later, Annie and I still share a laugh about Betty's birthday dress.

* * *

Betty had cataract surgery in 1984. She left the hospital on the day of the Reagan vs. Mondale election. Mary Jean Tully and I went to get her. When we arrived, she was already dressed and ready to go, but she was agitated. Convinced (as were we) that the Mondale-Ferraro ticket was doomed, she was in a particularly lousy mood. But when we opened the door to her Lincoln Center apartment, she brightened. She walked through her apartment as if she had never lived there. *How did you get these carpets cleaned so fast? I was only gone a day and a night.* I insisted the carpets hadn't been cleaned, but she didn't believe me. Mary Jean backed me up. Betty grew quiet. *Everything is so colorful, the carpets, the walls, the pictures. I didn't realize I was that blind.*

Remembering that day, I thought of our many times at the movies. Betty loved to go to the cinema and went regularly with friends. I enjoyed most going to movies in Sag Harbor, but we also went to films in Manhattan and Los Angeles. But seeing a film with Betty was an ordeal. She sat in the front row so she could see. She snarled at people she didn't know who invaded her privacy. She would make comments during the show, though eventually I broke her of that habit. We often discussed movies together. After the release of *An Unmarried Woman*, Betty admitted she was let down by the ending. I said:

"Isn't that the way we want it to end? The woman pursues her own life and doesn't get sucked into a romantic fantasy? I think it's a feminist ending."

She gave me the Betty look, the expression that said: Exactly whom do you think you are kidding?

Then she replied: *Don't tell me you aren't disappointed in that ending.* I waited to answer. I couldn't pretend with Betty. Then I confessed my own disappointment with the film's ending.

"I did want Jill Clayburgh to live with that dreamy Alan Bates. But I'm also pleased the movie ended the way it did. After all these years of the women's movement, we need to evolve. I'm a romantic and I'm not proud of it."

She shook her head in irritation:

Being a romantic and a feminist are not in conflict. There's no reason you can't be both.

She had forced me to an inner truth.

OK, Betty. I might as well call myself a romantic feminist before others accuse me. When people ask how that's possible, I'll refer them to you.

Betty didn't see a conflict between wanting love and romance and being a leader of the women's movement. She was reluctant to say she was a *feminist* with the same zeal the rest of us did. But claiming a position as the Mother-Of-It-All made refusing the feminist label problematic. Not being in love, not having a man in her life, being deprived of a committed relationship made Betty grouchy, unhappy. She talked about wanting to remarry and would sometimes obsess why a particular man didn't want to become her lover. For a short time she was fixated on an internationally famous scholar who had taken an interest in her. But soon enough, Betty learned his interest in her was not a romantic one. She was hurt and furious, and I became exasperated with what I saw as inappropriate whining. I told her to focus on her accomplishments, her role in the women's movement in America and in the world. I told her I wished she wasn't so concerned about potential love affairs.

She growled.

Don't start that crap with me. All this feminist stuff came too late for me. I want to be with a man!

The tension broke and we both laughed. "Betty, what are you talking about? You helped start all this feminist stuff."

She looked at me knowingly and lovingly, head slightly to the side, one hand touching her face.

Maybe feminism came too late for you too, Alida. Sometimes you're as bad as I am.

* * *

In the weeks following her death, journalists and representatives from organizations asked me to comment on her life. I tried to say something they had not already heard from the others. I emphasized that in my experience she was a good friend to women. I demurred on the *lavender menace* story, because I wasn't there and had not lived a lesbian life. I said it was an unfortunate blunder and a grave error, and that I believed she regretted it, perhaps more than any other misstep. One journalist asked specifically what I thought was her biggest disappointment. I did not cite the numerous public sorrows she experienced from the ERA defeat to the political fights within the movement, to not maintaining leadership, to the unfavorable reviews of two of her books.

I said only this: "Love eluded her."

Betty Friedan had thrown a huge rock into the ocean of women's lives and the resulting waves went from coast to coast and around the world. But she was not immune from the dilemma of independence versus attachment. Betty had also trapped herself in the miserable "will he choose me?" game. There are those of us who, though we may claim feminism proudly, and assert it as our primary identity, also want (or feel we need) to be chosen by a man. We fight that desire. Sometimes we lose this inner battle quickly, and give into the romance bit in the worst ways. Sometimes we gain self-esteem and decide to choose for ourselves. In the years I knew Betty well, I think that's what she attempted. She did choose men for herself. It was never a problem to find a man to escort her to events, or to come to a dinner party, or to take her out. Many men were flattered to have her court them, and they enjoyed the social privileges that came with being her companion or escort. But few of them were interested in a committed relationship.

I observed Betty in an instance when she allowed herself to fall in love. When speaking of it to others she referred to the relationship as a great infatuation. Years later in her memoir she called the liaison a *great crush*. But to me and a few other friends she talked about the possibility of a lasting relationship. She confessed to me she loved him. I thought that this man, who was a distinguished publisher, made sense for her. He was unafraid of her temper, was smart, powerful, and literary. He didn't bore her, a major plus because Betty became impatient when a man couldn't keep up with her ideas and interests. I liked him well enough, but far more important was how Betty acted when they were together. She was still herself, and certainly didn't regress into re-enacting the *mystique*. Secure and comfortable with him, Betty became much softer.

In a random occurrence, I learned this man was simultaneously seeing another woman. I knew the woman's daughter, who in a most casual manner told me about her mother's wonderful new romance. I thought her mother (the other woman) a strange choice, but she did live in a lavish apartment and had considerable amounts of money, the outcome of a favorable divorce settlement. I assumed these things appealed to him. Betty and this woman weren't part of the same (or even overlapping) social circles, nor did they share similar interests. Gambling that Betty wouldn't find out, I chose not to destroy her happiness with what I knew. And she never did find out.

Though their relationship quieted down, he and Betty remained friends. She told me his heart condition was the reason for the change in their status from intimacy to just pals. (And maybe it had been). He died more than a decade before Betty, and she grieved his loss.

* * *

My mother did not die in February of 2006. A few days after Betty's death, Mother recovered from her mysterious ailment. Her health crises, accidents, surgeries, psychological collapses, and assorted medical episodes began when she was seventy and continued until her death. At times, her needs and fears overwhelmed me. She was consumed with worry over what might happen to her in the future as well as obsessing about what was happening in the present. I devoted much emotional and physical energy to her as well as providing financial support, always in the hope it would ease some of her suffering, real and perceived. So it was a shock when my mother had to comfort me when Betty died. With all the vexing medical dramas, I had not expected this would be a part of our mother-daughter experience. She was significantly older than Betty. I had assumed Betty would take care of me when Mother died, and would have said precisely the right things to me. I hadn't seriously considered the possibility Betty would exit first. I should have though, given that she had been failing faster than my mother.

Mother's response was wise and tender when I told her Betty was dead. She was impressed that Betty left the world on her eighty-fifth birthday. She thought the simplicity and symmetry of it appropriate for a great woman of the 20th century. I gave her the obituary I had written. After she read it, she said: "She did so much for so many of us. What she wrote back then in *The Book* was brave." Mother talked vividly of the day more than forty years before when she had first read *The Feminine Mystique,* and then followed Friedan's advice. With effort she walked over to her bookcase and pulled out a paperback copy, the 10th anniversary edition. She handed it to me, reminding me that Betty had given it to her one Christmas at my East Hampton home.

"Look at the inscription. I don't think you remember what she wrote," she said as she opened it to the dedication page to the new women and the new men, underneath which Betty had written:

Christmas 1990
For Ida,
My dear friend Alida's mother—
Who has evolved beyond this herself, a new woman in her own
right—as a token of my delight in her daughter's being—
L'chaim! Betty Friedan

Mother died exactly one month before her 101st birthday, on the 4th of February in 2009, and coincidentally, Betty's birth and death dates. If I believed in the supernatural, I would say my mother chose to die that day because it was Betty's day. Mother died without the drama that had characterized much of her life. She left peacefully, at home and within the gentle embrace of her very old "New Man," whom she had loved for nearly seventy years. Love had eluded Betty Friedan, but it had not eluded my mother. Although much else had.

Ida Helen Brill lived a fairly ordinary life, but experienced remarkable changes for women, which took place over the span of her long life. She had the intelligence, insight, and imagination to appreciate most of it. My mother was born twelve years before the Nineteenth Amendment granted women the right to vote. In the last year of her life, she enthusiastically witnessed Hillary Clinton's run for the presidency, and was bitterly disappointed (and furious) that she did not become the nominee.

My mother really never found a place at the women's table that feminism set for us, but she urged me to find my own place there. She never stopped believing a woman was entitled to do and be anything, and unfailingly encouraged me to keep going, never to give in to the illness that had compromised my life. Together, Ida and Betty were the warp threads in the tapestry of my life.

Betty was a life force. If you chose to include her as a friend you had to understand you had no choice but to take her as she was—Betty Friedan could not be fine-tuned. There were occasions when I contemplated taking an extended vacation from Betty-land. But notwithstanding her legendary pride and ego, when our squabbles moved into serious disputes, it was always she, with one or two exceptions, who first returned to relight the flame of our friendship.

In the beginning, she was just a girl from Peoria, a smart Jewish girl who became the woman whose very name has been and continues to be iconic for generations of women. Peoria shaped and influenced Betty's development. It was there, in that Midwestern town, where she first observed the rigidity of women's roles, starting with her mother's. Throughout Betty's life, Peoria held symbolic significance. As a girl, she read books and dreamed dreams that were bigger than her hometown could accommodate. Betty Naomi Goldstein was not a candidate for homecoming queen or prom princess. And maybe this afforded her the mental solitude to contemplate other ways to live. Husbanding her early experiences and dreams, she would go on to combine them with research and her personal experiences as a suburban wife to write of wider worlds for women.

The intensity of the criticisms about her and her work (which wasn't perfect) is such that I wonder if it has a sexist base. Was she held to a higher standard because she was a woman leader of a women's movement? Was jealousy involved? It is only human to presume that, though she was the first, surely she wasn't the best. There lurks in many of us the hunch that we might have been the first, and if we had been, we would have been better and kinder. Was the ferocity against Betty because she was obviously Jewish?

If Betty Friedan had been glamorous or even just thin and elegant, essentially polite, and decidedly not Jewish, she probably could have gotten away with exhibiting such power and even anger. She wasn't tactful and she wasn't considered pretty. But was she so much more difficult than many other powerful people? Was she so disagreeable that her legacy should be shadowed and reputation eclipsed by tales of social lapses? And if she had written the same book, with its inherent limitations and exclusions, but had a pleasing personality, was possessed of a gentle persona, how different an outcome might that have yielded?

12

Not a Fairy Tale

I was no longer standing at the corner of Arbor Road and Downey Avenue in Lakewood, California, no longer a teenager, or the girl who had written a love-struck note to an upcoming princess. I was a middle-aged woman trying to hail a cab at the corner of 86th and Park Avenue—a self-identified public feminist who had just delivered a keynote breakfast talk at the New World Foundation about censorship and the book burning occurring in some Southern states. I was wearing the best dress I owned—a black and white print with a scoop neck. Around my neck hung my Grandmother Rosina's cameo, which I always wore for good luck when I gave a speech. I was on a Cytoxan protocol to contain the Wegener's; there were perhaps a dozen hairs left on my head, and I was wearing a fanciful wig in an updo that was more costume than camouflage. But it seemed to work.

A man from the breakfast meeting joined me at the corner and began to talk as if he had known me his entire life. I was annoyed to see him again. He had interrupted my remarks midpoint during my talk, and I had almost lost my way. I had paused for a moment, looked straight at him and said: *Would you mind terribly if I finished my remarks before you add your comments?* His face reddened and the blush covered his well-shaped bald head. He was tall, appeared physically fit, and formally dressed, even for New York. It was the middle of winter but he had a dark natural tan. It surprised me he wanted to talk. He offered to share a cab, but we were going in opposite directions. He introduced himself—Steve Scheuer—and looked astonished when I didn't recognize the name.

He apologized—hadn't meant to be rude but thought my remarks were so compelling he wanted to join in. He intended to buy my book immediately. Then he said he was involved in a major civil liberties project. Would I be interested in being a consultant? I cheered up; I was making a living as an independent consultant and speaker. I handed him my card but he didn't reciprocate. One of the flossy Manhattan real estate agencies owned an iconic London cab, which they used to squire around rich clients. Just then the London cab drove by us. I said spontaneously:

Oh there's that London cab!

Do you like London?

I do, very much.

I've just returned from London.

Really? Is that where you get such a good tan in the dead of winter?

Has anyone ever told you that you look just like a cameo come to life?

Really? Has anyone ever asked whether you are the sweetest man in Manhattan or the biggest womanizer?

Would that matter to you?

A cab pulled up, he opened the door for me, and I was off. I thought he was arrogant and interesting. My day was packed with obligations, meetings, and later a birthday party for a dear friend. I had left my apartment at 7:30 a.m. and didn't return til after 10 p.m. A beloved doorman, Frank, who was an alternate father to me, greeted me soberly: *Alida, a Gentleman was here and left some things.* He went to the lobby desk and from the cabinet below pulled out a large, double-blooming red azalea, a bottle of Lafitte Rothschild, and a book written by the man from the morning. It was inscribed: *Reds for a Glorious Red.*

I was amused. I had never met a man of such lavish gestures, let alone before a first date. I went upstairs and checked the answering machine. My earlier amusement changed to alarm.

He had left six messages during the course of the day. Clearly, he was a stalker. (This was before the era of instant Google search and the sleuthing crawl through Facebook.) I was at a loss. I called friends and colleagues but I couldn't find anyone who knew him. Some knew about his family—prominent, politically active, and influential. So he wasn't a stalker. He was smitten but not dangerous. Nevertheless I suspected he wasn't calling to offer me consulting work on a civil liberties project.

The next morning he called again, early. I was playful and biting. *You must have some civil liberties emergency on your hands if you needed to call six times and leave gifts.* He asked me to dinner. I agreed to lunch. We began to see each other often, always over lunch. There wasn't any consulting in the offing. He cared about civil liberties, but he wasn't involved in any project. It was a ploy—a lie.

Betty Friedan and I had lunch at the Carlyle Hotel a few times a year. She enjoyed being there and invited me to be her guest. It hadn't occurred to me to ask her if she knew Steven Scheuer, but it turned out she knew him quite well. She listened to my story of the friendship up to that point, and expressed concern. He had a reputation with women. But Friedan was quick to say these were rumors and that she had no first—or even secondhand—information. We spent the lunch discussing him. Betty thought there were too many potential risks to my career, and she didn't see him as a good bet for a partner. *Break it off now, before it gets complicated.* I agreed that I would. It was one of the few times Betty was cautious in matters of the heart.

Walking back to the apartment I felt sad, only then admitting to myself how much I looked forward to the calls, the lunches, his enthusiasm for life. In a world where most things were: *No, or Not Yet, or Never,* he was *Yes! Why not?* I was leaving for a consulting trip and promised to give him my contact numbers. But I left without doing so, and kept him far from my thoughts when I was away. When I returned to New York, Betty called.

She had been thinking about our lunch. She was recanting: *Go for it. He's a good man.* Steven had left numerous messages, many of them expressing concern, but the last messages were different—his tone was annoyed. I called. Although clearly glad to hear from me, he made it clear I had been rude. It was the first flash of what would be a pattern. I was required to be on call and available. He was permitted to be elusive, unavailable, and mysterious about his whereabouts. There was never a balance of power. I was too naïve to see that.

He charmed me. We graduated from lunches, to dinners, to theater and late dinners followed by a round of downtown jazz clubs. I found him unusual and fascinating. He was great fun. It seemed he knew everyone and his familiarity with the city was as intimate and comprehensive as if he were operating within a studio apartment. I rarely let him see me up to my apartment. When I did, I offered him mint tea and showed him to the door before he got an idea that anything else might happen. He didn't seem to mind. It did not occur to me that I was out of my depth. I still believed I was the one controlling whatever sort of friendship this was (or would turn out to be). It was the first of many myths I created over the next years.

I spent about a week a month in Phoenix consulting for the national YWCA. A few months after we had met, Steven called late one night to inquire when I was returning and on what flight. I told him and asked why. He said he was trying to figure out schedules. Abruptly he hung up. The next night (pre 9/11— therefore more relaxed airport security) I got off the plane to find him waiting at the gate—wearing a chauffeur's cap, holding a large printed sign that said: BRILL, and armed with roses. We got into a cab and he gave only my address. When he opened his briefcase I saw a change of basic clothing folded into the case— underwear, socks, and a shirt. His intentions were obvious but I said nothing. As I unlocked my door, he said: No more mint tea. He had caught me off guard and I liked it. I didn't resist him. It felt romantic.

Our relationship moved forward. He planned trips abroad and also to his favorite country inns on the East Coast. Money and time didn't seem to count. Periodically he would vanish. I assumed his work demanded it. He wrote a daily syndicated newspaper column about television, supervised a staff producing his annual books on television, and had a weekly public television program. I wasn't falling in love as much as I was falling under his spell. Eventually I learned that he lied about things large and small. Much later, I said: *his lies had lies.* It's a funny remark, but painful to say about a man who had become a husband. In his courtship of me he had lied about his age (and got away with a ten-year subtraction), his marital status, his family, and much more.

I could write a separate book about this marriage. Were I to do so I might call it: *The Memoir Of A Feminist Hypocrite.* After all my work on women and economic independence, women and power, women's liberation, the value of the single life, the sanctity of solitude—after all of that—I had been seduced into returning to the older model of an all-consuming relationship. In the words of Charlotte Brontë, at the conclusion of *Jane Eyre*: *Reader: I married him.* I had every opportunity not to, but that's what I did. We had a small luncheon wedding upstairs at the Box Tree restaurant in Manhattan. Four women held the poles of the chuppah that covered us during the ceremony. Betty was one of them. Later, I thought my insistence on four women was *faux feminism.* Was I trying to kid myself, my friends, all of us? I have a photograph, taken after the ceremony—it's a candid snapshot of Betty and Steven. He is seated and she's standing next to him wagging her finger. I can only imagine now what she was telling him.

Betty stayed loyal to me through all the troubles that followed and counseled me to be calm and to carve out a life of my own—and to write more. She also urged me to stop being a

WIFE. I knew what she meant. In a futile attempt to reduce the money he spent each month, I started cooking whenever we had company. Steven packed his East Hampton home with houseguests and lunch and dinner guests. He preferred catered events or someone to come in and cook for us. I am an excellent cook and it has always been therapeutic for me. It didn't save any money, because there were always new pressing demands for the funds, but it did gobble up my time. He didn't appreciate that I cooked. It embarrassed him. A friend from those days said he loved to spend weekends with us because I made wonderful food. Only years later did he realize that I was doing all the cooking and serving, while everyone else had an enjoyable time. I had mugged myself, and none of Betty's many lectures brought me closer to my senses. Betty never took Steven's side. She did not warn that if I left him or he left me, someone else would grab him. None of these things she was notorious for saying to other friends did she say to me. I was in deep and troubled waters and she swam the distance with me. The Glover Street house again became a refuge, and Betty was nonjudgmental and welcoming.

Friends are eager to give me a pass on a flawed marital decision. They point out factual and practical points of reference—love, increasing instances of illness, his repeated promises to me that marriage to him meant freedom to write, my elderly parents, the absence of siblings or other family, presumed financial security, our shared political values—the list of reasons is long. But I do not offer any rational reason or an alibi, because I suspected more than I cared to admit to myself before we wed. Once married, I was mired in solidifying emotional cement. One aspect of the entrapment was the seduction of being liked—we were a popular couple. For a time it appeared (even to feminist friends) that ours was an egalitarian form of the fairy tale. They weren't any more connected to reality than I was. Somewhere deep within many of us is the belief that the fairy tale is possible.

I would rather not write about this and I wish it were possible to write this memoir as a romantic feminist and omit any mention of this particular trip to the wedding canopy. But, if only a handful of women who are in marriages that are emptying their souls read this and recognize some part of themselves in these paragraphs, it's worth my exposure here.

Steven absented himself from the reality of my illness after we were married—at the onset of my first flare. He was angry. How could I possibly get sick when I was with him? He believed he had given me a perfect life, a life that did not permit a woman to be ill. At first, he hurt me so deeply I thought I could not go on, but then I persuaded myself his view was only a foible, or a phobia about illness and hospitals. I tried not to take it personally. After years of being single, I had a network of friends who would help me. I asked a few to continue as before, and didn't emphasize to them Steven's behavior. I lied about the trips he took when I was in the hospital, trying to persuade friends that his absences were unavoidable. Years later I learned he often used my illness (with tears flowing forth upon command) as an excuse for myriad things he couldn't execute. The marriage was profoundly disappointing almost from the beginning. His behavior veered far from that of the man who had courted me. Or perhaps it was the same, but now I saw it up close.

I approached my problems and crises with the same determination that I had confronted a lifetime of chronic disease. Eventually I came to realize that comparing a marriage to a disease was an ominous symptom of despair. We wasted many words and much money in individual and joint therapy. Nothing helped, nothing changed, and I chose not to leave the marriage. Instead, I wrote in my journals. And unlike Anaïs Nin the outpouring of words did not find their way to print. I should have used the energy and the time to write more articles, books, and essays, and not chronicle my grief. But, I was paralyzed.

Chaos is the word that adequately describes my life then.

He had excessive lifestyle requirements, the need for obsessive luxury travel, and he demanded my attention over anyone and everything else. And there were lies, lies, and lies. I tried to pretend this was normal for a man who had been raised in privilege and had achieved considerable professional status. I tried to reconcile his public views, his generosity of funds and spirit to help others, with the personal nightmare I was living. I looked vainly for the moment when his life might have changed, or for the moment when he became an uncontrollable bully. How could a man educated at the New York Ethical Cultural Schools have so loose a connection to truth and loyalty in his personal life? He had many friends who loved him and extolled his virtues. For a time I wanted to believe it was my fault. I was the wrong spouse. He had achieved much professionally, and so I also tried to write off the aggression and bullying as part of male power. I tried to blame patriarchy. Then one day, at a lunch in East Hampton, I tuned in and really listened to what he was saying and how he was saying it.

He was talking without stopping, barely taking a breath. He had a fascinating series of thoughts about a new world of hundreds of television channels and almost limitless on-demand viewing (still not then available). But there was also something frightening about him—the velocity of his language, his choice of words, his gestures, the urgency in his voice, the grandiosity of all he said. As our guests left, a dear friend, Dorothy Nelkin, asked me if had I read a book, *An Unquiet Mind* by Kay Redfield Jamison. She suggested I should read it.

Dr. Jamison describes in detail her battle with bipolar disease. Of interest to me (as Dot suspected) were the vivid descriptions of Jamison's own manic episodes. The book sent me on a new quest. Steven appeared to be a unipolar manic. A doctor was later to diagnose him as *hypomanic*. In Jamison's words, I found a portrait of Steven's many unrealistic plans, the flights of fantasy, his grandiosity and boundless energy—physical and intellectual. Suddenly my husband made sense to me. There must be a cure—a drug or a different kind of therapy that would help. I gave him the book to read during a particularly miserable patch in our marriage. He read it eagerly, marked it up in red ink, and wrote comments in the margin, such as *YES!* and *True for me too!!!!*

For the first time I was encouraged. With his consent, I contacted the psychiatrist and author Dr. Ethel Spector Person, a close friend. She recommended a colleague she thought would suit Steven. At the doctor's request, we went together to the first appointment. Within moments my hope collapsed. Steven talked excitedly about the Jamison book, saying it was the reason we had come. But then he told the doctor that what mattered for him were the portions of the book where Jamison wrote that she would rather have a life with mania than a boring one. While Jamison makes the point that one may function well despite mental illness, this was not the primary message *I* took from the book. Steven's mania was obvious to the doctor from the first session. He prescribed an anti-mania drug, but it didn't help, even with a considerably increased dose. Nor did other drugs help. Nothing helped. He was, quite literally, unstoppable. But I soldiered on—convinced he could be *fixed*.

Living with him on a daily basis was impossible, as anyone who has ever been around someone with mania well knows. I never knew what was coming next. Legal entanglements, unfulfilled promises made to others, financial commitments, threats, and things I wouldn't learn about until years later. The problem with Steven was that his intelligence, his vision, and a certain brilliance had kept him from getting proper treatment earlier. It probably wouldn't have mattered because his professional status and the prominence of his family would have worked against finding ways to control his behavior. He almost always made sense, but the proportions and the scale of his plans were unrealistic. His mind was a racing demon, and that seemed to delight him. It had me thinking about suicide more than once.

An aspect of Steven's pathology (whatever it was) involved a particular form of retaliation when I disagreed with him. If I tried to stop him from pursuing an idea that would certainly have led to further grave consequences, legally and/or financially, he would phone friends or visit neighbors to get help, saying I was *nuts*. He learned that using that word didn't persuade anyone, and that calling women who had been my friends for decades simply led them to call me. (Some of them asked what on earth I was doing with my life.) Steven then perfected what he saw as a better scheme. He kept a detailed ledger on me called W-Lash (whiplash) in which he recorded my presumed crimes against him. These he recited to those he wanted to convince, to gain their cooperation. He had coined a new phrase, reporting that I was proven to have *deep-seated psychological problems*. Apparently, I was no longer merely *nuts*. The psychiatrist told Steven to stop making lists and calling people. Steven insisted to the doctor that he had stopped, and that I was (of course) also delusional.

His various strategies didn't work as he had hoped they would. Too many people knew too much about what he was doing and, out of concern for me, they called. But not everyone saw through him, or analyzed with any care what he was saying and doing. Steven continued to fool some people with his charm, his ebullience, and his largess. A few women were jealous of what they saw as my enviable life. They encouraged him to see what could be done about me. He happily reported what they said, as an open threat. I was frightened. I had read too much 19th-century literature about women and madness, and I knew what a man with power, status, and money could do, even in the 20th or 21st century. I was now less rational and more apprehensive. I felt I was spinning, going anywhere. A few strong women friends tried, and mostly succeeded, in keeping me sane and steady.

Some years earlier, Steven had been diagnosed with a brain tumor, which turned out to be benign. His neurologist, a woman, had become a friend and ally to me and a wonderful physician for him, but she had since left clinical practice. The experience of brain surgery, of course, was traumatic, but it was a successful operation. Although both she and the neurosurgeon at the time of surgery had said the tumor had no effect on his behavior, at that point, I was eager to get another neurologist's opinion. I persuaded myself the previous tumor must have been at the root of his aberrant behavior and aggression (another moment of my handcrafted magical thinking). Eventually, we were referred to a new neurologist for a consultation.

This neurologist was older and wise. He was seasoned at dealing with all sorts of brain dysfunctions and the troubled spouses that came along with them. He saw through my façade to the despair I felt. He carefully explained that the placement of Steven's tumor (in the cerebellum) had not damaged the frontal lobe and the tests he ordered confirmed that. The tumor could not be the cause of the behaviors I described (and which Steven willingly related). The new doctor saw Steven several times. He examined him and spent a great deal of time talking to him alone. On a follow-up visit, when Steven was getting dressed after a physical exam, the doctor asked me to come into his office. He told me to give up my search for a remedy. Firmly, tenderly he said: *Your husband can't be reformed or changed. My reading of this is that he has narcissistic personality disorder and there's nothing that can be done for that. Even Freud knew that. For all I know he might be a sociopath. At the least, I would say he exhibits sociopathic tendencies.*

It was hard to put the doctor's words out of my mind, especially the label *sociopath*. Perhaps it was an overstatement; nonetheless it resonated and helped me translate my past. Trying to control Steven's excesses was almost a full-time job. What the neurologist told me was of enormous help. His diagnosis and medical opinion enabled me to put together some of the pieces of the marital puzzle. Attempts to cajole or force Steven to be reasonable were futile. And always had been. At first, I was angry that therapists and shrinks hadn't seen the narcissism and the grandiosity for what it was, but I also understood his mania was a camouflage. The fact that medications hadn't slowed him down might have been a clue that the problems were largely those of his character and not his psyche. But at last, the question of what was wrong with my husband no longer intrigued me.

I now understood my life was not his life. The search for a peaceful life was over. Life inside the Scheuer-Kaleidoscope had taken its last rotation. My internal world would no longer change each time Steven geared up for action. I would no longer put myself between him and the inevitable outcomes when his ideas and businesses fantasies went up in financial flames.

I had kept a mental ledger—how could he do this, or that, or the other? The lists of an aggrieved spouse are likely pretty similar, whatever the underlying causes. The hardest thing for me to accept was that I had saved his life three times (once from a swarm of wasps that had stung him repeatedly, another from a potentially fatal heart arrhythmia episode while driving, and finally, my dogged pursuit to arrive at the original brain tumor diagnosis). And throughout our marriage he had ignored my illness and sabotaged my writing whenever he could. I understood what he could not. My essential question became how to compose my own life. That was my job and my business. I tried to organize financial and legal safeguards, and warned people who cared about Steven not to encourage his pursuit of multiple business plans. Most of the damage had been done, but it saved my apartment from the debris heap.

Business ideas were the source of his most dangerous adventures. He went down the rabbit hole and landed in Wonderland with Alice. His judgment as a parent, and his concerns and compassion for friends (both young and old) were legendary, and his intellectual acuity on other matters was in place and functioning. But his obsession to become a mogul (although his professional success was substantial) was insatiable, and it made him quite literally insane. He came to see me as an enemy because I stood in the way of his dreams. He wanted to become one of the giants of the television industry, to become International T.V. Czar, and to live in opulence. He was willing to do anything, risk everything, and even hurt me to achieve his fantasy.

When I tried to make him face the increasing drain of money he would say it was his money. Who was I to tell him what to do? When our houses were sold suddenly, and valuable possessions vanished to sustain his fantasies, I was less than understanding. He had also found a devious way into my own funds. And there were personal betrayals, which I might have seen coming, but didn't choose to acknowledge until late.

Why didn't I divorce him?

I think there are as many reasons for a spouse to stay as there are for one who leaves a marriage. Mine were practical as well as emotional. Perhaps they were flawed reasons, but simply stated: I did not divorce. We came to an accommodation and I tried to reclaim my identity and my life. I was helped by the support of friends, and by the loyalty of my parents, who although frail and elderly, were still sharp. I ghost-wrote three books, which gave me an income and the ability to provide some care for my parents. One of those books changed me.

I was hired to write the memoir of Lola Leiber, a remarkable woman who had survived the Nazi era with her husband because of her bravery and intelligence. I understood it as a woman's story. Lola was an ultra-orthodox Jew. At first I was reluctant to take it on, because I didn't think I could handle being inside that enclave of Judaism with its anti-woman approach.

Fortunately, the man who hired me (a relative of hers by marriage) lived a more secular life. He convinced me Lola and

I would understand each another. He was right: Lola stole my heart and her story empowered me. When we met she had been a widow for some years. From the beginning of her life in New York she had found a way to navigate the ultra-orthodox community in Brooklyn. She was the only woman ever to own her own art gallery inside this strict religious community. She wore the traditional wig—but hers was blonde. Although she was well into her late 80s, she was glamorous and feisty. I privately told her she was the Ultra-Orthodox Hasidic Zsa-Zsa Gabor.

She relished the remark but lamented she could never tell anyone because everyone she knew would disapprove. We became close friends. I told Lola the whole story of my marriage. She listened for hours without interrupting. When I finished, Lola took my hand: *Dahling, dahling, men...men... men...what can I say to you?* She then reached up to her head and pulled off her wig—a heavily constructed helmet—and tossed it onto the sofa. *You see? What is this? We are all always doing things for men. It's too much. Don't be so hard on yourself.* Even though we were alone in her apartment, what she did and said to me was a radical act for her. Without her wig, she looked a great deal like my own mother. Lola had been able to be a working artist by defining terms for herself. Within the confines of a rigidly controlled religious existence what she had accomplished might have seemed impossible—but Lola had been undeterred.

When I was hospitalized with a bad flare of my illness, she sent foods, fruits, and flowers. She called constantly. One Friday as the sun was setting, a young chaplain came into my room. I politely told him I was not interested in spiritual counseling. He smiled. *I'm on a mission. The rabbi here begged me to come in to give you the Sabbath candles. He can't come in here because you are a woman alone. But he told me he's going to be in big trouble with someone named Lola if you don't have your Sabbath lights.* We both laughed. The young chaplain was a Lutheran, and we had a long talk about faith and religion. I told him the highlights of Lola's survival story and about her present life.

When it was time to publish Lola's book, *A World After This: A Memoir of Loss and Redemption*, she insisted my name be on the front page. It reads: Lola Lieber Schwartz/Written by Alida Brill. It is rare for a ghostwriter's name to appear so prominently, if at all, in a book for hire, and it certainly wasn't part of the contract I had signed. Lola knew the importance and value of work for women. It was the essence of who she was along with the rest of her identity as a traditional Jew. In the Acknowledgments, she wrote: *I am deeply appreciative to Alida Brill who was able to find my voice and project my feelings. She gently took me through the difficult and indescribable memories of the six years told in this book.* Lola would never accept that it was she who had given me back my voice and guided me onto a new path. Writing Lola's story and becoming her friend allowed me to place my marriage in a different context. People had managed to survive far worse conditions than I had. And more important, I had learned that I was in better shape than I had recognized.

For a period of time I functioned without the constant worry about what Steven would do next. I regained a sense of self-esteem and independence. Then, Steven's health failed totally. During the last years of his life his brain really did take leave of him. His mind was still active and there were fantasies, but now they were sad and meaningless. Often he insisted we were on a boat and not in the apartment. His athletically trained body, which had served him so well, crumbled. He could no longer walk more than a few steps. It was a grim ending to an exuberant life. There was nothing remaining for Steven to give me—emotionally, financially, or spiritually. Now I was the one who had something to offer us both—forgiveness. To the extent possible, I forgave him and myself. I cared for him and made sure the caregivers were loving and kind to him, which they were, unfailingly. He died of congestive heart failure.

After he died I came to compassion, forgiveness, and acceptance. I was able to separate the husband he wasn't from the man who had an accomplished career and had been generous to many. Letters from those who had known the public Steven consoled me. There was goodness in him, generosity of spirit, and the desire to be of use in the world. Fans of his work—the movie and television books, and his public television programs—wrote to share how much they had relied on his media criticism through the years.

The marriage consumed me far longer than I wish to remember. But the marriage and the man did not define me. He was not the last word on my life. I took myself out of his story. He wasn't my tragedy. He was his own. I faced what I had done to myself. In love with the concept of being in love, I wanted to be chosen, and had continued to want it into my forties. He really hadn't seduced me. I had seduced myself. I paid an enormous price for being selected by a powerful man with a limited vision of relationship and marriage. A man who was a public feminist yet a private tyrant. He had me fooled, and I had fooled myself into believing that *happily ever after* could ever be true.

Had I taken anything from my years in the women's movement? Was I still partly that little girl with blind faith in fairy tales writing to Princess Grace? How could I have become so entrenched in a fantasy marriage? Marriages are never fairy tales. But in order to survive in mine, I had created one, without admitting the stark truths of my life with him.

I take important lessons rather than bitterness from that marriage. From those years, I gained a resolve that strengthens me as I have gone forward. In one of the most dismal passages of that time, I confided to feminist friends in the movement my line that I should be appointed *Head Hypocrite of the Feminist Movement*. One famous sister replied without blinking: *Don't be ridiculous, Alida, the line for that job forms to the left.*

Before Lola and the second neurologist—both of whom helped to free me—I had an earlier awakening that proved to be the beginning of my renewal. Steven and I were in Copenhagen (it would turn out to be our last trip together). I was on my way to Venice. Given my health, Venice was a risky choice, but I was eager to be in the city that always seemed to revive me, and where I had research and restoration projects in progress. Steven was on his way to London where he had other interests, personal and professional. It was a dreary and cold day, but I was determined to visit the house of the writer Isak Dinesen, whose birth name was Karen Blixen. She is so revered by the Danes that in the pre-Euro days her image was on their paper currency.

I was recovering from a flare and my stamina was low. To make the trip via public transportation involved a train ride, a walk from the train station to the museum-house, and then another walk back to the train station. It was neither wise nor possible. I asked what a car and driver would cost, and was told it would be expensive. I was in the anguish of acknowledging I was mired in a marriage more damaging to my soul than my disease was to my body. Steven extracted a deal from me. If I promised to delay writing another book, he would pay for the car and driver. He resented my writing, which he said took time away from our marriage—what displeased him was that writing took time away from my undertaking tasks he felt entitled to demand. I agreed verbally to his conditions. It was an extravagant decision on my part, not on his. He still had money. I had bargained away time, my only precious asset.

Surely the spirit of Karen-Isak did not miss the irony of the arrangement. But something compelled me to go. I needed to stand in the room where she wrote after she left Africa—where she used words as the weapons to fight against heartache and poverty—despite disabling chronic illness. In a perplexing last-minute gesture of togetherness, he decided to accompany me on my pilgrimage—perhaps for a simple reason: Copenhagen bored him. Now I would be encumbered by his impatience and overbearing opinions on this excursion, as in my life. I had desired the luxury of solitude.

When we arrived, I went directly to the room where she wrote. However limited my gifts, as I stood in her writing room I knew the only thing that would save me was to put my own work first. I would block out the noise of his relentless and increasingly pointless demands. I would laugh with amusement or ignore him when he referred to my *so-called writing career*. Most importantly, I would write for light against the cold shadow of my illness.

Not surprisingly, Steven quickly lost interest in all things Blixen, and found his way to the small restaurant on the grounds and had his lunch. I got my solitude after all. I stayed in her writing room, and I was alone, for there were no other visitors. Karen Blixen had refused to be erased by disease, financial circumstances, or heartbreak. She did not allow herself to be diminished further by a brother who plundered the family business, and almost cost them her home and land. She was not swept away by waves of bitterness toward the husband who had given her syphilis. She harnessed the pain of loss from the death of her lover and turned it into creative fuel. Writing could cure neither her illness nor her grief, but it was a tangible victory while she lived.

From the far end of the room, I watched the rays of sunlight scamper across her writing table, making prisms. I vowed not to be taken down in defeat. I would not be doomed because of a crippling and complex legal relationship. I spoke to the spirit of Karen Blixen-Isak Dinesen. I confessed how fearful I had become from the last bouts of illness and even more terrified of upcoming treatments. And I feared I wasn't good enough to claim an identity as a writer. She spoke back not in words, but in the ways the light moved in her room. When I left the Blixen house, I felt her spirit presence accompany me. I felt renewed confidence. I had regained focus. I walked past the luncheon café, waving at Steven as I headed for the gift shop. There I purchased a photographic guide to the Karen Blixen Museum.

This small book has accompanied me—to my writing desk, to my bedside table, to the Infusion Room where I have had chemotherapy treatments, to hospital rooms when I was admitted, and also tucked into my carry-on luggage. Blixen became a guardian angel, an additional light to the lamp on my writing desk. Blixen was mostly alone, even as her publications increased, and her disease worsened. She wrote: *All sorrows can be borne if you put them into a story.*

Not into fairy tales but into stories. When I felt my resolve weakening or self-esteem taking leave, I would repeat the line to myself, and then her writing room would return. I would be transported back to that Danish afternoon at Karen's house. The memory would bring again the peace I had found in the spiritual and physical dwelling of a writer who had reclaimed her life. It was there I began to realize there was nothing to do but write off the lost years and begin again. The only strategy was to move forward independently. I could right my mistakes by getting on with life. I asked for an extra helping of allotted time, and the ability to reside within the healing world of words.

Wedding reception, Box Tree Restaurant, New York City
November, 1991

13
Toward Romantic Feminism

I cannot quite cure myself of the conviction that if we could
discover a word that meant "adventure" and did not mean
"romance" we in our late decades would be able to free ourselves
from the compulsion always to connect yearning and sex. If an
ancient (by American standards) woman finds herself longing
for something new, something as yet not found, must that
something always be sex or till-death-do-us-part romance?
— Carolyn G. Heilbrun,
The Last Gift of Time: Life Beyond Sixty

During a time when I was watching too much television,
a particular AARP commercial aired often. Despite
the meaning of the acronym—*American Association of Retired
Persons*, the word retirement was assiduously avoided. Actors
portraying aging boomers were filmed in a variety of settings.
They revealed what they hoped to do when they grew up. One
man wanted to build houses; a woman dreamed of travel to
exotic places; someone else wanted to play in a band. Others
expressed a desire to help change the world as best they could.

In one of the last images a silver-haired woman who is
decorating a wedding cake pauses. Looking straight into the
camera she says: *I want to fall in love again.* She was luminous and
beautiful. I was sure she was speaking directly to me. Dismayed,
I let out a sigh. It was a knockout punch to my Princess Grace-
Gigi-heart.

Romance is a cornerstone of our culture. Notwithstanding
the women's movement, protests, consciousness-raising, women's

studies programs, feminist publications, women's publishing houses, two generations of feminist mothers, and all the talk in public and in private as well as the endless rounds of meetings and research panels leading to advocacy projects and conferences about independence and autonomy, in spite of all of this and none of this, we still reside in a world obsessed by romance.

We cling to a storyline that says we are better off in pairs, even as we sail off into our sunset. We can't seem to move beyond this fantasy. I imagine a pier where luxury ships receive passengers for the *Last Chance Voyage for Romantics*. A cruise barker stands on the shoreline and shouts out a razzle-dazzle pitch: *Lonely People, come this way. Don't miss the opportunity to win the Sweepstakes Prize for The Final Voyage on Noah's Human Ark. Just one chance left to come aboard. Happiness guaranteed.* He's only a make-believe huckster, but I wonder: Are we really doomed if we are in a solitary life? Is the single life so dreadful?

Most solo lives are not spent totally alone, but in companionship with others; frequently this includes an assortment of family members and friends. Singles engage in lasting intimate relationships though they might not fit the happily-ever-after endings of romance films. A life lived on one's own terms could be described as being *with yourself* rather than the prejudicial *by yourself*. Historically, women without partners have been assigned the status of *ladies in waiting* for their princes, aging kings or just that ordinary guy down the street or down the hall. The unmarried U.S. Supreme Court Justices Elena Kagan and Sonia Sotomayor received free passes by reason of their brilliance and achievement.

There are numerous presumptions about women who don't have husbands or families. Alternative life choices are not promoted or regularly portrayed in film, fiction or television. Paul Mazursky's *An Unmarried Woman* stands out as an exception. For my generation, a single woman's life was seen not as a preference but as the result of disappointment or rejection. This conviction lingers into the 21st century, although statistical reports indicate increasing populations of single people enjoy satisfying lives in urban settings as well as in small towns or rural villages. A woman determined to compose a meaningful life that also includes marriage faces daunting obstacles. I myself was frustrated and ultimately defeated in my attempts to combine the two. In *Writing A Woman's Life*, Carolyn Heilbrun handled the dilemma of love and marriage with stinging wit, intelligence, and a sobering dose of realism:

For women, the only sane way to live through a romance is to live through it without closure. Marriage to a lover is fatal; lovers are not husbands. More important, husbands are not lovers. The compulsion to find a lover and a husband in a single person has doomed more women to misery than any other illusion.

I don't remember my reaction when I read the book twenty years ago. Now I always burst into laughter. *Of course, that's right.* Then, I modify my thoughts. *Well, Heilbrun was right about me!* Some of us are unsuited for the responsibilities perpetuated in the stereotypical universe of *Wifedom*. Many of us know this about ourselves, yet we insist on entering into the sacrament of marriage or its civil versions. Inevitably, our authentic selves collide with the many mythologies surrounding marriage. The result is domestic combustion and volatile behavior. Some of us leave our vows and the men behind, or wake up to the fact that we've been left.

We try it again, fervently hoping for different results. We often reach the same outcome, but with a different man. If we don't have the guts to face the fact that marriage doesn't work for us, we grow increasingly alienated. Some of us become trapped in lies and act monstrously toward our spouses. Or we bury the pain so deeply we become ill. The late Dr. Albert Grokoest, a distinguished and beloved physician, is credited with the comment that in the animal world it is *fight or flight*, but that humans invented a third option: *stick around and get sick*. I add this: Leave a destructive marriage, but rather than move forward to a renewed life, wallow in paralyzing guilt.

Some of us treat marriage as an achievement test. Even with dismal scores, we sign up for a retest. When a marriage ends we frequently say it failed. If our marriages fail, then by extension we are failures at what is our most highly regarded institution. Margaret Mead's view on the topic is worth noting: *I have been married three times and not one of them was a failure.* If a marriage doesn't endure for a lifetime, it doesn't constitute a failure. If separation and divorce were described as *completions*, perhaps we would not remarry as often or as quickly. Many women hold fast to the dream of finding their true prince. Even into our older years we are determined to find a more comfortable glass slipper. Women who should know better enter into multiple remarriages, including ones that are suspect from the beginning. Over the last decade the divorce rate for first marriages has hovered between 40 to 50 percent. Divorce rates in second marriages are above 60 percent. Third marriage divorce rates remain at a stubborn 70 percent.

In *Heartburn*, Nora Ephron wrote:

The desire to get married, which I regret to say I believe is basic and primal in women is followed almost immediately by an equally basic and primal urge which is to be single again.

I embellish it to:

Apparently followed by a need to marry again and again. Why don't we decide instead to buy new dresses, throw great parties, drink champagne and dance? At least then everybody knows when the party is really over.

Our fixation on romance ensnares women more than men. In *A Room of One's Own* Virginia Woolf employed the visual metaphor of men gazing into the mirror that women provide for them. In this glass the men who are confident of a wife's approval are able to see themselves as larger than life before they must enter a difficult and competitive world. A reverse mirror exists for women. When we glimpse ourselves in male mirrors our singleness looks unattractive, perhaps pathetic. If we would only believe and think otherwise, it would help diminish our perception that men hold all the power and the secret to a meaningful life.

Frequently women are too eager for perfect endings, sometimes without a specific man in mind. I too have longed for the high drama of an elaborate courtship. While consumed by the experience, I pretended it was genuine love, but I managed to go on extremely well when those love affairs dissolved. Women are conditioned to desire a romantic high because we've been told that sensation alone represents the *real thing*. We've been persuaded there's but one great love out there. After all, we were taught from girlhood that _HE_ is supposed to exist and whatever it takes we are destined to find him. This distortion is handed down as revealed truth from generation to generation of girls, who then as women get sucked into a narrow interpretation of love and relationship.

We write men into our plots without their knowledge, and as we age we edit and revise our fantasies. Women's desires are fueled by the movies and stories we saw and read as girls but usually these wants retain recurring elements. The *Rescue Me* theme is an oldie but goodie: Here a man whisks us away into coupled paradise, where presumably we leave all our woes behind—illness, financial worries, unhappy family relationships, boring jobs, crummy apartments. The list is endless because the *Rescue Me* fantasy knows no limits. This particular theme ignores the details of how married life might work out with a specific man. Instead, we create a scenario where the man is only the back-story—it is a tall-tale that says that getting married will cure all that is wrong in our lives. This fantasy puts the entire burden of a happy relationship on the man—the hoped-for-husband. Long-term compatibility, a sense of shared values, to say nothing of chemistry, all end up reduced to subservient details.

The experience of being madly in love is all consuming and sometimes mindless. The word *madly* is an apt description. *Crazy-in-love* drives us to destinations we regret later with disastrous and unimaginable costs, financial as well as emotional. When it's over some of us reflect on our sanity. I certainly have. Obviously, positive intuitions and practical reasons make us desire lifetime commitment. Good marriages work across many dimensions—sexual and sensual compatibility, raising children, the joy of each other's company, a goodly number of shared interests, mutual respect and patience, taking care of one another, financial partnership, an appreciation of humor and laughter, a shared lightness of mood and spirit, courage in adversity. These are only a few of the attributes that contribute to sustaining happiness and satisfaction. These are the relationships that make us feel content and secure. And this is a large part of what marriage should do for men and women. It should make us feel stronger and safer in the world and within our minds and bodies. Once married, some of us do well, but many of us do not—whether or not we divorce.

When a marriage doesn't work, the poison it produces trumps most other forms of emotional distress. Often marriages don't just stop working, but are broken beyond repair. The spouse who initiates the ending need not be identified as a villain, culprit, betrayer, or monster. If we ended before describing our spouses in pejorative terms, healing could become part of the *marriage-finis* cycle. Some of us fear confronting separation and divorce and the guilt over breaking up a family. Paralyzed, we stay until there's little will or energy to go forward in life. Being miserable and staying together is dishonest and unfair to both spouses and to children. Falseness has yet to make friends with intimacy.

We have the capacity to embrace sadness and can invite it into our conversations and senses as a valid and even a welcome presence. It would be worthwhile to cultivate a place where we can accommodate sorrow and loss unaccompanied by the assignment of blame. Such an approach is rarely chosen over the default responses of rage and retribution. In wedding ceremonies couples write their vows or recite ancient ones. We sign prenuptial agreements detailing financial arrangements that foreshadow the possibility of a divorce before we've begun a marriage. Separation agreements involve post-nuptial financial contracts that often become concurrent with divorce settlements. We might wrestle over custody of children, although many parents work together cooperatively to keep joint custody schedules moving smoothly.

I suggest a new tradition, which could be called the *vows of parting*. Even in the challenging circumstance when only one spouse wants to end a marriage, our divorces and separations could become humane and compassionate.

Rilke's lines in XIII of *Sonnets to Orpheus* resonate:

Keep ahead of all parting, as if it were behind you, like the winter just now passed. For in winter you are so endlessly winter that only by wintering through it can the heart survive.

We could do well to learn to *winter through* our partings. As part of the grant of living, we all suffer and all must endure endings. Hearts do survive loss. Recrimination and bitter accusations erase memories worth preserving. Most marriages could end in gentle and accepting ways. But instead, we resist acknowledging that it usually isn't only one person's fault. Instead of facing our own responsibility, we allow anger to rob us of an opportunity to share the pain of a joint loss. We have the power and intelligence to choose how we leave our vows. But this isn't the *romantic* part. It's not like planning a wedding event, trying on designer gowns, choosing flowers, selecting music, or sampling from menu options. But our endings linger longer than the ephemera of a wedding day. How and in what manner we exit is of paramount importance to the continuity of life beyond marriage.

Despite well-intentioned efforts at resuscitation, some relationships are better ended. If we took completed marriages off life support and moved forward with compassion and tenderness, we could make quite a revolution. The effects would be lasting and not just for couples but also for the future of our families. The customary forms of how we take our leave are rigidly defined and could stand revision. If we did so we might create a space before separating where we affirm our spouse as a person, even as we untie the bonds of marriage. There would be fewer damaged children and bruised adults, though the divorce lawyers would lose.

In the run-up to a wedding many women get swept away by their girlhood daydreams, and so when a marriage is over the Prince is decried as an imposter or worse. But everyone and everything has played the role of imposter—the husband, the wife, the entire machinery that fabricates the way we wed and how marital unions are depicted. Nothing is perfect forever. If we are honest we know it isn't perfect when we begin the adventure. We don't know how to back out with civility and kindness when our marriages as healthy entities die. How could we be expected to know? We have crafted our marriage rituals from vats brimming over with pastel shades of spun sugar. I have participated in those weddings and I have been that kind of bride. When the *happily forever and ever* assumptions do not hold, we are distressed. Men and women suffer in the same ways and in different ways. We are unwilling to accept the idea that even as each of us will enjoy a different life span, so it is with marriages.

The desire to cling to a simplistic personal plot is not unlike being cast in a musical comedy for the rest of your life. I appreciate the *Great American Songbook*, and as a girl I was taken to musicals and I listened to the soundtracks of many of them on vinyl. After a glass or two of wine and a forgiving crowd, I can still belt out "Some Enchanted Evening." I go to the best revivals on Broadway. The lyrics are good, the musical scores even better, and they are a part of our theatrical heritage, but I know now they don't represent real life, and this is what I could not accept as a child. Musical-comedy love is appealing because it is make-believe; it takes us out of ourselves. If I'm having problems or recovering from a flare of illness, a musical comedy will transport me from the trials of everyday life. It's a fine form of self-medication as long as I remember to leave the floating feeling at the theatre's exit doors.

If there's a consistent message in these plays it is this:

In a magical instant one man or one woman will banish all things terrible and from that moment forward everything will be gloriously romantic and everyone will be happy. Even the darker ones, such as *Carousel* or *West Side Story*, bestow forms of romantic redemption before the curtain comes down. The worlds inhabited by these characters are filled with music and dancing, beautiful costumes and lavish sets. The 1950s classic musicals are versions of the traditional fairy tales. It is the same old story of Prince Charming.

Clinging to the ideal of a princely husband all but guarantees disappointment to a woman and probably leaves a man feeling perplexed and then defensive. I've listened to many a dissatisfied wife tell stories of ruined birthdays, inexpensive engagement rings, inadequate restaurant choices, ugly flowers, lousy presents—the lists continue, only the decades and the century change. Women who consider themselves feminists also complain about husbands and their disillusionment with marriage. Becoming a wife transmogrifies some of us. A woman previously capable of arranging celebrations and events and enjoying those arranged by friends wants her husband to make the celebrations perfect. She wants her husband to make the plans, surprise her, spoil her, and treat her like Princess Grace just prior to the royal nuptials.

But idealizing what a husband should be and do is unfair

to men and it harms marriages. Men who are scolded about their *mistakes* or inadequacies and face disapproval will probably not be receptive to finding a deeper intimacy. It's a destructive model for any couple. The dynamic dissolves and the outcome is a disappointed wife and a resentful husband. Both spouses claim the right to be called *the aggrieved*. Men are not exempt from being taken for granted or neglected. They feel defeated when their wives are unhappy and are told (or assume) it's their fault. A common response is to do nothing, further reducing the opportunities for trust and companionship.

Wives who think they have made their desires clear become angry because we're convinced our husbands willfully chose to make us miserable. Men shouldn't be held to mythical standards of a storybook Prince Charming or a handsome actor in a feel-good romantic film. Nor should women play the role of perfect wife or princess bride. But when we trap ourselves in a traditional marital script, that's exactly what happens. Disappointments based upon unnecessarily high expectations and fueled by the corrosive ideology of gender roles eclipse the people we once loved and the marriages we cherished. In this environment, misunderstanding is all that thrives. When we stay too long in these marriages the damage can last and find its way into future relationships.

Carolyn Heilbrun wrote of a brave way to be married and stay married.

The sign of a good marriage is that everything is debatable and challenged; nothing is turned into law or policy. The rules, if any, are known only to the two players, who seek no public trophies.

The overhyped *rules* of romance impair our ability to make lasting connections. We're hoodwinked by phony commercialism that works against reciprocity and equality between men and women. Finding the appropriate influences in our marriage is at the heart of Heilbrun's comment. A good marriage is controlled by each spouse and not by external forces and artificially constructed courtship patterns. I doubt couples writing their vows use her quote. Romantic feminist love asks that equality and compassion exist as primary vows, along with the others. Heilbrun provides the blueprint to follow. If I ever found the courage or the hubris to marry again, I would look to her words as a guide.

* * *

As a child I was permitted the occasional box of "Cracker Jacks." The caramel corn was OK, but it wasn't my thing. I have more a salt than a sweet tooth, but I would root around in that box eating the corn as I searched for the prize inside. My father caught me in this act. He asked which I liked more: the candied popcorn or the surprise inside the box. My immediate answer: *The surprise, of course!* I admitted I didn't like the taste of the corn or its texture. That afternoon we went to the local Woolworth's. We walked up and down a few aisles filled with small *surprises*—all were nicer than the ones buried in the sweet and sticky popcorn. We looked as long as I wanted, and when I was ready I chose two things that I liked best, although I can't remember what they were now. My father emphasized there was plenty of time to devote to this quest. The message was that I should take my time. I didn't have to eat "Cracker Jacks" to obtain a crummy little surprise.

It took many more years to realize the deeper meaning of his lesson. A girl, then a woman, can select her own treats and make many other independent decisions. We have the option to think about who and what we want to include in our lives. No need to fritter away precious time digging inside a box hoping that the buried prize might be something we want. Designing an equitable relationship with someone is a readily available prize if we would accept this option as an article of faith. Rather than rushing headlong into romances and toward weddings, girls and women could learn to say: *Not Yet* or even *No* to the coupled life. I suspect disappointment and personal misery would be reduced significantly. Life generally affords us enough time to select our own *prizes*; they are what I call *treats along the way*—if we are liberated from the obsessive hunt of finding a *one true love* at the expense of so much else.

I do not know the writer Mary Gordon, but I feel we are contemporary feminists together on a journey toward the understanding of men and women, romance and attachment. In her 1981 novel, *The Company of Women*, Gordon wrote of the price of being chosen:

> *I wonder what abuse a woman has to go through at the hands of a man before she gives up the inner flicker of delight, like the click and flame of a cheap cigarette lighter, at being chosen? Where did we learn that definition of honor? As long as it is there, we are never really independent.*

I kept that quotation pasted to the inside of my front door as a reminder of what mattered whenever I left my apartment. I called it my Feminist Mezuzah. I've also placed it underneath my desk mat to give me courage when writing. I have given copies of the quotation to younger women to assist them through sexism, break-ups, and a variety of harsh encounters. When I do, I acknowledge that I too sometimes still feel that lurking danger of longing for the familiar flicker of excitement when a man chooses me. Most of my battles against the desire-demon are now over. Thankfully, I've defeated the foe. But I still remind myself that choosing to be chosen and choosing to choose are human desires, and not a male birthright.

Mary Gordon spoke again about choosing in her 2011 novel, *Love of My Youth*. Miranda, the central character, is as an older woman who speaks of being loved and who has loved. Miranda's view could represent the future for women who love men, but who choose not to be defined by them.

> *... maybe it was based on the anxiety that you might not be chosen, that you might miss out on something essential if you weren't listening in*

the right way, if the man didn't feel you were. Yes, she thinks it is about being chosen. An older woman has either lived with not having been chosen or learned that having been chosen doesn't shape a life as much as she'd once thought.

For some men, the pursuit and *conquest* of a happily single woman is an ego boost. Meeting a woman who doesn't need a fairy tale ending can be refreshing. It's a dominant theme in numerous self-help books that presume to teach women how to catch a man. Many of these authors proffer techniques to help a woman act like someone she is not, including strategies to appear as if a serious relationship is of little consequence. Twisting yourself into a human pretzel as you pretend not to want something you emphatically do want isn't a promising way to begin or sustain intimacy. A woman is encouraged to be coy and to develop a dating persona that is a false presentation of her own self. Is it any wonder many of us grow weary of the search for *Mr. Right* and become discouraged by the phony games and elaborate deceptions? Such techniques insult our intelligence and are a cheap trick to play on men.

Skim a table of contents in one of the many relationship advice books and you will see my point. An all-time attention grabber for me remains: *Why Men Marry Bitches: A Woman's Guide to Winning Her Man's Heart.* It's the *trifecta* of everything we should not want our romances and marriages to be. But there it is, with many more like it. If men truly want tough and unkind women, why would any of *us* want *them?* Are men so shallow and stupid they can be played, ensnared, and then caged? These find-a-man programs trivialize us as human beings.

It's risky enough that the route to a lasting marriage is still based on antiquated courtship mythologies. But we further endanger happiness by placing relationships on the shaky foundation of deception. It's the prelude to the subsequent horror of realizing you've revealed yourself to the wrong man or woman. This gets worse as we get older. Rather than just being heartbroken when love hits the ditch, we, as older people, feel numb and humiliated. There's a certain battle fatigue, accompanied by the sense that maybe love doesn't matter any longer. I've heard women and men say versions of: *Why should I bother at my age?* And I've felt that myself.

At a certain point we've heard most of the pickup lines, exit speeches, and participated in a series of false starts and ultimately hurtful finishes. What began in hopeful anticipation too often concludes with attitudes of *us (women) versus them (men)*. This is the language of sexual polarization and it doesn't help men or women find the way into healthy relationships. There's all too little in the heterosexual approach to partnering that is romantic. And it's decidedly not feminist. Viagra and its brother drugs make men candidates for sexual activity into their later years in ways not previously imagined. But sexuality is not the same as sensuality. True intimacy can thrive without sexual acrobatics into our late eighties and beyond. Women and men deserve better than the routine rubbish we're fed by drug companies and the formulaic romance industry, both of which pervade much of what we read, hear, and see.

We ought to be smart enough to know all this before we recognize ourselves in the AARP commercials. Romantic feminist love isn't dry, boring or humorless. It doesn't exclude great passion and excitement. It doesn't preclude the satisfaction of being appreciated by and appreciating your partner. We have the capacity to experience an almost limitless range of sensual feelings for one another. However, most of us choose to exercise self-restraint rather than engage in the pursuit and sexual consummation of every attraction one has over the course of a lifetime. But for many of us assuming an obligation of absolute monogamy for life is hoax turned into farce. The almost inevitable *lapses* (as the religious call them) or *interludes* (a more neutral term) a person experiences during a lifetime are tagged with the ugly description, "cheating." Too often it is entering into marriage too early, with the wrong person, or at all, that cheats us of living fully and loving completely. Marriage as the ultimate outcome, the *sine qua non* of human identity and personal success, marriage as the only plausible response to loving someone, has been at the root of much unhappiness and pain.

In some cases, marriage is primarily a legal decision based on the benefits granted to couples by the Internal Revenue Service, and marriage can often provide spousal health insurance coverage. The vow to spend life together until death surely shouldn't be based on taxes or health insurance. But tax codes and insurance policies are designed for the residents of the Couples Ark. The persistence of these laws and rules affords another opportunity to punish those who are not onboard.

Women alone are not portrayed often enough as role models for the young (unless perhaps as members of celibate religious orders). Yet it is the case that women who live more solitary and independently—according to their own truths—are also productive and many content and happy with their lives. An inclination toward kindness and compassion is not reserved for the married or coupled. The stereotypical notion that the *barren*, the unattached, or differently attached woman is selfish, brittle, impatient, mean-spirited, and sexually empty has never been empirically validated. There are married couples (and married women) who cling to the opinion that unmarried women are in a perpetual state of longing to achieve couple-longevity or at least marital survival. Over the decades I've heard unhappily married people proudly proclaim the number of years they've been married. And I was one of those wives. It would have been more honest to have described my marriage as *years served*.

Before middle age an unmarried or unattached woman becomes a concern to family and friends and is viewed as a social liability or a financial burden. Women today are given the cultural license to be unmarried, but not to live alone most of the time, all the time, or for extended periods of their lives unless in widowhood. A woman who does so still risks society's judgments. If we are also strong, successful, and self-reliant, then perhaps we're man-haters, or just too difficult to have been chosen. It takes fortitude and considerable self-confidence to stand in opposition to the tired old idea that womanly fulfillment only comes through marriage and children regardless of work, love liaisons or profession.

The harsh punishments of past eras have largely disappeared. The Scarlet Letter "A" for adulteress is no longer tattooed onto our foreheads or sewn on our clothing—at least in secular or tolerant communities, but retribution remains robust among numerous denominations of the religiously orthodox. Across continents a nonconforming female risks banishment, torture, and death. Even in the United States unmarried women of *a certain age* who maintain active intimate relationships with men can be made to feel unwelcome in what passes for modern polite society.

We still don't have a neutral or affirmative glossary for women who choose *not* to say: *I Do! Thank God! Today I am a WIFE.* There are sexist words for women who reject marriage or full-time cohabitation as incompatible with their needs and personalities, but no words that illuminate a complexly textured existence. We don't know how to describe attributes of independence, freedom of person and movement. Here are a few historic ones (and too often still used) that barely scratch the top layer of the lexicon: sinful, promiscuous, wanton, loose, easy, cheap, and immoral. The nouns include: prostitute, slut, whore, jezebel, harlot, strumpet, and tramp.

A woman who has lived without marriage or a permanent partnership with a man but is in the arts (or exists in an intellectual environment) can fly under the radar as an interesting woman with a *history*. Read: She's had too many lovers but because of her status as *une femme des lettres*, she is forgiven. She's interesting enough and perhaps dramatically entertaining at a dinner party. This category is reserved only for those women whose artistic achievements allow them to slide into this place of historical precedent. In the heterosexual world, there's a limited number of *character* roles that exist for a woman who has *missed out* on marriage—but a prejudice remains that it is marriage alone that offers life's greatest adventure.

When a woman chooses to make a life with a man she loves, it is usually assumed she desires to become his wife sooner or later. Our communal imagination leaves little else to consider. We not only merge our lives but we transform men into *The Husbands*. In same-sex marriages, both persons hold the same title and have the same status—i.e. husband and husband, wife and wife. In my opinion, the distinction of nouns in gay marriage may have significance beyond the semantics. At the very least these marriages suggest the possibility of a more level playing field in the challenging sport of domesticity. But the suspicions linger about a heterosexual woman of my generation who doesn't want a husband or no longer wants to be a wife. *Who or what is she: An incomplete or unfinished woman; a victim of childhood or domestic abuse; a narcissist; a failed or bad ex-wife; or just plain crazy?*

I recognize only now how ill suited I was for the *happily ever after dreams* I had as a girl. After decades of believing enough of the hype to keep trying, I finally came to understand why I was not a good candidate. First, most men are frightened by my chronic disease. Those who pretend they can handle it might remain physically but become remote and emotionally absent. One spouse left me because of my illness, but in his exit speech reconsidered his previous comments and insisted my disease had nothing to do with it. Second, when I experienced a loss of autonomy of mind and spirit in marriage I became anxious, and then angry. I felt stultified and suffocated. In my much later life marriage, I denied all those feelings and became overly solicitous. I sacrificed my own well being, damaged my financial security, and hindered my career in the attempt to make an unhappy and troubled husband happy and trouble-free.

Yet, there she was before me on the television: the beautiful AARP woman of a certain age staring at me during the vulnerable hours of late night. Decorating that damn wedding cake and telling me she wants one more run at it. *Shouldn't I want that, too?*

Many years ago I was annoyed at a man who told me over dinner that I was a romantic. I took it as an insult, which was not his intent. Several years later, over another dinner, he said something different. He said he had underestimated me and that I was rather extraordinary. Maybe all he said was that I was somewhat remarkable, but I remember it with more romantic overtones. I wasn't upset. I didn't ask him why it had taken so long. I thought at least he had the honesty and integrity to reveal this to me when he realized it. By then our friendship had evolved into a nurturing and comforting relationship, a real companionship.

But in that moment I felt gratitude. I was on Gigi-Automatic-Pilot. Did I hear him humming? *Oh Gigi! Have I been standing up too close or back too far? … Oh! What miracle has made you the way you are?* He looked nothing like Gaston, and we were enough past our prime to appear in our own AARP commercial. I gave an understated response: *Yes. You did.* What's stunning about this exchange is I had underestimated how much the importance of his delayed approval meant. Being taken seriously by colleagues and friends wasn't enough. I wanted it from *him*. The record of my feminist positions suggests a woman who wouldn't and shouldn't need what he offered in that *Gigi* moment.

An authentic relationship offers the possibility of a positive bond between a man and a woman, but not if we trap ourselves inside prescribed gender roles. At its essence, being a romantic feminist means we choose to love in mutually understanding and accepting ways. This is a love negotiated through the hairpin turns of distrust and false assumptions. I've learned to embrace the possibilities that emerge when a man and a woman discover their mutual trust in each other. A truly equal relationship requires both people be able to trust. When we permit the intrusion of stereotypical illusions, our ability to maintain trust diminishes. Romantic feminist love has the power to move us beyond the preoccupation with our own vulnerabilities and singular histories (the proverbial baggage). It gives us the chance to engage fully and to transcend entrenched cultural roles. But before we can do that, we must acknowledge their uniformly destructive impact on the nature of intimacy. Once we free ourselves from cultural constrictions, men and women can reach a reciprocity of caring.

It is not required that feelings be identical or of the same intensity. Acts of loving ought not to be recorded in a quid-pro-quo ledger. We can pledge instead to be involved with another person based on what and who we are and not on expectations of what we might be or should become. We need to commit to authenticity and have no tolerance for falseness. As women we should require of ourselves that we choose men who want the same. There are men who are (or can become) ready to discover new forms of attachment and caring. I envision relationships whose terms are so nurturing and accepting that they are usually limited to descriptions of unconditional maternal love. Perhaps this is the next step for men and women who are unafraid. It is possible to sustain relationships, even marriages, without the whizz-bang trappings created by everyone except the couple. This is brave and radical love.

The romantic feminist's approach to love requires courage because we must break with so many stereotypes and media-fueled images. It is essential if we are to form lasting bonds that do not impose unrealistic conditions. Such love encompasses a willingness to be attached without manipulation or agendas, either hidden or open. This is the hardest part of the reinvention of romantic love, because women so often perform a self-sleight of hand: we insist a relationship is equitable when it isn't. One of the first steps toward romantic feminist love is that we invite honesty in as an equal partner. It isn't easy, but the alternatives condemn us to years filled with accusation and betrayal.

Is what I describe real love? For me the answer is *absolutely,* and in profound and surprising ways. Romantic feminist love is the experience of loving someone while standing firmly on one's own two feet, of caring deeply but at the same time knowing your head and heart are paying attention to what is now, not what may or may not transpire. This reality-based intimacy is more satisfying in the long run than the *jittery-obsessive-in-love-choose-me-or-I'll-die-dramas* that fill our screens and invade our own stories about how love went wrong.

I've had a challenging time describing and justifying romantic feminist love to some friends. I'm asked if it's as meaningful as being *in love.* That question suggests a wariness that this love isn't the *real thing* and therefore doesn't count as much. We've been conditioned to trust only the most familiar forms of being in and experiencing love. I am convinced we can reach deeper forms of intimacy. It might feel impossible at first, but it can become as natural as breathing.

After a late night with friends when I failed utterly to explain what being a romantic feminist meant, I had a dream. I was a guest on the old Piers Morgan CNN interview show. In the dream, Piers Morgan asked, as he routinely did during the years of his show: *"Have you ever been properly in love?"*

That dream catapulted me toward clarity. This is what I now say to the dubious: We've had a slow food movement, designed to move us away from the quick fix of junk food filled with too much salt, sugar, fat, and artificial flavorings. No question that prepared foods and fast foods are satisfying, but only for a brief time. We're soon famished again and want more. We grow fat as we continue to eat more, but we derive less joy from the act of eating. We've become addicts to *feel-better-right-now* food. So it is with love.

Romantic feminist love is a slow love.

It takes time to develop new relationship tastebuds. We must learn to savor experiences with another person. It is a challenge, but in time we learn to appreciate that each and every bite won't be scrumptious but there are plenty that will be delicious and enough that will be tasty. Long-term contentment in a relationship is more than worth the patience it takes because it's a love that nourishes the heart and the mind. Living as a romantic feminist won't leave you constantly hungry to be wanted and always eager to be chosen. It will take us to attachments that are based upon authenticity, trust and equality. This is small bites love.

I call it the *Slow Love Movement.*

I was fairly old before I was willing to risk this kind of loving. It was hard in the beginning, but then the focus shifted and it wasn't about how difficult it was, but instead how complete it became. With a newly cultivated awareness (and especially with a commitment to patience) women and men can discover whether our initial instincts about each other were correct. My own long learning curve illuminates for me why popular culture remains stuck. In an episode of *Grey's Anatomy,* a leading character, Meredith Grey, says to her boyfriend, Derek Shepherd, a leading male character: *Choose Me. Love Me.* The words and the way the actor Ellen Pompeo said them proved so popular that a clip of that scene ran regularly as a promotion for the program.

The popular quasi-reality show, *The Bachelor,* makes a more disturbing statement. Stabbing one another in the back for the chance to be chosen, several women contestants compete for one man. When Barbie turned fifty, I wrote her a birthday message in an article I wrote for the Women's Media Center. It ended this way:

Sometimes to remind myself I can't retire from the advocacy part of my life, I force myself to watch "The Bachelor." [While watching a season finale] ... I fell asleep. In my dream my Barbie kept watching as the others waited for the final rose. The real women looked more like Barbie than my Barbie. Their lips quivered in fear—would Ken choose them? I mean, The Bachelor. My Barbie screamed, Alida, get me out of here! What's happened? In the morning I looked over at my original Barbie, high heels on her feet, earrings still in her head. I noticed her arm was extended defiantly in a gesture telling me to fight on to empower girls and women.

After decades as a self-defined and publicly identified feminist, I finally worry far less about what men think about me. And I hope that young girls set their sights on a dream that isn't about being a princess or a bride. Princess Grace wasn't happy forever and ever, and she lost a great deal of her identity in the bargain she made to be chosen by a prince. Happy-forever-and-ever is never possible. A decently happy life and a degree of contentment are best achieved by intelligent personal decisions that bring girls and then women to the realization that our personal lives are under our own control, and not in the hands of any man holding a glass slipper.

This is what I want to say to them, after I pull off their tiaras and take away their fairy godmother magic wands:

That's it! No more coaches and white horses, girls! No more pretending. No more fairy tales—the coach always turns into a pumpkin and those horses into white mice. Real women and real men are not princesses and princes and don't need coaches and horses.

A girl's and then a woman's sense of herself need not rest with the evaluations of boys and men. We have the power to stop dancing to the tune of *Will he or won't he want me.* Personal honor is maintained and independence achieved when we claim the right to shape the contours of our own lives. We can choose to include a man some of the time, most of the time, always, or never. We can choose partners inside or outside structured or legal arrangements. We will enjoy lovers. We are in same-sex relationships openly and proudly, and now under legal entitlements and protections. Some of us will reside in solitude, which is to say *with ourselves, not by ourselves*.

However we compose our moments, hours, days, weeks and years, all these choices are decidedly ours.

Additional Copyrighted Sources and References:

The Feminine Mystique by Betty Friedan, copyright © 1997, 1991, 1974, 1963 by Betty Friedan; W.W. Norton & Company, Inc, NY

Life So Far by Betty Friedan, copyright © 2000 by Betty Friedan; Simon & Schuster, Inc., NY

The Company Of Women by Mary Gordon, copyright © 1980 by Mary Gordon; Penguin Random House

Love Of My Youth by Mary Gordon, copyright © 2011 by Mary Gordon; Penguin Random House, NY

The Last Gift Of Time: Life Beyond Sixty by Carolyn G. Heilbrun, copyright © 1997 by Carolyn G. Heilbrun; Penguin Random House, NY

Writing A Woman's Life by Carolyn G. Heilbrun, copyright © 1988 by Carolyn G. Heilbrun; Penguin Random House, NY

"Growing Old In The 90's" by Nancy Mairs, copyright © 1993 The New York Times, c/o PARS International Corp., NY

"Marilyn, The Woman Who Died Too Soon" by Gloria Steinem, copyright © 1972 by Gloria Steinem c/o East Toledo Productions